Let them Eat
PANCAKES

ALSO BY CRAIG CARLSON
Pancakes in Paris

Let them Eat
PANCAKES

One Man's Personal Revolution
in the City of Light

CRAIG CARLSON

PEGASUS BOOKS
NEW YORK LONDON

LET THEM EAT PANCAKES

Pegasus Books Ltd.
148 W 37th Street, 13th Floor
New York, NY 10018

Copyright © 2020 by Craig Carlson

First Pegasus Books edition July 2020

Map of Paris copyright © 2020 by Masako Bando.

Interior design by Maria Fernandez

Library of Congress Cataloging-in-Publication Data is available.

ISBN: 978-1-64313-440-6

10 9 8 7 6 5 4 3 2 1

Printed in the United States of America
Distributed by Simon & Schuster
www.pegasusbooks.us

For Julien

CONTENTS

Paris

1. Luxembourg Gardens
2. Gilets Jaunes (Yellow Vests)
3. The Pigeon Man
4. The Anarchist
5. French Tax Office
6. La Tour d'Argent Restaurant
7. Madame Hubert
8. Mayor's Office (4th arr.)

PROLOGUE

"Of all the diners in all the towns in all the world, she walks into mine."

—Rick from *Casablanca*, if he'd owned
a greasy spoon instead of a gin joint

s it possible to order pancakes at this hour?" a preppy Parisian customer in his early thirties asked *en français*, his voice hushed, as if conspiring to do something naughty.

"*Mais, bien sûr!*" (Of course!), I said. "Why would you think otherwise?"

"Because pancakes are for *breakfast*," he said, leaning forward the way French people do whenever they're making an important point. "And right now it's 2:00 P.M.—*lunch*time."

"But you're in an American diner, *Monsieur*," I flashed a devilish grin. "Here, you can have breakfast *anytime* you want!"

"*C'est vrai?!*" (Really?!) the customer perked up in his chair, rubbing his hands together like a rebel who'd found his cause. "*Formidable!* I'll take a tall stack then!"

Seeing the customer's reaction made me think of the French expression: "*Ça s'fait pas.*" Roughly translated: "That's *not* done." For example, as my French husband, Julien, constantly loved to remind me, snacking between meals was "not done" *en France*—except for 4:00 P.M., the hour of *le goûter*.

Knowing what was considered acceptable behavior among the French was enough to drive a person crazy. Fortunately, as the owner of the first

American diner in Paris, Breakfast in America, I was fast becoming an old pro at navigating cultural differences.

As I went to take the next order, three of the most important people in all of Paris stepped into the diner: *les éboueurs* (the sanitation workers). If these guys weren't happy and went on strike (which seemed to happen at least once a year), it was a disaster for business. Garbage would pile up on the sidewalk for days—sometimes weeks—resulting in an apocalyptic rat free-for-all.

"*Salut les gars!*" (Hey, fellas!), I said, shaking the workers' hands.

As I served them their daily complementary drinks—two espressos and a pineapple juice—I did a quick scan of the room. The place was hopping. Nearly every one of the fifty seats was full. With its fire engine–red booths and classic décor—including a mini jukebox, American movie posters adorning the walls, and toasters at each table—the diner could've been located in Anytown, USA. But the best part was, when you stepped out the door, you were back in Paris.

The makeup of the diner's clientele had evolved over the years. It now consisted of about 70% French, the rest American students and expats, with a sprinkle of international tourists. Surveying the room, I noticed a group of French customers using a knife and fork to carefully cut their burgers into bite-size morsels, dipping a piece of bun, meat, and lettuce into their *sauce ketchup* before eating it.

Another French customer was unwrapping her wrap, using her utensils like a surgeon does when performing a delicate operation. (According to Julien, it was considered "bad education" in France to touch your food with your hands.)

By contrast, a group of American students grabbed their breakfast burritos and shoved them into their pie holes. Another American customer used his finger as a knife, pushing his scrambled eggs onto his toast.

I was happy to see a lot of our regulars in the diner that day. There were the four African American basketball players from the States who'd been recruited to play on France's national team. They were so tall they could barely squeeze into the booth, ordering enough food to feed a dozen people. They finished it all off without having to ask for a doggie bag, or the official, much more elegant-sounding name in French, *le gourmet bag*.

Off in the corner, our resident French artist—a comic book illustrator—was doing his daily artwork on the paper place settings. He loved to draw panels of otherworldly characters invading the diner, such as a mutant Donald Trump who, after transforming into a monstrous-sized pancake, smears butter all over himself as he wreaks havoc across the city.

Then there was the group of female students from the nearby Sorbonne. They met at the diner once a week for their "Pancake Club." They would film themselves for social media, hamming it up as they drenched their pancakes with maple syrup. Not satisfied with their performance, they would do take after take. By the tenth take, I had to look away as all of my profit margin *drip drip dripped* out of the now empty syrup container.

Lastly, there was Savannah, my waitress from Mississippi. A blond bombshell with a deep Southern drawl, she'd startle French customers half to death with her big, booming voice. "How y'all doin' today?" she'd say. "Can I get you a dessert? Or are you sweet enough already?"

Without fail, by the end of her shift Savannah would have piled up *beaucoup de propositions* from French guys—like this one from Armand, a model/actor who left a handwritten note on his business card, next to a photo of himself, half-shaven, as he gives his sexiest Casanova gaze.

"*In case you think about divorcing,*" Armand wrote on his card. "*Call me. Like Ghostbusters, I'll come to the rescue!*"

On the surface, it might look as if it were just another day at Breakfast in America. (Except for Armand; since when did a French *dragueur* [player] wait until a woman was divorced before pursuing a *liaison amoureuse* with her?)

But behind the scenes, it was a different story. I wasn't actually supposed to be working on the floor that day. For the past thirteen years, I'd been trying to step back from the day-to-day operations and direct things from on high—like a regular business owner would do. But as Al Pacino famously said in *The Godfather Part III*: "Just when I thought I was out, they pulled me back in!"

Earlier that week, the waitress who opened in the morning had gotten an *arrêt de travail* (work stoppage) from her doctor, which allowed her to be out sick for five straight days, even though the document didn't indicate what she was actually suffering from.

As I suspected, the waitress' illness turned out to be "spring fever," because the next day, she'd posted pictures of herself on Facebook having a picnic with her friends on the Canal Saint-Martin. (This kind of thing always happened when the weather forecast in Paris called for a week of sunshine after a month of rain.)

Of course, since I was in France, I couldn't just fire her—even with her guilty-as-hell photos. Instead, I'd have to put a *dossier* together, which could take months, if not years before a verdict was reached—which 90% of the time ended up favoring the employee.

On top of my server woes, I was also on the verge of losing another cook. A couple days earlier, right in the middle of the lunch rush, Fikadu put his spatula down and said, "I want what Kyle has."

It took me a moment to figure out what he was talking about. Kyle, a fellow cook at the diner, had just started a year's worth of paid leave after siring his second child.

"Oh . . . do you mean *paternity* leave?" I asked, putting two and two together.

"Yes, that."

"Well, Fikadu, to get paternity leave, you have to have a child first."

"But I *am* having a child."

This was news to me. With all the gossip flying around the diner, I knew a lot about my staff's personal lives. Sometimes too much.

"But doesn't your girlfriend live in London?" I asked. Fikadu nodded. I chuckled slightly as I stated what I thought was the obvious. "Well, I'm pretty sure to get French paternity leave, your child has to be born in France."

Just to be safe, I called my accountant. She was my first resource when it came to all questions involving France's complicated labor laws. "Looks like your cook is more on top of the latest developments than we are," she said.

After consulting the government's website, my accountant discovered that a new law had just been passed with very little fanfare. Not only did Fikadu *not* have to live in the same country as his baby in order to get paternity leave; he didn't have to be the biological father, either.

"He can declare himself the '*concubin*' of the baby's mother," my accountant said, "and *still* qualify for full benefits." (Apparently in France, concubines come in both male *and* female.)

All this, and much more, was swirling around my head when *she* walked in.

"I'm looking for Craigie!" a kindly voice said to Savannah.

I turned around to see a woman in her eighties standing in the doorway. She was wearing a flowery blouse, her ashen hair cropped. I recognized the Irish glint in her eyes immediately.

"Mrs. O.?!"

"Boy, am I glad I found you," she beamed.

"Me, too!" I said, giving Mrs. O. a big American hug. At that moment, I felt so thankful my waitress had faked being sick. Otherwise, I might have missed one of my favorite teachers of all time.

"Can you believe it's been thirty-five years?" she said.

"No, I can't," I said. Although after my rough week, I was starting to feel my age. "What brings you here?" I asked.

Mrs. O. explained that she was in Paris for a kind of mini family reunion, meeting up with her daughter and son-in-law who lived in Spain. In her hand was a rolled-up copy of my hometown newspaper, the very same one I'd delivered as a paperboy. She flipped to the page where there was an article about me.

"You've become quite the celebrity back home," she smiled. According to the article the whole town was abuzz ever since they learned I'd be coming back for a presentation of my book, *Pancakes in Paris*, in just a couple of months. "Your story is such an inspiration!" Mrs. O. continued. "Did you ever imagine that one day you'd be in Paris—living your dream?!"

Just then, there was a loud crash in the kitchen. After a moment, Savannah's voice could be heard shouting across the room, "I'm all right, y'all! Nothing's broken!" Then there was a pause. "Not on me, anyways . . ."

I looked at Mrs. O. and smiled. If only she knew . . .

That night over dinner, Julien and I talked about our upcoming trip to the States. The thought of going back to my hometown conjured up old feelings from my tumultuous childhood. Julien seemed to pick up on it right away.

"*Ça va?*" (You okay?), he asked. "You seem a little anxious."

"Yeah, maybe a little."

"Why?"

"Back when I was a kid, nobody liked me."

"Why would you say that?"

"Because Todd Ferguson told me so."

I recounted the story of when I was in the fourth grade. Having come from the wrong side of the tracks, from a neighborhood that was ironically named Frenchtown, I was convinced that the other kids in my class hated me. But my sweet, maternal teacher, Mrs. Robataille, said I was being silly. "Everybody likes you, Craig!"

I really wanted to believe her. Then one day during recess, I stood on the sidelines while all the other kids played kickball. I wanted to join them so badly, but was afraid to ask. I then recalled what Mrs. Robataille had told me, building up the courage to ask Todd Ferguson if I could play with them.

"No," he said.

"Why not?"

"Because nobody likes you, Craig. Mrs. Robataille just told us to be nice to you!"

I turned and ran away from school, hiding out in an empty church until a kind stranger found me and brought me back home.

"Wow, that's harsh," Julien said.

"Yeah, but the craziest part is, after the article came out in the newspaper, Todd Ferguson sent me a friend request on Facebook."

Julien and I couldn't help but laugh at that one. After a moment, my *chéri* took my hand and looked at me with his deep brown eyes. "Forget that Todd guy, *mon petit*," Julien said. "He's an *imbécile*. Besides, you're not the same person you were back then. You're *practically* French now!"

Was I really? I wondered. And if so, how had living in Paris all these years changed me? And more importantly, would I ever be truly French?

PART ONE

LIVING IN FRANCE

ONE

The Cobblestone

T he French love their revolutions. This was never more evident than in the spring of 2018, when all throughout Paris exhibits were set up to commemorate the fiftieth anniversary of the student protests of May 1968—or *"Mai soixante-huit,"* as it's referred to here. To mark the occasion, I went into the diner's cellar and retrieved an actual remnant from that tumultuous time: a two-hundred-year-old cobblestone. As I picked up the heavy chunk of rock, I could literally feel the weight of history in my hand. Like a meteorite that had fallen to Earth from some distant time and place, the cobblestone was a direct link to that seminal period when French society radically changed, seemingly overnight.

The story of how I came into possession of the cobblestone began in 2001. I'd just returned to the States after working for a year on a kids TV series coproduced in Paris. Knowing how much I loved breakfast (my nickname was "the pancake kid" after all), my friends took me to my favorite coffee shop in downtown LA. The moment the waiter brought me my ham steak and eggs, hash browns, buckwheat pancakes, and sourdough toast, I stared at my breakfast feast and said, "This is the one thing I missed in Paris!"

That's when I had an epiphany and decided to open the first American diner in Paris.

My friends who were with me that day thought I'd completely lost my mind. They gently pointed out that: a) I'd never owned my own business before, let alone a restaurant, the riskiest business of them all; and b) I chose to open my diner in a foreign country, with a foreign language, which also happened to be the culinary capital of the world.

"Yeah, yeah, whatever," I said, undeterred. "And the French don't eat breakfast, and I don't cook. Your point being . . . ?"

After a year of slogging to raise the seed money, I spent at least that much time in Paris searching for the perfect location for my diner. Just when all hope looked lost, I stumbled upon a café in the Latin Quarter owned by an elderly French couple, the Marins. But before I could seal the deal, the real estate agent told me I'd have to convince the owners that I was the right person to take over their place.

Turns out, for the past several years Madame Marin had been gently trying to push her husband out the door so they could retire. But Monsieur Marin had no intention of leaving. (The café was his baby.) Fortunately, the Marins and I hit it off right from the start. Not only did they like my idea for Breakfast in America (aka BIA), they also took me under their wing, treating me like the son they never had.

On the day we signed the documents making it official, Monsieur Marin, with a tear in his eye, handed me the keys to his place. He then ran down to the cellar and came back a few minutes later holding a square object wrapped in crinkly old newspaper.

"*Voilà.*" he smiled. "*Un cadeau pour vous. De la révolution.*" (A gift for you. From the revolution.)

Monsieur Marin handed me the object. It was surprisingly heavy for its size. I carefully removed the newspaper revealing an old gray stone.

"What's this?" I asked. "A brick from the Bastille?"

"No, not *that* revolution," Monsieur Marin said. "The revolution of *Mai '68*. It's a cobblestone."

Living in France, I'd heard a lot about May '68—the legendary period when French students rallied against, among other things, capitalism, consumerism, and France's antiquated institutions. But I'd never heard of the protests referred to as "*la révolution.*"

"Oh, they weren't just protests," Monsieur Marin said. "They were *riots*. Riots that went on for weeks, right along this street." Monsieur Marin pointed out the window to rue des Écoles on which his café sat. The aptly named "Schools Street" ran from the Sorbonne on one end to the *Campus Universitaire* of Jussieu on the other.

Monsieur Marin recounted his memories from those turbulent times. While Paris burned, rioters dug up the cobblestones that had once covered the majestic, tree-lined streets of the Latin Quarter, including boulevards Saint-Germain and Saint-Michel—and closer to home, rue des Écoles.

With thousands of cobblestones at their disposal, students creatively devised different uses for them. First, they stacked them on top of each other, forming massive barricades, like a stone snow fort, to ward off the advancing riot police. This action led to one of the movement's most popular slogans: "*La barricade ferme la rue, mais ouvre la voie!*" (The barricade blocks the street, but opens the way!)

Next, with so many cobblestones at their fingertips, students had stock-piles of ammunition, which they hurled at the police like lethal snowballs. As the number of protestors grew, so did their anger, resulting in one last use for the cobblestones: smashing them through nearly every shop window along their path. Photos from that era showed large swaths of destruction throughout the Latin Quarter, transforming it into a veritable war zone.

Back in the café, Monsieur Marin stepped over to the façade and pointed to the huge sheets of pane glass that ran from the floor to the ceiling.

"The cobblestone smashed through the window here," he said, pointing at the exact point of entry. "Then it continued across the room until it came to a stop over here." Monsieur Marin was now standing in the back of the café.

Madame Marin looked at her husband who had to be at least thirty feet away. "Imagine how hard the protestor must have thrown that cobblestone for it to have landed all the way over there?"

I almost made a joke about how he would've made a great pitcher for the Red Sox, but then remembered that the French knew nothing about baseball. Instead, I asked if they had been in the café when it happened.

"Ah, *oui*," Monsieur Marin said. "It was late at night, when we were just about to close the place."

"We ended up sleeping over there," Madame Marin said, pointing to a booth with a thin, worn-out cushion. "The worst part was we had to sit up and face the broken window all night long, so the *racailles* (delinquents) would see us and not loot the place."

I looked at Monsieur Marin who stood there, quiet and still. "Were you scared?" I asked.

"Oh, please," Madame Marin answered for her husband, dismissing the thought with a wave of her hand. "We lived through World War II. In Normandy. On D-Day!"

Monsieur Marin turned to me and said softly, "Yes, we were *very* scared."

As I stood there, transfixed, it suddenly dawned on me that I'd never met anyone who had been a witness to *Mai '68*. Could it be that I was in the presence of what the French famously called a *soixante-huitard*, literally a 68er?

Not quite. I learned that to be given that vaunted title (or *reviled* title, depending on which side of the political spectrum you fell), you had to have *participated* in the protests, not just witnessed them. In other words, the person who had thrown the cobblestone through the Marins' window in 1968 was a proud *soixante-huitard*. But Monsieur Marin, who had had to sweep up the mess afterward, was not.

Back in the present, I looked at the cobblestone, realizing that if I ever wanted to meet a real *soixante-huitard*, I'd better hurry. Their median age had to be at least seventy-five. And with each passing year, my chance of meeting one was becoming more and more remote. But that was about to change in the most unexpected way.

I first came in contact with Mary Harris in 2016 shortly after the launch of my memoir, *Pancakes in Paris*. One of the stops on my tour was Chaucer's Books in Santa Barbara, California. The moment I entered the shop, the owner smiled and handed me an envelope. "Looks like you have a fan already!"

It was a lovely handwritten card from Mary. In it, she explained that she had seen my book on display and, intrigued by the subject matter, decided to buy it. After reading the book in one sitting, Mary insisted that we meet. "We have so much in common!" she wrote.

As circumstances would have it, we kept missing each other. But then at the beginning of 2018, Mary wrote to tell me she was coming to Paris in May. We arranged for a rendezvous at a café near my apartment in the Marais. Even though I had no idea what she looked like, I was able to pick her out of the crowd immediately. At seventy years old, Mary exuded the same youthful energy that came through in her letters. As we chatted away over our *kirs*, it became clear that she was right; we did have a lot in common. Like me, Mary had been a student at the University of Connecticut, where she'd jumped at the opportunity to study in France as an exchange student. And like me, she immediately had *un coup de foudre*, falling in love with all things French—so much so that the country would play an integral role in her life, just as it had done in mine.

"Believe it or not," Mary said. "I took part in the very first study abroad program at UConn."

"Really? What year was that—if you don't mind my asking?"

"1967 to 1968."

"Wait . . ." I said, half believing my luck. "Does that mean you're a—?"

"Yes," she said with excitement. "I'm a *soixante-huitarde*!"

It wasn't a coincidence that Mary was in Paris for the month of May; it was a pilgrimage. For years, she had promised herself that if she were still alive and kicking, she would make it to the fiftieth anniversary of *Mai '68*.

"What was it like?" I asked. "I want to hear everything!"

Turns out, Mary had pretty much seen it all. The riots. The burnt-out cars. The cobblestone barricades. And the biggie: the student takeover of the Sorbonne.

"Mai '68 changed my life forever," she said. "So much so that when I returned to UConn I wrote my thesis on it. Would you like to read it? I brought the original copy with me."

"Mais bien sûr!" I said.

That night, I devoured Mary's report. I was so impressed with how mature her observations were. At barely twenty years old, she had written a thoroughly researched and balanced account of those controversial times. But to truly appreciate the impact of Mai '68, Mary argued, it was crucial to understand how rigid French society was back then. For example, before 1968 university students had no direct contact with their professors. They were required to sit in total silence in large lecture halls as *les profs* droned on from the podium.

"When I told French students how different it was at American universities," Mary said, "they kept asking me, 'You mean, you're actually allowed to ask your professor a *question*?!'"

Outside the ivory towers of *les universités*, the rest of French society was just as stern. Before 1968, women weren't allowed to wear pants to work. And if that same working woman wanted to open a bank account, she had first to get written permission from her husband (or father). On a personal level, I was shocked to learn that homosexuality was a crime in 1968. And as a business owner, I had no idea that back then workers could actually be fired.

"Things were so different in 1968," Mary said. "You couldn't even sit in the chairs at the Jardin du Luxembourg if you wanted to."

"What do you mean?"

Mary went on to explain that if you sat down in one of the iconic green metal chairs scattered around the park, an old lady with a ticket machine would suddenly appear out of nowhere and charge you twenty *centimes*. "We students said, 'Enough is enough!'" Mary exclaimed. "'After a long day in class, we should be able to sit in the park for free!'"

I couldn't help but think of the valued tradition in France of being a *flâneur*, which is the art of sitting around for hours doing absolutely nothing. No wonder French students were outraged; messing around with their right to be idle was bound to backfire. Like the British colonists in Massachusetts and their fondness for tea, sometimes it's the little things that can lead to a revolution.

This got me thinking: Was it possible for an American to be a *soixante-huitard*, or was that distinction reserved for the French only?

"Oh, all of us students were *soixante-huitards*, no matter what country we came from," Mary said. "You have to realize, we were part of an international movement. Protests in the U.S. influenced protests at the Sorbonne—and vice-versa. After *Mai '68*, I returned to the States as an activist, protesting against the Vietnam War and fighting for women's rights."

But the movement wasn't without its casualties. Mary recalled an American student who, after having been hit by a rubber bullet near the Sorbonne, was blinded in one eye for the rest of his life. "How can anyone say that American student wasn't a true *soixante-huitard*?"

Talking with Mary, it was impossible not to feel the impact that that period had on her life—as well as the lives of countless others. All the more amazing considering how short-lived the *révolution* was. By May 30, the demonstrations had reached their peak. However, this time they weren't led by rioting students or the striking workers who had joined their ranks. Instead, over 500,000 *pro*-government, *counter*-protesters marched down the Champs-Élysées, culminating in a landslide reelection victory for President Charles de Gaulle in June.

Just as quickly as it was ignited, the flame of revolution was extinguished. Life in France, as they say, returned to normal. Or had it?

Opinions on this subject are as varied as the number of cheeses in France. Jean-Paul Sartre, the famous French philosopher, said that what was important about *Mai '68* was that the action had actually taken place at a time when "everyone judged it to be unthinkable."

By contrast, the renowned French sociologist Jean-Pierre Le Goff, who had been a militant *soixante-huitard* as a student, eventually had a change of heart, lamenting that, "After *Mai '68*, we lost a sense of collective responsibility, leaving behind a legacy of narcissism and cynicism."

Others called the monthlong clash between students and police "a case of French psychodrama." My French mother-in-law who was living in

Dijon at the time, formed her opinion from reading newspaper articles, since there was very little TV coverage of the protests on the national news. For her and many of her generation, (including my landlords, the Marins), *Mai '68* was nothing more than *une crise* (a tantrum) by a bunch of spoiled children.

That said, nearly everyone in France agreed on one thing: after *Mai '68*, France was never the same. A journalist summed up the revolution's legacy this way: "In just four weeks, France underwent a radical political and cultural revolution. An archaic society was swept aside (and) all institutions were transformed: the workplace, the university, the family and the couple."

Today, I'm aware of that legacy every time I make my way to work. With my diner sitting squarely in ground zero where most of the action took place, I think about *Mai '68* as I step onto the dark asphalt covering rue des Écoles, imagining the beautiful cobblestones hidden underneath. I also see that legacy when I stroll past the nearby *Université* at Jussieu, where a thirty-foot-deep dry moat was dug out around the buildings, creating an impenetrable fortress to hold back students should they ever try to storm the campus again.

I also think about *la révolution* as anti-Macron demonstrations heat up in the city, led by the *gilets jaunes* (yellow vests). As French riot police hop out of their vans like storm troopers in a Hollywood movie, guns in holsters, mace and billy clubs strapped to their bulletproof vests, American tourists stare at them—freaking out—while stoic Parisians go on about their business, as if it's just another day.

Watching the demonstrators march past, carrying signs and chanting slogans against the tiniest of President Emmanuel Macron's economic reforms, a thought occurs to me: *How ironic that in 1968, protesters marched for radical change. But in 2018, they march to keep the status quo.*

I continue to think about the legacy of '68 when I arrive at my diner and see the long line of customers, most of whom are French. Back in 2003, when I first opened Breakfast in America, there was a clear generational difference between French customers who were thirty-five years and older versus those thirty-five and under. The younger generation seemed much more willing to give American grub a try, whereas French people over thirty-five would stop in the doorway, see that my diner was an American joint, then promptly turn around and leave.

As I'm wont to do, I did the math. Sure enough, thirty-five years before I opened my diner just happened to be . . . 1968. I know it's a stretch, but could it be that the breakdown of French society brought about by the events of *Mai '68* helped pave the way for Breakfast in America?

I think about this as I enter my diner and find out that my cook hasn't shown up for work for the sixth straight day. Thanks to the events of June '68, when the French government secretly negotiated with labor unions, granting workers unprecedented wage hikes, generous benefits, and strict job protections, I'm unable to fire him.

As for my personal life, perhaps the greatest legacy of *Mai '68* was how it opened the door for gay rights, which now allows me to go home after work and bitch to my French *husband* about how screwed up French labor laws are.

With the commemorations for the fiftieth anniversary of *Mai '68* in full force—and with Breakfast in America located smack in the middle of where it all happened—it only made sense that, as an entrepreneur, I come up with a way to join the two: the *révolution* and my diner.

I decided to return to the cobblestone for inspiration.

As I carefully unwrapped the brittle newspaper encasing it, I noticed that the old chunk of rock seemed to have aged considerably since Monsieur Marin had given it to me fifteen years earlier. It was now all pocked up and dirty, not at all like I'd remembered it. Having been cooped up in the basement for so long, the poor cobblestone hadn't had the chance to be cleansed by a refreshing Paris rain.

Holding the cobblestone in my hand, fond memories of Monsieur Marin came flooding back, and I suddenly found myself tearing up. Alas, my kindly landlord didn't make it to the fiftieth anniversary of *Mai '68*, having passed away nine months earlier. In homage to him, though, I believe I've finally come up with something that would make him proud.

With the world spinning out of control, mired in extremism and dangling on the edge of uncertainty, I've decided to put Monsieur Marin's cobblestone on display in my diner. It will be housed inside a plexiglass box, with a little metal hammer mounted on the side. And underneath it will be inscribed an important message, both in the language of my adoptive country, as well as my own:

En cas de révolution, brisez la glace
(In case of revolution, break glass)

TWO

From Frenchtown to France

I grew up listening to immigrant stories. My Grandma Lizzy loved to regale me with tales of how she and my grandpa's family were the first, and only, Finnish people to settle in northern Connecticut. As a kid, I never imagined that one day I would have an immigrant story of my own, albeit in reverse, with my running away and going back to the old country, if not exactly the same one.

But my reasons for leaving were different than theirs. *Weren't they?*

Stored in an old cedar chest, my gram had boxes and boxes of memorabilia that brought her family's adventure to dazzling life: exotic turn of the century postcards from Viborg, a Finnish city that was later annexed by the Soviet Union after World War II; lovely, handwritten letters containing the longest, most incomprehensible words I'd ever seen.

But by far my favorite items were the old black and white pictures. These weren't your typical images of immigrants as seen on the History Channel—of huddled masses, in tattered clothes, yearning to breathe free. Instead, they were of my great-aunt and uncle looking remarkably like "swells," replete with top hat and cane, posing in their spacious home—not on a set.

What stuck in my memory the most was the frilly lace everywhere; on the curtains, the lamp stands, the regal wooden chairs on which the couple sat stiff and stone-faced. There was even a creepy photo of a lace-adorned coffin inside which was an unnamed relative dressed to the nines, as if he were itching to hit the town on the other side of the veil.

If my Grandma Lizzy were alive today, I'd ask her why my Finnish family had left such apparent opulence for America, especially knowing how their lives turned out. My great-grandfather became a penniless drunk who was struck by a streetcar as he stumbled out of the local saloon. His wife, my great-grandmother, was locked up in an insane asylum shortly thereafter. (My Grandma Lizzy said it was probably due to grief, but judging from certain members of my family that followed, I suspect she may have already been a little *coo-coo* to begin with.)

With both his parents gone, my Grandpa Hans and his four siblings were placed in an orphanage. Continuing with the Dickensian nature of my family, my grandpa, who was barely in his teens, managed to escape, moving from one squalid city slum to the next, with no frilly Finnish lace in sight. This instilled in him a restlessness that would continue for the rest of his life, culminating during the Great Depression. After fathering two boys (my father and my uncle), he abandoned my Grandma Lizzy, never to return. She ended up raising both kids on her own, working two grueling jobs in order to provide for them.

After hearing my Grandma Lizzy's stories, I came to the conclusion that our family should have stayed in Finland. Especially now, given that the country consistently ranks at the top of the list for best places in the world to live.

As for my Polish grandmother on my mom's side, sadly her immigrant story was buried with her. Unlike my Finnish grandmother, my Grandma Mary did not want to talk about her childhood in Warsaw, having come to America with her parents in 1910 when she was just five years old.

"Tell me about Poland, Gram?" I'd ask her.

"Bullshit Poland!" she'd say in her thick accent.

Whenever there was something my Grandma Mary didn't want to discuss, she would quickly shoot it down with her favorite word. But that didn't stop me.

"How about Warsaw? Any memories of your childhood there?"

"Bullshit Warsaw!"

"Okay . . . Can you tell me where Grandpa Frank came from then?"

"Bullshit Grandpa Frank!"

Clearly, this conversation was going nowhere. Time for a new tactic.

"So, Gram . . . I really want to learn Polish. Can you teach me to say something?"

"Bullshit Polish!"

At least she was consistent. But I was persistent. "Guess what, Gram? Mrs. Ciszewski down the street taught me a funny Polish expression: What does *ja cie kochem* mean?"

"Bullshit *ja cie*—" My grandma abruptly stopped talking, a tear welling up in her eye.

Ha, gotcha Gram! I thought to myself, knowing full well that *ja cie kochem* meant . . . I love you.

With no pictures, postcards, or stories to share, my Grandma Mary's life in the old country would forever remain a mystery, although her favorite expletive offered a pretty good clue. Years later, my mother would tell me that one of my gram's favorite things to eat as a little girl was stale bread covered with lard. Knowing how poor her family had been, I couldn't help but wonder if that was because it was the *only* thing she'd had to eat.

Contrary to the Finnish side of my family, it was a good thing my Grandma Mary left Poland.

Following in the footsteps of my Grandpa Hans, one of my own earliest childhood memories was when I was four and living in an orphanage with my three older siblings. Being a rather traumatic period in my life, I could only recall three episodes from that time: first, being dropped off at "the Home" (as we ironically called it) and promptly making a run for it—with my big brother leading the escape. Unfortunately, my tiny feet weren't fast enough; the authorities had no problem scooping me up and plopping me back into the Home. My brother, on the other hand, got away and would later boast about how he'd gotten to taste a full day of freedom.

My second memory involved an unfortunate incident with sweet potatoes, which I prefer to forget. And my final remembrance: leaving the orphanage after a year. That's when I realized my siblings and I were different from the other kids at the Home; we still had our parents.

Although my family wasn't aware of it at the time, my mom had started to show symptoms of bipolar disorder. Thinking it would help her to have a break from us kids, my dad and Grandma Lizzy decided to check us into the children's home—a rather unorthodox approach to the concept of "maternity leave." Although they believed they were doing the right thing, my family could have saved me thousands of dollars in therapy years later if they'd simply taken a moment to explain to me where they were taking us—and for how long—instead of dumping us off at a big, cold, gated complex, then driving off.

In the end, my family's plan did not work out as, well, planned. Shortly after we got out of the orphanage, my parents split up, and my mom spent the next several years in and out of a mental hospital. Instead of having the stable and nurturing home I'd always dreamed of, I found myself living alone with my dad in the bad part of town, the curiously named Frenchtown.

Surrounded by abandoned factories that had been slowly crumbling to the ground for decades, Frenchtown was nevertheless a lively and colorful neighborhood—full of druggies, dropouts, and deadbeat dads. Strangely enough, not a single French person lived in Frenchtown.

Of all the inhabitants of this tiny, fringe *quartier français*, no one was more colorful than my dad, Fast Eddie. At first I thought he'd gotten his nickname from the bright yellow racing stripe he'd painted on the side of his rusty station wagon. But later I learned it had more to do with his reputation as a *tombeur de femmes* (a ladies' man).

Despite his thinning gray hair, beer gut, and bright purple varicose veins, Fast Eddie fancied himself to be the mirror image of his idol, Elvis. Wearing only boxer shorts, a sleeveless muscle T-shirt and knee-high compression socks (for his varicose veins), Fast Eddie would get down on one knee in the middle of the living room, point his finger in the air, then belt out every song from his favorite Elvis album, *Aloha From Hawaii*, as it played on his stereo in the background.

"I'm just a hunk, a hunk of burning love. Aaaah! A hunk, a hunk of burning love. Aaaah!"

But, of course, Fast Eddie thought of himself as much more than just a hunk of *amour enflammé*. He prided himself on his mind, too. Not only did he watch public television (when he wasn't watching *Charlie's Angels*), he also read up on all the important issues of the day, regularly citing articles from his favorite periodicals, *Playboy* and the racier *Lui* magazine. ("That's French for *Him*," Fast Eddie would say.)

For wooing the ladies into his lair, Fast Eddie loved to display his sensitive, romantic side. He scotch-taped cutouts of French Impressionist paintings by the likes of Monet, Renoir, and Van Gogh (his absolute favorite) all over the walls of the apartment.

As time went on, though, I saw my dad less and less. Sometimes he'd stumble home late at night, the smell of beer on his breath. Other times, he'd mysteriously disappear for days, *sans* explanation. In his mind, my father truly believed that at twelve years old, I was perfectly capable of taking care of myself.

"That's what I had to do when your Grandma Lizzy was away at work," he'd say. "You'll manage."

And he was right.

On my own, I became completely self-sufficient, taking on two paper routes and saving up enough money to buy myself a bike and a telescope. Every day I'd read articles in the newspaper and stare at the breathtaking pictures of exotic places from all over the world. It fostered my wanderlust. Soon, I couldn't wait to get out of the wasteland that was Frenchtown.

On the eve of my thirteenth birthday, it looked as if I'd finally get my chance. One of the newspapers I delivered, the *Hartford Courant*, was offering a one time only opportunity for paperboys to go on an educational trip to Germany for the summer—all expenses paid!

With much excitement, I gathered all the items for the *dossier*. First, I got letters of recommendation from my teachers. Next, I wrote a statement of purpose, saying why I wanted to go on this trip. And lastly, I needed a written consent from "a parent or guardian."

Everything was going great until part *drei* (three). When I presented the application to my dad for his approval, he read the recommendation letter from my guidance counselor, zeroing in on this one line: "*Craig has a unique home situation and has to overcome tremendous adversity just in order to survive.*"

"I am *not* signing this!" Fast Eddie said, furious.

"Why not?"

"Because you're just trying to get attention by making me look bad."

My dream trip to Europe would have to wait until another time.

With no way to escape Frenchtown, I turned to escapism. Using my paper route money, I bought a Super 8 camera and directed a series of films using Frenchtown as the backdrop, the most popular being *Invasion on Chapel St.* (the name of the street I lived on). In that film, I created my own special effects, superimposing an alien spacecraft, then putting scratches directly onto the film, generating a laser beam that would zap the neighborhood kids into oblivion.

Next, to bring some *joie de vivre* into my 'hood, I created a Haunted Fun House in the backyard of my building. Using a series of strings and pulleys, I made brooms fly through the air and plastic skeletons pop out from behind gravestones marked with the names of the very same kids who'd been vaporized in my Super 8 *œuvre*.

To enter the Fun House, I charged kids a nickel. ("To cover expenses," I told my clients' parents.) The attraction turned out to be a huge success. That is, until a couple of punks, the Beavis and Butt-Head of the neighborhood, took a tour of it.

"Your haunted house isn't scary," Beavis said. "Just stupid!"

"Yeah," Butt-Head said. "We got a way better idea that'll make the kids shit their pants!"

The two punks found an old French door in a nearby alleyway, then propped it up against the fence in my backyard. Next, they ran an extension cord from my apartment, hooking it up to a desk lamp.

When the kids entered the Fun House and passed by them, the punks turned on the lamp. Through the broken windowpanes of the French door, Beavis could be seen lying on the ground, his shirt torn open and covered with blood/ketchup. As Butt-Head pinned him down, he air-stabbed him with a fake knife. "Where's the fucking money!" he screamed. "I gave you your dope, now pay up!"

When the parents in the neighborhood got wind that the updated version of my Haunted Fun House now included a drug deal gone bad, they swiftly forbade their kids from ever going back. Sadly, my first business venture—and primary means of escape—ceased operations shortly thereafter.

By 1977, after seeing *Close Encounters of the Third Kind*, I wanted to get out of Frenchtown so badly, every night I would ride my bike down to the edge of the Connecticut River and beg for aliens to abduct me. *With their higher intelligence*, I told myself, *I'm sure they'll understand me.*

One cloudless night, with the brightest full moon I'd ever seen lighting up the landscape, I noticed a flash of yellow on the other side of the riverbank. It was the racing stripe on Fast Eddie's pimped-out station wagon. I ducked behind a large boulder, making sure he didn't see me. I then peeked over the top, watching him as he slowly downed a twelve-pack of Schlitz beer.

So that's where he's been hiding, I thought. I tried to imagine what Fast Eddie could possibly be thinking about for hours on end, gazing at the river. Years later, my brother would tell me that when my dad was in the air force in the 1950s, he met a Japanese woman while on leave in Tokyo and became completely enamored with her. (It was the first and only time he would ever leave the U.S.) Could it be that, as Fast Eddie stared at the water, he was thinking about his long-lost love on the other side of the ocean?

Looking back now, I realized that, in a way, my dad and I were two kindred spirits. Two lost souls, staring at the river flowing by, longing to be somewhere else. As it turned out, only one of us would get away.

I never knew it was possible for a guy like me to go to college. Then French came along and changed everything. It was during my senior year of high school, on the first day of class, when my French teacher smiled and said, "Did you know that this is an AP course?"

"It is?" I said. "Wow, *incroyable!*" (I had no idea what an AP course was.)

Sensing my ignorance, my French teacher explained that AP stood for Advanced Placement. "And since this is an advanced-level French class," she said with pride, "it allows you to earn free college credit!"

That was a major turning point in my life; I began to focus on what could be possible beyond graduation in June. In short, French got me out of Frenchtown. One thing led to another, and before I knew it I was a student at the University of Connecticut, studying journalism. One night, when I was alone in my dorm room, an envelope got slipped under my door. Intrigued, I stepped out into the hallway to see who had delivered it, but whoever had was gone.

I picked up the envelope. It was an invitation to a meeting about the Junior Year in France program. *How strange*, I thought, since I'd already fulfilled my language requirement two years earlier thanks to my AP course. Although French was not on my agenda at the time, something inside me said I should go to the meeting anyway.

After an impressive slideshow of the most famous sites in Paris, I was tempted, but not yet convinced that the study abroad program was for me. I began to reconsider when I noticed two guys sitting off to the side—one an American who'd participated in the program the previous year, and the other, his French friend who'd come to visit. The two sat closer to each other than I'd ever seen two guys do before, speaking with a passion and intimacy I craved.

I want that, I thought, although it would take me years until I understood what *that* was.

I signed up for the program immediately.

During my very first week in Paris as an exchange student, I met an angel. It was 1985 and I'd just arrived with the junior year abroad program. With nary a *sou* in my pocket, I couldn't afford the price of an elevator ticket to the top of the Eiffel Tower. Instead, I opted to climb the 674 money-saving steps up to the second level.

I barely had a chance to catch my breath when I noticed a bunch of stage lights and a crew scurrying about on the level below. Moving in for a closer look, I discovered it was a film shoot. And the star of the production: Cheryl Ladd, best known for her role on *Charlie's Angels* (or the bizarre title in French, *Drôles de Femmes*—or "Funny Women"). Cheryl was the first Hollywood star I'd ever seen in person. And even more beautiful than on TV.

Suddenly, my mind went back to the late '70s, when I was still living in Frenchtown. As Fast Eddie and I watched an episode of *Charlie's Angels* on his huge color console (which he'd just won in a poker game), I asked, "Who's your favorite angel of all time, Dad? Mine's Cheryl."

"Nah," Fast Eddie shook his head. "Farrah is by far the sexiest angel. Hands down. But I *will* say this about Cheryl," Fast Eddie took a long drag off his cigarette, his beer gut hanging over his boxers as he adjusted his junk. "She's definitely the *classiest*."

Back at the Eiffel Tower, I must have had the dumbest look on my face, because one of Cheryl's handlers came over to me and asked, "Would you like to have your picture taken with Miss Ladd?" I could barely squeak out, "*Oui!*"

I couldn't believe my luck! In the picture, Cheryl Ladd is wearing a chic, fuchsia-colored fedora, her hand propped elegantly under her chin. She sports a warm smile as I crouch down on one knee beside her, clearly starstruck.

I couldn't wait to tell Fast Eddie the news. Turns out he'd been right; Cheryl *was* the classiest angel of them all. For years afterward, my dad would carry that picture with him wherever he went, showing it off to anyone who would care to look.

For me, it was a sign that France was where I was meant to be.

After a month in Paris, immersed in intensive French language courses, it was on to Rouen, in Normandy, to study at the *université* for a year. For me, though, one of the best selling points for the exchange program was having the opportunity to live with a *famille française*. French or not, I was so excited to get a second chance to experience a genuine, bona fide family for the first time in my life.

But as luck would have it, I was assigned to Mme. Yvart, *une vielle fille* (old maid) who lived by herself in a narrow, four-story townhouse not far from the city center. Her walls covered with crucifixes, Mme. Yvart was a devout Catholic and a music professor at the *Conservatoire*. Half mad artist, half schoolmarm, she reminded me of a bespectacled Margaret Thatcher—if her finger were stuck in a light socket.

I'm guessing that due to some unfortunate incident in the past, the university required host families to sign a detailed contract before paying them to take in students. According to the contract, Mme. Yvart had to house and feed me, but only a *petit* breakfast and dinner, Monday through Friday. The rest of the time, I was on my own.

Each night, the menu at *Chez Yvart* was the same, consisting of World War II–style rations, such as a bowl of soup as a starter, followed by the main course, usually a hard-boiled egg (sometimes two) or a cold chicken leg, accompanied by a bed of wilted lettuce, tossed with an intense, nasal-cleansing vinaigrette. That was it.

But the worst part was no matter what I did at the table, or how I dressed or carried myself, Mme. Yvart would shout at me, saying I was "*mal élevé*!" (badly raised)

"*Oh-la-la*, look how you're holding your fork. And chewing your food! And slumping in your chair! *Comme vous êtes mal élevé!*" (How badly raised you are!)

If my French had been good enough, I would have shouted back, "You're wrong, Madame. I'm not *mal élevé*. I'm *non-élevé*, meaning I haven't been raised at all! In fact, I wished I'd had the luxury of being badly raised!"

Adding insult to injury, I soon learned that not all French family dinners were created equal. Other students in the program would tell me stories about their delicious three, four, and sometimes *five* course meals.

"By the time my family rolls out the cheese cart," my fellow exchange student said. "I'm so stuffed, I can't hardly eat another bite!"

"Stop it, you're killing me!" I said. "How come I don't get to have a cheese cart?!"

I got my answer one morning when I was suddenly awoken by loud banging coming from the ground floor of the townhouse. I got dressed and went to investigate. Inside the narrow hallway, workers were ripping layers of old paint off the walls.

Nothing unusual at first. I made my way into the kitchen and nibbled on some dried-out biscuits (my breakfast), washing them down with a bowl of watered-down coffee. As I stared at my tasteless *petit déjeuner*, I suddenly put two and two together. There was a reason why I'd lost nearly fifteen pounds since moving in three months earlier. Instead of using the money the university was paying her to feed us, Mme. Yvart was using it to renovate *chez elle*!

That night after "dinner," I mentioned my little discovery to Mme. Yvart. Her face turned beet red, her glasses fogging up as she pointed to the door. "Out! Now!!"

Later that evening, as the grandfather clock struck midnight, I stood by the front door, my suitcase by my side, waiting for the director of the study abroad program to pick me up and bring me to a new home.

A week later, with the TV blaring in the background, I sat at the dinner table and smiled awkwardly at my new French family. I'd been relocated far from the center of town to a posh area called Bois-Guillaume (William's Woods). The mere mention of *le Bois* would illicit "*Oh-la-las*" and "*C'est chiiic!*" from the locals. But you wouldn't know it from the modest, working-class home of my new family, the Lerouxs. A retired couple in their seventies, their place was located on the fringes of the *Bois*—at the end of a dead-end street.

Although the Lerouxs had no cheese cart, it was definitely a step up from *Chez Yvart*. Dinners now consisted of *post*-WWII grub, meaning, now that the war was over, there was no need to ration anymore. Occasionally, the Lerouxs would allow themselves to splurge on frozen meat and vegetables—however blandly prepared.

Monsieur Leroux, a retired train conductor, always wore his striped conductor's uniform and matching cap around the house, including at the dinner table. A tiny, hand-rolled, filter-less cigarette was forever dangling from his lips. It seemed to defy gravity, bobbing up and down as he mumbled incoherently.

Across from the train conductor sat the rotund Madame Leroux. Donning a housecoat and big clumpy shoes, she reminded me of a classic French extra you'd see in the background of movies like *An American in Paris*. I noticed that whenever I looked away for a second, Madame Leroux would swat her husband.

"Josef!" she'd say before rattling on in a Normandy patois of which I only understood an occasional word or two. *Something, something*, imbécile, *something, something, hiss, hiss.*

Josef would respond in kind. *Grumble, grumble*, casse-couilles (ballbuster), *grumble, grumble, hack, hack.*

I would stare at the old couple, trying to figure out what the hell they were saying. When she caught me looking, *Madame* would suddenly stop arguing and smile innocently—as if nothing were going on.

By the time dessert was served (which was often a yummy *tarte aux pommes* made by Madame Leroux herself), Monsieur Leroux would turn the volume on the TV way up, getting ready for his favorite program to come on. Then he'd adjust his conductor's cap, light up a smoke, and sit back and enjoy the show.

Cocoricocoboy was a one-hour variety program geared for the entire French family. I'd never seen anything like it on prime time TV in America. It featured a bevy of buxom, topless women dancing to disco music.

Monsieur Leroux was in seventh heaven as he sat there ogling the sea of naked breasts bouncing up and down on the screen, giving new meaning to the term "boob tube." When Monsieur Leroux caught me staring with my jaw hanging open, he grinned a tobacco-stained grin and slapped me on the back. "Betcha don't get to see titties like that in your *puritain* America!" he said in French.

"Josef!" Madame Leroux snapped, swatting him again. *Something, something*, vieux pervers (old pervert), *something, something, hiss, hiss.*

As I watched the old couple quarrel, I thought about my own parents and the much more heated scrapes they used to get into. I then looked at the dancing boobs on the TV screen, imagining how thrilled Fast Eddie would be to be in France right now.

Although not the stable and nurturing family I'd always longed for, the Lerouxs and I did become close. For years, we'd write each other letters and send Christmas cards. And whenever I returned to France, I'd pay them a visit. Eventually, not long before their passing in the late 1990s, I was finally able to understand their witty repartee—deliciously mordant insults smothered in rich Normandy cream—the kind of *français* that's not taught in schools, such as Madame saying that her husband was dumber than a blood sausage and Monsieur countering that she was lazier than a dishcloth and should go fry an egg (i.e., get lost).

That's when I knew I was on my way to becoming a true Frenchman.

Craig reuniting with his French teachers after more thàn 35 years.

THREE

Le Gift du Gab

"Y ou obviously have a gift for languages."

People have been saying this to me for so long, I've actually started believing it. I've mainly received this compliment from American expats who've lived in Paris for decades but have given up trying to learn the language of their adopted country. Their main excuse: "Unlike you, learning a language for me is *hard*!" When I've challenged them on this point, most eventually get around to the real reason they've said *non* to *le français*: "I hate sounding like a six-year-old!"

Of course, there's no way to avoid this. Even French people don't start off speaking like a twenty-one-year-old. They have to pass through each year—from toddler to tot to adolescent—before they become hands-on-chin-intellectuals who've mastered *le bon mot*. Why should it be any different for us Americans?

Still, I've been speaking it for so long, it's easy to forget how *difficile* learning the language was for me, too. Even after taking French in public school for six years—from the seventh to the twelfth grade—I came out of it barely able to form a coherent sentence. This became particularly apparent when I tried to speak to the French exchange student my sister hosted one summer, Chantal.

Thinking it might help their troubled marriage, my sister's husband had the bright idea of inviting a young French girl into their home. After picking Chantal up at the airport, he put her straight to work babysitting their one-year-old son. This allowed the bickering couple to go out on the town, filling their weekdays with date nights, hoping to rekindle the flame.

Of course, this is not what Chantal had signed up for. As she heard stories of her fellow exchange students being pampered by their host families—going to barbecues and county fairs, visiting historic sites throughout New England—poor Chantal stayed holed up in my sister's ultramodern glass house in the middle of nowhere, gazing through the windows at the wooded hillside and the Connecticut River far below, a crying baby in her arms.

Given my own experience with host families in France, I sympathized with Chantal. One day over lunch, as the baby wailed in the background, my sister and her husband hurled insults at each other with poor Chantal caught in the middle. "*Sauvez-moi*" (Save me) she mouthed to me in French.

"*J'ai très désolé*" (I have so sorry), I said, struggling with my limited French.

When my sister heard me speaking French, the fact that my vocabulary consisted of a few dozen words was enough to convince her that I actually spoke it fluently.

"ISN'T IT GREAT THAT MY BROTHER CAN SPEAK TO YOU IN YOUR NATIVE TONGUE?" my sister shouted at Chantal.

"Glad someone can," her shithead husband chimed in. "Her English is atrocious!"

Chantal looked at me with tears in her eyes, having no idea what anyone was saying. I gave her a reassuring smile, then said in my Pidgin French, "Don't sad, Chantal. I save you yesterday." (Of course, I meant "tomorrow.")

The next day I took Chantal into town. We laughed and made fools of ourselves as we talked baby-talk over milkshakes at the local Friendly's restaurant. That's when I learned that you could actually get by pretty well with just a couple dozen words. And that the most important part about language was making a human *connection*.

All that I'd learned about language was put to the test when I arrived in France for the first time with the Junior Year Abroad program. I was surprised to learn that Parisians, who moved about freely and weren't holed up in glass houses in the middle of the woods, weren't as patient and forgiving as Chantal had been. They spoke quickly. Very quickly. And even when I was able to get a Parisian to slow down, I still couldn't understand what he or she was saying.

What the hell? I thought.

Adding to the mystery, in our morning French classes in the dark and dank basement of our youth hostel, I seemed to be fluent—on paper at least. Especially when it came to verb conjugation. (Man, I *loved* that stuff!) But for some reason, once I crawled out of the dungeon and entered the real world, the language on the streets sounded nothing like what I learned in class. Oh, how I would have given my left *boulette* just to be able to speak *half* as well as a French six-year-old!

Gift? What gift? The truth was I had no such thing. Thankfully, I was about to take a pair of classes that would help take *mon français* to a whole new level.

Before arriving at the Université de Rouen, I had never heard of *la dictée* before. It turned out to be the first class in nearly nine years that truly helped my *français* reach a respectable level. Not surprising since *la dictée* is one of the ways French kids learn French, which made me wonder: *Why wasn't this method part of the language curriculum back when I was a student in the States?*

Basically, *la dictée* works like this: The teacher chooses a text to read out loud to the class, such as a poem or an excerpt from a classic French novel. The students must then write down what they hear, a next-to-impossible task given that so many letters in French are completely silent. For example, as the teacher read the text, a student might ask, "How do you spell *houleux* (stormy)?" to which the teacher would snap back, *"Comme ça se prononce!"* (The way it's pronounced!)

But of course, that's absurd since half the letters in *houleux* are *not* pronounced. Undaunted, the teacher would stare at the student and say, "Watch my lips. I will articulate the word for you: *ou-le*. Voilà! Now you can write down *houleux!*"

Within a few months, though, something magical happened. For reasons I still can't explain, a light bulb suddenly went off in my head, and I started seeing the words in my mind as they were spoken—even with all those silent letters. On top of that, *la dictée* forced me to decipher where one French word ended and another began—no small feat considering that, in addition to all those silent letters, the French language has no stressed syllables. That's why to the beginner, every French sentence ends up sounding like one long, incomprehensible monotone. And don't even get me started on those bloody *liaisons. Très dangereux!*

Which brings me to perhaps the best French class I've ever taken: *Phonétiques* with Madame Bâtard (which, *oui*, means "Bastard"). With her flaming orange hair and hoarse smoker's voice, Madame taught us that the secret to speaking French was training your ear to hear the subtle differences among the forty or so phonemes—or individual sounds—that exist in the French language. It was a lot like learning music. But as anyone who has tried to learn French knows, if your pronunciation is just slightly off, nobody will be able to understand you. Or even worse, they *will* understand you. But not in the way you intended.

Of course, this can lead to a lot of embarrassing situations. Once during Bastille Day celebrations, I confused the word for "firecracker" (*pétard*) with a similar sounding word, *pédé*. I couldn't understand why my French friends were laughing hysterically when I yelled out, "Careful everybody! Gay people are exploding in the streets!"

In our phonetics class, Madame Bâtard was such a frightening presence, she'd often send students into tears, never letting up until our pronunciation was absolutely perfect. Heaven help us if we didn't croak out our *r*'s from deep inside our throat, or if we failed to snuff out "nasal vowels" from deep inside our nose. (An example of a nasal vowel is the *en* in Rouen. The *en* is similar to the sound of being kicked in the gut—*uunh*!—but with the *n* being silent.)

Monday's class was the worst. Madame Bâtard would make students stand up in front of the room and recount what they'd done over the weekend. Of course, it was already hard enough to come up with the right vocabulary, the right verb conjugation, and that ol' ballbuster—masculine and feminine. But having Madame on the sidelines, ready to pounce at the slightest mistake, made the situation unbearable.

Madame Bâtard seemed to take particular pleasure in riling up Cara, a straight A student who, much to her dismay, found herself in a country that didn't give out A's in class. *Ever.* (In the French grading system, students are lucky to get what amounts to a D in America.) Worried about tarnishing her perfect grade point average, Cara was always on the verge of an emotional meltdown. Wrong class to be in.

"Miss Cara," Madame Bâtard said one rainy Monday morning *en français* as she took a long drag off her cigarette. "Would you give us the pleasure of recounting your grand adventures in Rouen this weekend?"

"Well," Cara said excitedly in her best French, "Saturday I went to the museum! And then, *um* . . ."

"*Er!*" Madame Bâtard shouted.

Cara looked confused, but soldiered on, speaking in short nervous breaths. "And then . . . after the museum . . . I ate a *croque monsieur* for lunch and . . . *um* . . ."

"*Er!* Repeat!"

"*Um* . . ."

"*Er!*"

"*Um . . .*"

"*ER! ER! ERRRRRRR!*" Madame Bâtard growled as she pounded her fist on the desk. "There is no *um* in French! Only *errr!*"

Madame Bâtard's wrath was so all-encompassing she wouldn't even let us stammer incorrectly. But despite a few psychological scars, for me, Madame Bâtard was a blessing—albeit with a few inconvenient side effects: To this day, a *frisson* (chill) runs down my spine every time I hear an American say *um* instead of *er* as they valiantly struggle to speak the language of Molière.

Looking back now, I realize why it took me so long to learn the language. And why it was so painful. French is a bitch. (Or in the case of my phonetics class, a bastard.) But it can also be tantalizingly fun. Even more, studies show that speaking a second language can actually change your mind for the better, helping to ward off progressive diseases like Alzheimer's. (Although I wouldn't mind a little dose of that as far as Madame Bâtard was concerned.)

Anyway, nowadays the number one question American customers ask me at my diner is if I speak French.

"I'd better!" I say. "Since I've been living here for fifteen years."

"Yeah, well, I've been here for *twenty* and still can't speak the damn language. Do you have any tips that can help me?"

Actually, I do. For what it's worth, here are a few things I've picked up over the years, and that I wish someone had told me. Follow them and before long—once you've put in your ten thousand hours of practice, of course—you'll get to hear people say: "Wow! You obviously have a gift for languages!" It's up to you whether to tell them the truth or not.

The five-minute rule. As a beginner, it can be very intimidating to speak French with a real French person, especially one who chatters on as if they've just drunk five espressos. Or even worse, speaks better English than you speak French. Once you've managed to get them to "*parler lentement s'il vous plaît*" (speak slowly, please), resist the urge to default to English just because it's easier than struggling with French.

I've seen this happen with many of my expat friends; they simply give up too soon. I'm convinced that there's a part of the brain that needs at least five to ten minutes to warm up before it gets into the groove. Once it does, French words will start popping into your head, which will give you a slight rush, encouraging you to keep going, which in turn fills your brain with even more vocabulary, round and round, ad infinitum. It's a win-win situation!

Learn a French song (*ou deux ou trois*). It makes sense since learning a new language is a lot like learning music. There's a rhythm and tone that's picked up and processed by a sensitive ear. And much like with music, it takes a lot of practice.

Try memorizing a classic French song. Or if you're feeling especially daring, a *risqué* song you've picked up from your French pals after downing a few cognacs. I've found that such songs are the most fun way to learn *argot* (slang), that all-important, and surprisingly practical side of everyday language that's rarely taught in school. My favorite "dirty ditty" starts off, "*Un dimanche matin, avec ma putain, sur ma mobylette . . .*" which is about a sexy Sunday morning drive on a scooter with a lady of the night that only gets more R-rated with every refrain.

Memorizing a French song will not only help with your pronunciation, it will improve your comprehension, too. Soon, in everyday conversation you'll find yourself saying, "Hmm, that doesn't sound right." That's much more organic than saying, "Hmm, is that the correct conjugation of the third person subjunctive of that irregular verb?" Sure, language rules are important. But honestly, did you learn to speak your mother tongue by looking at a chart of verb conjugations? Do most people even know what the subjunctive tense is? Yet we learn our native language as toddlers through songs and rhymes in nursery school, so start singing!

For millennia, human beings communicated by verbal language only, long before some egghead caveperson decided that language needed to be written down and imposed with strict grammatical rules. I have a theory that the reason why there are so many irregularities in language (especially with verbs) boils down to what *sounds* best. Only afterward did professor caveman determine that a rule (which he or she imposed in the first place) had been "broken."

Recite a poem, a piece of literature, or my favorite—make up your own script. As a former screenwriter, I would often write up a scene in French, such as shopping at an outdoor market or desperately trying to get a waiter's attention. After supplying the scenario with questions and potential answers, I'd memorize it and then try it out in the real world. As Shakespeare said, "All the world's a stage," so start learning your lines!

French in action. There was a great show on PBS years ago that was called just that—*French in Action*. I'm convinced that a relatively small percentage of learning a language comes from sitting down, either in a class or with a tutor. Instead, get off your butt and *live* the language. You're much more likely to remember vocabulary (and especially verbs) when you're active. I can recall many moments in my life when I was either shopping or visiting a museum with a French friend and learned a specific word or fun idiom.

By getting out and living, I learned the French expression for a snobby person: someone who thinks he or she "farts higher than their asshole." Or when a customer is being unrelentingly nitpicky, they're trying to "sodomize house flies." (Think of how unfeasible that is and you'll get the idea.) And finally, thanks to French in action, I'll never confuse a firecracker with an exploding homosexual ever again.

Learn phonetics. Just to be clear, when I say "phonetics" I mean the forty-plus individual sounds in the French language—not the funny way those sounds are written up in the dictionary. Learning to pronounce a small number of phonemes correctly is way less intimidating than learning how to pronounce thousands of French words individually.

Before Madame Bâtard, I never knew there was a subtle difference between the *ay* sound in *j'ai* and the *ay* sound in *parlé*. That tiny distinction will do wonders for your pronunciation and comprehension. And just wait until you see the miracles that'll happen once you learn the three ways to pronounce those pesky French *R*'s—not to mention my favorite: the difference between *ou* and *u*. (Think of how a Cuban pronounces their country, Cuba [like Coo-ba], compared to how a gringo does.)

Learn the dreaded "masculine and feminine" the French way! It's already crazy enough that words in French have a sex. But what they never teach you is that French people don't *memorize* gender; for them, it's part of the word. This is where "language as music" can be so helpful. I learned from Julien that I should never ask if a noun is with a *le* or *la*.

Instead, ask if the word is with *un* or *une*. For example, "*Est-ce que c'est un table ou une table?*" (Is it *a* [masc.] table or *a* [fem.] table?) The reason for this is French people learn the gender of a noun via *un* or *une*, not *le* or *la*. If you make this subtle shift, soon your well-trained ear will be able to hear what sounds right and what doesn't. "*Mais bien sûr,*" you'll find yourself saying. "It's *une* table not *un* table!"

Le "Red Pen" Is Your Friend. The French *love* correcting you. Especially when you mess up their language. Many Americans are put off by this. They think it's rude. Or they take it way too personally. (*Why are they being so mean to me?!*) Here's another way of looking at it: *You have a French teacher for free!* Everywhere. When a French person points out that a vagina is masculine, ("*C'est* un *vagin!*") and the male equivalent is feminine ("*C'est* une *bite!*") simply smile and say, "*Merci.* I stand corrected." Then stand there, happily corrected. Rinse. Repeat. Until one day no one corrects you anymore.

Another important point: language is *cultural.* Since France is a completely different culture, it's important to accept the fact that: *You will never be 100% French.* Get used to it. Celebrate your American-ness, your Canadian-ness, or your whatever-ness. From the first day I arrived in Paris, I dreamed of passing as a Frenchman. But as a half-Finnish, half-Polish, six-foot-three Scandi-slav, it didn't quite happen that way. Inevitably, a French person would hear me screw up a phoneme or a gender, and the jig was up.

No problem. Have fun with it. Play with the inevitable clichés that the French have about you: that you're a Coke-swilling, burger-munching cowboy with a machine gun. Then have fun surprising them by flipping their stereotypes on their head. Sing one of the Édith Piaf songs you've memorized. Quote Molière. My favorite is from *Candide* since the oft-cynical French already consider Americans to be hopelessly naïve: "*Tout est pour le mieux dans le meilleur des mondes possibles.*" In English: "All is for the best in the best of all possible worlds." Say this cheerful phrase to *un français* and watch him quiver. Optimism is a Frenchman's Kryptonite.

Which leads me to my last and most important tip:

Embrace your inner six-year-old. Throw out your critical mind. Bury your ego, your pride. Allow yourself to feel vulnerable. After all, that's how we evolve and grow, *n'est-ce pas?* Don't be ashamed to make horrendous mistakes. Talk baby talk. Play. Just like a six-year-old. Heck, look at it this way: how lucky you are to get to live your childhood all over again. For someone like me, whose formative years weren't exactly "La Vie en Rose," having a second childhood is a wonderful opportunity to get it right the second time around.

That said, I understand how badly you want to converse intelligently about deep, Important-With-A-Capital-*I* subjects like politics, religion, and the arts. But be patient. That day will come. But for now, get rid of the hang-up of sounding like a six-year-old. I hate to break it to you, but to much of the world, Americans already sound like six-year-olds. ("We're number one!" "Build the wall!" "It's *my* money!" Need I say more?) From my own experience, I've found that the French will actually be impressed to hear you sounding like a six-year-old, because you'll be doing it in another language—*their* language.

A French friend of mine who's been living in the States for years loves telling this joke: "What do you call someone in America who speaks a second language?" Answer: "A tourist."

Prove that snarky Frenchman wrong! Learn his language. If you do, you'll happily remind him that, compared to other countries in Europe (Finland, for example), the French are far less likely to speak a second language.

Then sit back and gloat like a six-year-old.

FOUR

The Pigeon Man of Paris

After a decade of running a successful business in Paris, it looked as if I was finally going to have a real home of my own. But first I needed to sell *beaucoup de* pancakes before I saved up enough money to put a down payment on a place. Only problem was, given the skyrocketing prices of real estate in Paris, I barely had enough left over to afford what amounted to a large walk-in closet.

But as is my nature, I chose to look on the bright side of things. Located in the hip and historic Marais district in the center of the city, the two-hundred-plus-year-old apartment had a cozy, functional fireplace (although I wasn't sure if it was legal to use it or not). Best of all, it included a large rooftop terrace, the kind that was extremely hard to find in Paris. Adding to the Old World charm, the only access to the terrace was by climbing up a ladder through a hole in the wood-beamed ceiling.

Now that spring had sprung, Julien and I couldn't wait to lounge on our rooftop oasis and grow organic vegetables in big box gardens. But before we had a chance to pick out which seeds to sow, a loud rumbling noise came from the street below. I ran over to the window to take a look. Six floors below, a brown Mercedes sedan pulled up to the curb, barely visible through the huge cloud of smoke spewing from its fractured tailpipe.

The driver parked in front of our building and shut off the engine. As soon as the smoke cleared, I got a better look at the Mercedes. The once luxury vehicle was now a banged-up, twisted heap of metal that would fit nicely in the modern sculpture garden at the nearby Pompidou Center museum.

After a moment, the driver's side door opened and out stepped an old man who had to be in his seventies. A cross between Quasimodo and Santa Claus, he was hunched over, sporting a bushy white beard and tattered gray trench coat. His yellow-stained fingernails were so long I could see them from six flights up. As if on a mission, the old man rushed over to the back of his car, opened the trunk and pulled out a shopping caddy. He then stuffed it with a burlap bag and raced off down the street.

Julien joined me by the window just as the old man disappeared around the corner. "Where's he going in such a hurry?" I wondered.

Bright and early the next morning, the roar of the Mercedes's engine jolted me awake. I crawled out of bed to see if *le vieux* (or the "old guy" as Julien and I now called him) was leaving. He was not. Instead, he kept his engine running for about twenty minutes, revving it up from time to time. A stream of suffocating blue-black smoke poured out of the exhaust pipe, rising up the façade of our building. I shut the windows just in time as the hazy cloud continued climbing up, finally settling like a thick bowl of soup atop our rooftop terrace.

I looked over at Julien who was sound asleep. Tall and debonair, Julien had Cary Grant good looks and impeccable style, his wardrobe never having known a wrinkle. *Oh, how I wished I could sleep like him*, I thought as I looked at my *chéri* lying there peaceably. But I'd always been a light sleeper, and the old man and his smog-spewing Mercedes weren't helping any.

And it only got worse from there.

Over the next several weeks, I noticed that *le vieux* had a very precise routine. Every morning at 7:00 A.M. sharp, he'd stand outside his Mercedes, getting ready for what I deduced was his day job. He'd open up the trunk and pull out his shopping caddy, stuffing it with a couple of burlap bags filled with God knows what. By 6:00 P.M., he'd be back at his car again, this time the burlap bags empty. Strangely, by the next morning, the bags would be filled up again.

As the mystery deepened, I decided to investigate. Approaching the Mercedes, I noticed two letters in the upper left-hand corner of his license plate: *I* and *T.* I guessed that they stood for Italy. Next, stuffed under the driver's side windshield wiper were dozens of unpaid parking tickets. *How strange*, I thought. Paris was very Draconian when it came to parking violations. Normally after just a couple of tickets, the car would have been towed. Why hadn't the Mercedes? Did *le vieux* have an in with the cops?

The detective in me continued. Viewed from up close the Mercedes was in even worse shape than I'd thought. Three of its four tires were flat and the windshield cracked. In true hoarder fashion, nearly every inch of the car was crammed with his personal effects. Judging from the evidence, it certainly looked as if the old man was living in his car.

At that moment, I felt sympathy for *le vieux*. I knew firsthand what it felt like to be homeless. When I was sixteen, my dad sat me down in our living room, lit up a More cigarette and said, without a hint of warmth or remorse in his voice, that he was leaving the state to move in with his blond-wigged girlfriend, Linda. "You're on your own, kid."

Fortunately, my friends let me couch hop until I graduated from high school. But by my freshman year at UConn, my situation had gotten much worse. Unbeknownst to me, once finals were over, all the dorms closed up for the summer. Suddenly, I had nowhere to go, which meant I was homeless again. I ended up squatting in an empty frat house and collecting cans off the street, which I would cash in for five cents a pop. It allowed me to earn enough money to buy a jar of peanut butter and a loaf of bread to feed me for the week.

Back in the present, I looked at the banged-up Mercedes and felt a kind of kinship with *le vieux*. With his flat tires and unpaid parking tickets, clearly he wasn't going anywhere soon. Sure, there'd be a few inconveniences, such as the days when the old man ran his car engine. The degree to which Julien and I suffocated from the exhaust fumes depended on the weather. During the spring months, there was often a cool and refreshing breeze that would blow the toxic cloud away. But by the summer, just as our garden was taking hold, the air turned muggy and still, making it difficult to breathe.

But no matter. I refused to be like one of those NIMBY schmucks I'd heard about back in the States. As a progressive who came from humble beginnings, I found their acronym, "Not In My Back Yard" to be extremely intolerant to those less fortunate. But, of course, that's because I'd never been in their shoes. Continuing with the same analogy, it wouldn't be long before the shoe was on the other foot—so to speak—and my strongest, most compassionate beliefs would be put to the test.

"Hey, Julien, take a look at this," I said, my voice low.

Julien climbed down the ladder from our rooftop garden, washed his dirt-stained hands and joined me by the window.

"See that lady down there?" I pointed. "She and *le vieux* have been talking for over an hour."

Standing by the Mercedes was a thin woman in her forties. She wore bright red and white zebra-style glasses and talked passionately with the old man.

"Is she a social worker, you think?" I asked Julien.

"Probably not. Too nicely dressed."

Good point. I hadn't noticed the woman's designer dress and matching handbag. So very bourgeois—yet with a touch of a certain "*je ne sais quoi*."

"Maybe she works for the government then? The upper echelons?"

"*J'sais pas.* Have you ever seen a *fonctionnaire* with that much energy?"

Indeed, I'd never seen a civil servant so animated, ever. But still, a part of me was hoping she was there to help. Maybe find *le vieux* some housing. Or at the very least, a shelter with a shower and a hot meal.

I stared at the woman, searching for more clues. There were none. After a moment, she made a quick gesture with her head indicating she was done with their conversation. She shook the old man's hand, spun around on her heels (Gucci, I think) and was gone.

Julien looked at me as I stared out the window and laughed. "Careful, kiddo," he said. "I think you might be becoming a tad obsessed."

"Hmm, you think?"

A few days later, as I headed home after work, I sensed that something was different. It took a moment to hit me: The Mercedes was gone! I couldn't believe it. After so many months of having *le vieux* as a neighbor, I was filled with a myriad of emotions: elation that Julien and I would be able to breathe fresh air again; a strange melancholy left behind by the man's absence; and finally, a sense of relief that perhaps my intuition had been right—that the bourgeois woman had found the old man a home after all.

That turned out to be only partially true.

The next day, parked in the exact same spot, the Mercedes was replaced by a brand-new, shiny white van. The old man stood next to the open sliding side door, supervising a young carpenter who worked away inside.

All week long, with the din of a buzz saw and the whirr of a Makita, the carpenter completely pimped out the van, filling it with custom-made wooden shelves and cabinets. Once the renovations were complete, the old man placed rows and rows of empty shoeboxes on the shelves, each one punctured with small round holes. Next, he stuffed the cabinets with as many burlap bags as he could squeeze in.

Settled in now, the old man got up bright and early the next morning and went straight to work. He grabbed one of the burlap bags and reached inside. For the first time I could see what was in them: birdseed. The old man grabbed a handful and started scattering it everywhere: on the sidewalk, on the street, and even underneath his vehicle.

Pigeons must have an extraordinary sense of sight and/or smell because within minutes, dozens of them had swooped down from on high and landed beside his van, excitedly pecking away at the birdfeed. Being a creature of habit, the old man kept to the same routine as before, except with one slight change: before heading off to his secret 9–5 job elsewhere, he now included *two* feeding times for the birds, one at 8:00 A.M. and another at 6:00 P.M.

Like *le vieux*, pigeons were creatures of habit too, prone to Pavlovian conditioning. With a free meal waiting for them every morning, it was only a matter of time before more and more birds began showing up—and right at the crack of dawn. They would perch themselves on the windowsills of the first floor apartment, overlooking the van, waiting for the old man to wake up and feed them.

Naturally, word-of-beak spread like wildfire. Soon, there were too many birds to fit on just the first floor's windowsill. They needed the second floor. Then the third, fourth, and fifth. And finally, the sixth—our floor. With no more windowsills left, the massive flock spilled onto the rooftops, including the zinc roof directly above the bedroom area of our small studio.

Until moving to Paris, I didn't realize how far north the city was—basically the same longitude as Nova Scotia. That means the sun rises *really* early in the summer, with the first light of dawn appearing on the horizon by 5:00 A.M. Not so coincidentally, that was also the time I was being awoken by the pitter-patter of little feet atop our zinc roof.

"Do you hear that?" I asked Julien.

As usual, he was fast asleep. I shook him once. Then twice.

"*Quoi?*" he mumbled.

"Pigeons. They're on our roof again."

Unfazed, Julien reached into the little drawer of his nightstand and pulled out a pair of earplugs. "Try these, kiddo." He rolled over, covered his head with his pillow then quickly fell back to sleep.

Of course, since I was a light sleeper, even with earplugs I could still hear the *click-click-click* of little footsteps—and worse—the sexed-up cooing of pigeons in heat. In just a few weeks, the pigeon man (as we now called him), had managed to attract hundreds of birds who were feeling quite at home roosting on every ledge, windowsill, and rooftop in sight. Sadly, the once beautiful zinc roofs and limestone façades of the 17th-century manor homes that made up our historic *quartier* were now covered with gooey white pigeon poop, which turned a crusty green-brown as it baked in the sun.

And did I mention the smell? Long gone were the cool spring breezes that swept the stench away. Instead, we were approaching the harvest season, when the air was at its haziest and most humid. No matter how many times we hosed down the *merde*, the smell didn't go away. How I longed for a summer thunderstorm and the cleansing rain that came with it. But, alas, Paris was in the middle of a record drought, with no relief in sight.

Between the mounting *merde* and not being able to get a good night's sleep, I was starting to reach the breaking point. But I wasn't alone. One morning, I heard yelling coming from outside. I ran over to the window. On the sidewalk below, a stout woman in her seventies was in the middle of confronting the pigeon man.

Fearless and in his face, the elderly woman let him know, in no uncertain terms, that she had reached her "*limite*" and was "blowing a fuse" because he and his dirty pigeons had "degraded the neighborhood" as well as the "tranquility of the *quartier*."

The pigeon man responded by growling like a dog and charging after her.

"*Vous êtes fou!*" (You're crazy!), the old woman screamed as she hightailed it down the sidewalk, just barely dodging the wads of spit the pigeon man was sending her way.

I was quickly losing sympathy for the pigeon man.

Unfortunately, *l'homme pigeon* was having a negative effect on my personal life as well. As the tension built, our tiny studio apartment began to feel even tinier. With no separate rooms for us to get away from each other, Julien and I found ourselves literally walking on each other's toes, like two birds in a cramped cage.

"What this relationship needs is a wall!" I blurted out one night, causing Julien to stare at me a moment, before we both burst out laughing, lest we break into tears.

Clearly, something had to be done. But what? I didn't want to sell the place; I'd worked too long and hard to finally have a home of my own. Plus, I'd barely put a dent in the mortgage.

"What if we start a petition," I said to Julien one day as the sound of cooing drowned out our conversation.

"Hmm, not a bad idea," Julien said. "But check with the *syndic* first. Get their advice."

In France, the *syndic de copropriété* was the equivalent to a building association (HOAC) in the States. As a business owner in Paris, I knew how important it was to follow the proper procedures. That night I sent an email to the *président* of the *syndic* to set up a rendezvous.

Bearded and soft-spoken, Monsieur Potiron (which meant "pumpkin" in French) met me in front of my building the following morning. With the pigeon man working away in his van across the street, I filled Mr. Pumpkin in on all that had happened over the past four months. He didn't seem surprised at all.

"Sounds like Giancarlo," Mr. Pumpkin said, his voice low so the pigeon man couldn't hear.

"*Giancarlo*? Is that his name?"

"Yes. But of course, you wouldn't know that. You're new to the neighborhood."

Mr. Pumpkin filled me in on the pigeon man's history. Originally from Italy, (hence the *IT* on his license plate), Giancarlo was a retired university professor. ("Liberal arts, I believe.") He'd been living in his Mercedes for years, most recently on the rue des Archives, just a couple blocks away.

"Why'd he move here?"

"Who knows," Mr. Pumpkin shrugged. "A change of scenery perhaps?"

I was curious to find out how a former university professor could end up living in his car—especially in France, with its generous and humane safety net.

"Oh, that's a looong story," Mr. Pumpkin said.

Turns out, after his retirement, Giancarlo had been living in an "HLM," a form of subsidized housing. HLMs were so in demand, people got onto waiting lists that took years before a slot opened up. Giancarlo had been one of the lucky ones.

Mr. Pumpkin couldn't recall when Giancarlo developed his love of pigeons, but it ultimately led to his getting deep in the *merde* with his neighbors. Literally.

"Giancarlo started feeding pigeons on his porch. Just a few at first. But soon the birds were everywhere; living with him in his apartment, invading his neighbors' balconies . . ."

I had no problem visualizing Mr. Pumpkin's story. All I had to do was look up at the hundreds of pigeons perched on my own building.

Mr. Pumping continued, "Eventually, the neighbors were so fed up they started a petition, stating that the pigeons were destroying their property. But that didn't work."

My heart sank. *So much for the petition I wanted to start.*

"Was there anything the neighbors could do?" I asked, afraid of the answer.

Mr. Pumpkin nodded and said that the tenants ended up taking Giancarlo to court on the grounds that the unsanitary birds were endangering their health. The case dragged on for years, but eventually the pigeon man was evicted.

"And to think," Mr. Pumpkin said. "All Giancarlo had to do was stop feeding the pigeons, and he'd still have an actual roof over his head."

Mr. Pumpkin and I looked over at the pigeon man. For the first time, I was able to see what was inside the shoeboxes. Baby pigeons. Not only did the van serve as Giancarlo's home, it had also become a mini *pigeonerie* where the old man could raise future generations of birds to poop all over the neighborhood for years to come.

"There's still one thing I haven't figured out," I said. "How'd he afford to buy a new van? Did he have a secret stash hidden somewhere?"

"Oh, *that*," Mr. Pumpkin chuckled. "You can thank the *bobos* for that."

Although I knew what a *bobo* was—an annoying cross between a *bourgeois* and a *bohémien* (aka the idle rich who liked to push their causes onto everyone else)—I still didn't see what they had to do with any of this.

"Well," Mr. Pumpkin explained. "A bunch of bobos—who don't even live in the *quartier* by the way—got together and decided to make Giancarlo their *cause célèbre*. They set up a Facebook page and a 'Fund-me' account to raise money to buy him a new van."

Of course! That explained the bourgeois woman with the Gucci shoes whom I'd only *half* figured out: the "*je ne sais quoi*" part was her *bohémien* side.

"Wait, it gets even more absurd," Mr. Pumpkin smiled as if getting a thrill out of telling me this. "The *bobos* also raised money to pay for Giancarlo's parking tickets, as well as his birdfeed, which they arranged to have delivered to his van twice a week."

I stared at the president of the *syndic*, dumbfounded. Before I had a chance to respond, Mr. Pumpkin said he had to get going. I couldn't let our meeting end without asking one last question: "Is there *anything* we can do?"

"Well, we could call a special meeting with the other homeowners and propose installing anti-pigeon wire on all the ledges. But before doing that, we'd have to commission a study that shows no pigeons will be harmed in the process."

"Uh . . . how about something that won't take *years*?"

Mr. Pumpkin stood there, stumped.

"You know what," I said. "Why don't I just talk to the pigeon man myself? Appeal to his humanity. In the end, we all have to find a way to live together in this crowded city, *n'est-ce pas?*"

"*Non, non, non, non, non!*" Mr. Pumpkin said, his face turning red. "Whatever you do, don't talk to Giancarlo. He gets upset very easily. If a *bobo* sees you getting him all riled up, they'll report you to the authorities for harassment!"

"Seriously?" I said, gesturing toward the hundreds of pigeons shitting on every available space in sight. "And what do you call this?!"

That night, when Julien came home I told him all about my meeting with the president of the *syndic*, and how I had suggested having a talk with Giancarlo.

"Oh, I already spoke to the pigeon man," Julien said.

"Really? When?"

"Just now. Before I came upstairs."

"What did you say?"

"I reminded him that he's not alone in this world. That he has to be respectful of his neighbors."

"And what did *he* say?"

"Nothing. He just spat on me."

The next morning I got up bright and early to go for a walk, to escape the nerve-racking sound of nonstop cooing. I hoped that if I emptied my head, a brilliant idea about what to do next would suddenly enter my mind. It didn't.

All day long I couldn't concentrate. Since it was a slow day at work, I decided to head home earlier than usual. I was so glad I did.

It was a little before 6:00 P.M. I was walking up rue des Archives, turned left onto my street, when something up ahead caught my eye. Like in a horror film, a huge black cloud rose up from behind the Pompidou Center. But this was no ordinary cloud. It was alive, darting left, then right, as if of one mind. As it got closer, I could finally make out what it was: a huge flock of pigeons heading directly toward my apartment building.

As if in perfect sync, the pigeon man rounded the corner just as the flock of birds swooped down to join him. *So that's where all the pigeons have been coming from*, I thought. Since I rarely got home this early, I'd never had the chance to see them from this vantage point nor the precise moment they arrived for their six o'clock feeding.

It was time for me to investigate further.

The next day, like clockwork, the pigeon man finished his 8:00 A.M. feeding, then grabbed his caddy and took off down the street, taking a right onto rue du Temple. I followed after him.

At the next side street, the old man made a stop in front of a Carrefour supermarket. There he dug into his burlap bag and pulled out several handfuls of pigeon feed, scattering them all over the sidewalk. He did the same thing at his next stop on rue du Renard. Like Hansel and Gretel with breadcrumbs, the pigeon man was leaving a trail of birdseed.

Moving along to a pedestrian street just north of the Pompidou Center, the pigeon man continued a couple blocks to his final destination: the northwest corner of the esplanade behind the museum. Under the shadow of the enormous vents popping out of the ground, the pigeon man opened the flap to his caddy. Right on cue, the familiar black cloud from the day before rose above the rooftops—but this time in the *opposite* direction—coming from my apartment building to join the pigeon man behind the Pompidou Center.

Holy merde! I thought. *Those are the exact same birds from* chez moi! But . . . if he was already feeding them here, why was he feeding them in front of my place, too? The more I tried to wrap my head around it, the more it didn't make any sense.

I looked back at the pigeon man as he reached into his caddy and began tossing birdfeed around like rice at a wedding. How could it be that I've walked past this spot a million times but never noticed that tucked away in the northwest corner was an old man surrounded by hundreds of pigeons?

Being a restaurateur, I noticed that the old man had set up shop directly in front of a row of family-owned cafés, all with huge outdoor terraces. I could only imagine how much Giancarlo and his avian friends were harming their business.

"How long has he been doing this?" I asked one of the restaurant owners.

"Ah, so many years, I've lost count."

"Have you tried to stop him?"

"But of course!" the restaurant owner said in exasperation. "In every conceivable way! Why, just last year, my *confrères* and I were sure we had the old man beat. We went to the mayor's office with a *dossier* proving that all the *merde* from his pigeons was destroying the vents of the Pompidou Center—one of France's most important cultural landmarks. But for some reason, no action was taken!"

I felt the restaurateur's pain. I knew firsthand how hard it was to stay afloat in the restaurant business. And here, through his actions, one man, the pigeon man, had the power to bring down an entire fleet.

There had to be something I could do to stop him. And not just for me; for my fellow restaurateurs and all my neighbors who shared in the misery, including the elderly woman whom Giancarlo had spit on, as well as my very own *chéri*. But what could I do?

I stared at the pigeon man as he spun around in pure ecstasy, feeding his feathered friends. At that moment, I was reminded of something from my childhood, something that I'd completely forgotten about: I used to love birds. I mean *really* love birds.

My avian *amour* started when I was nine years old and living with Fast Eddie in Frenchtown. Lonely and craving affection, my only respite was the yellow bus that took me to school every day. There my warm and caring teacher, Mrs. Robataille, had set up incubators in the classroom, placing a dozen or so duck eggs on top of a soft bed of straw. Each student was given the responsibility of taking care of an egg, making sure the heat lamp never got too close and that the egg was rotated periodically.

From the moment I saw my egg wobble and a little beak poke through the eggshell, I was hooked. A maternal instinct must have been unleashed in me because as I held the little duckling, I wanted nothing more than to take care of it. I even convinced Mrs. Robataille to let me take *two* ducklings home. But Fast Eddie was not having it.

"Our apartment's too goddamn small for those filthy birds," he said. "Get rid of 'em!" I nodded, then went into my room and hid the ducks in a box. Luckily, my dad passed out shortly thereafter so I got to keep them.

For their daily diet, I fed the ducklings watered-down morsels of Wonder Bread three times a day until they outgrew their box. By that point, my dad was so fed up with their incessant quacking he contacted Mrs. Robataille, who kindly found a home for them on a farm the next town over. As I watched her drive away with my babies, I tried to be strong, but the absence of the ducks left a void in me that I just had to fill. Thus, for the next year and a half I turned my bedroom into a mini bird sanctuary/way station for lost and injured birds, starting with a pair of baby robins who had fallen out of their nest—or rather, were *kicked* out by their heartless mother. (At least that's what I convinced myself had really happened.)

My bird-saving days culminated one afternoon when, in front of my apartment building, Damien Purdy, a pimply-faced punk I recognized from the *really* bad part of town, held up a BB gun and started shooting at a flock of pigeons flying overhead. "What are you doing that for?" I screamed. I tried to stop him but wasn't quick enough. I watched in horror as one of the pigeons dropped from the sky, hitting the ground with a thud. I rushed over. The bird was still alive, but its wing was badly injured.

How could anybody do something like that, I thought. With tears in my eyes, I gently picked up the bird, vowing to take care of him until the day he'd be able to fly again.

From her porch across the street, Mrs. Jaycox, an eccentric old lady with hairy armpits that spilled out of her sleeveless muumuu, had, unbeknownst to me, witnessed the entire incident. Seeing how upset I was, she went down into her cellar and came back a few minutes later with a rusty, pint-size birdcage. "Here you go, Craigie," she said, handing it to me. "So as you can take care of your little friend there."

Over the next several weeks, I nursed the injured pigeon back to health, carrying him with me wherever I went. We became quite the fixture around town. One of my neighbors, a middle-aged stoner living in his mother's garage, even gave my pigeon a name, which he would shout out every time the two of us walked past: "Hey! Tripperrr!"

Soon word of boy and bird spread beyond the city limits. One day as I was walking along the sidewalk with Tripper, a fancy car pulled up alongside me. Out stepped a reporter from the big city newspaper. She asked if it she could take some pictures.

"Sure," I said, excitedly holding up my pigeon as the reporter clicked away. Here I was, barely out of the fourth grade, and already I was eager to get my fifteen minutes of fame. Years later, when I stumbled upon the photo, what struck me the most was how pitiful I looked—like a street urchin in a Dickens tale. I wore a tattered blue flannel shirt, my wild mane of blond hair reaching down to my shoulders. The only thing in sorrier shape than me was the pigeon I held in my hands, its battered wing stretching out in an attempt to fly away. And yet, despite it all, I had the biggest smile on my face.

Back at the Pompidou Center in Paris, I stared at the pigeon man. With his wild gray hair, tattered clothes, and beaming smile, he could have been me as a kid—only sixty years older. Just then, a strange feeling came over me: *How could I have forgotten I used to love birds so much?* Was it simply due to the passage of time? Or had I blocked that difficult period out of my mind?

At that moment, I knew what I had to do: talk to the pigeon man, despite the warning from Mr. Pumpkin. Perhaps if I spoke from my heart—maybe, just maybe—I'd be able to get through to him and stop the madness.

With much trepidation, I approached Giancarlo's van. After only a couple of months, it already looked ready for the junkyard. Gone was the shiny white paint, covered instead with all the colors of the rainbow. But not because the van was parked in the gay part of town. Rather, it had been tagged and retagged *ad infinitum* by local graffiti artists.

I waited until Giancarlo had finished his 6:00 P.M. feeding and was back inside his van before heading over to the side door, which was wide open. With his back to me, the old man filled water dishes for his baby pigeons, which I could see bobbing up and down inside the shoeboxes.

"*Bonsoir*," I said hesitantly, not sure how much—or if—he spoke any French.

Giancarlo turned around and looked at me, not saying a word. He had a *sang froid* look in his eyes that was very unsettling.

"Sorry to disturb you," I said. "But I live in that building right there, which kinda makes us neighbors, right? Anyway, I was hoping, if you had a moment, maybe we could have a little chat?"

I'm guessing it was because of the soft and soothing tone of my voice, but the pigeon man seemed to let down his guard, becoming a little subdued even. Interestingly enough, it was the same voice I'd used as a kid when visiting my mom in the mental hospital. (It was the only way to keep her calm.) I never imagined that such a sadly acquired skill from my childhood would turn out to be so useful as an adult.

Sensing an opening, I told the pigeon man everything: how when I was a kid I used to love birds, just like him. How I'd raised them from babies, just like him. And how I'd nursed injured pigeons back to health. Just. Like. Him. Hell, I was such a bird lover, I could've been called "the Pigeon Kid of Connecticut!"

I detected a hint of a smile beneath the old man's beard. "*Monsieur*, I guess what I'm trying to say is . . . As much as you and I love birds, we have to remember that we live in a city. A very *crowded* city. That means we have to find a way to live together somehow, *n'est-ce pas?*"

After a long pause, the pigeon man finally spoke. "*Oui, je comprends.*"

"*C'est bon, monsieur!*" I said. "May I ask you a *petite question*: why do you feed the pigeons here, in front of my apartment, when you already feed them at the Pompidou Center?"

"No, no, no," Giancarlo said, starting to get agitated. "They're not the same birds." He pointed at the pigeons perched on the windowsills above us.

"These ones come from over *there*." Giancarlo pointed east, in the opposite direction of Pompidou.

Of course, having seen the cloud of pigeons with my own eyes, I knew this wasn't true. I also knew it made no sense to argue the point; it would only cause me to lose any ground I'd gained with the pigeon man. Thinking quickly, I said, "Then in that case, why not feed the birds over there?" I pointed. Coincidentally, it also happened to be the same direction from whence came the *bobo* lady in the Gucci pumps. Oh, how I wished I had her address so I could send the pigeon man to *her* place. To share the love.

The pigeon man looked to where I was pointing. He seemed to be considering the idea, as if all he needed was one last nudge. "It'll be good for the birds to take a little tour of the neighborhood, *n'est-ce pas*? One week over there. Another week *way* over there. You could even try another *arrondissement*! How fun would that be?!"

I could feel my face getting flushed with excitement. The pigeon man stared at me. From his blank expression, I realized I'd lost my soft and soothing voice. I took a deep breath, struggling to get it back.

"What I'm trying to say is: I need your help, *Monsieur*. Please. I haven't been able to sleep in months. It's slowly killing me."

The pigeon man nodded then grabbed the sliding door to his van. "*Bonne nuit*," (good night), he said, slamming the door shut.

"Well, at least he didn't spit on you," Julien said as he watered the box gardens on our rooftop terrace a short time later. "That's a start!"

"I'm serious, Julien. I really felt we made a connection. Just think of what this could mean; our nightmare may soon be over."

"Hmm, guess we'll see soon enough," Julien shrugged in that nonchalant French way that drove me crazy.

"You're unbelievable. How can you be so calm about this?"

Julien smiled, then stood up and put his arm around me, gesturing westward. The autumn sun hugged the horizon, glowing a bright pink and orange. "Take a look at that sunset, kiddo. *C'est magnifique, n'est-ce pas?*"

I nodded. It was indeed *magnifique,* the colors becoming more intense with each passing minute.

Just then, a flock of pigeons appeared on the horizon, swooping up and down like a school of fish, heading straight toward our rooftop garden. Ever so calmly, Julien removed his flip-flops and slapped them together several times, making a loud *plap-plap-plap* sound. The pigeons freaked out, did a quick U-turn, then flew off in the opposite direction, disappearing behind the Pompidou Center.

Julien smiled, satisfied with himself. "Works every time."

At 5:00 A.M. sharp the next morning, I was awoken by the familiar pitter-patter of pronged feet on our zinc roof. I sprung out of bed. *"Meeeer-de!"*

As I made my way toward the window, I tried to think of what large and heavy object we had in the apartment that I could hurl down at the pigeon man.

Oh, yeah. It had gotten *that* bad.

At the window, I looked down at the street below. I couldn't believe my eyes. The van was gone!

"Julien! Wake up!"

Julien yawned as he crawled out of bed and came over to the window.

"Look!" I pointed. "He's gone! I knew if I just appealed to his humanity . . ."

"Incroyable," Julien said, genuinely impressed.

"You know what makes me feel the most proud, though? Knowing that, as an American, I could use diplomacy to avoid conflict and find a peaceful solution."

"Even with an Italian!" Julien added. "Good job, kiddo!"

I looked down at the parking spot where the van had been. In its place was a bright red Volvo, the same color as the designer glasses worn by the *bobo* lady. I wondered if the car belonged to her.

"Look. There's a bunch of pigeons underneath the Volvo," I said to Julien. "And everywhere else for that matter."

"C'est normal," Julien said. "They've been conditioned. It'll probably take a while before they realize the old man isn't there to feed them."

"Yeah, well, I say we *de*-condition them. Starting right now. Gimme your flip-flops."

Julien handed them to me. I held them out the window and slapped them together. *Plap-plap-plap*! As before, the pigeons freaked out, leaping off the windowsills and flying full speed toward the Pompidou Center. I smiled smugly at Julien. But my victory lap was brief. I watched in dread as the cloud of pigeons circled back around like a boomerang, before heading straight back to our building, landing exactly where they had started.

"But— . . . Wha— . . ." I looked at Julien flabbergasted as I held up his flip-flops. "How come it works for you and not for me?"

Julien placed his hands on my shoulder and stared at me with his big brown eyes. "*Chéri*, I mean this in the nicest possible way: Nobody's a-scared of you."

"That's *afraid*, not a-scared. And besides, it's not true," I said, trying to block out of my mind all the employees who'd taken advantage of me over the years. "I can be *fierce* if I have to be!"

Julien rubbed my belly, causing me to melt like a popsicle. "*Bien sûr,* baby. *Bien sûr.*"

Later that morning, as I left my building and passed by the red Volvo where Giancarlo's van had been, I literally skipped with joy, humming the Seven Dwarves' infamous ode to capitalism: *Hi-ho, hi-ho, it's off to work I go!* I felt giddy just thinking about how much better my life would be *sans* the pigeon man: How I'd be able to open the windows whenever I wanted; lounge naked on the rooftop terrace if I chose to; and *sleep—mon dieu—*I imagined a deep, sweet sleep that lasted until well after the sun had risen.

But before any of that could happen, I'd have to be patient. The *de*-conditioning of the pigeons was taking much longer than expected. Days went by, but the birds didn't budge. Most puzzling, a bunch of pigeons still gathered *underneath* the cars that were parked where the van had been. Occasionally, one of them would waddle into the middle of the road and get run over by a passing car, leaving a flattened piece of pavement pizza *au pigeon*.

"Why won't they leave?" I asked Julien one muggy afternoon when I desperately wanted to open the windows. "It's like the pigeon man laced their bird feed with crack, and now they're totally addicted."

If only the problem had been an opiate dependency. It turned out to be worse than that. I made the discovery on my way home from work after a particularly rough day. I'd just found out that one of my favorite employees had been stealing from the diner. As if that weren't bad enough, she'd also been proudly posting pictures of her heist on Facebook. Of course, this being France, it *still* wasn't sufficient grounds to fire her.

As I rounded the corner to my street, I saw the familiar black cloud of pigeons circling above my apartment building. They seemed more excited than usual. *Oh, shit,* I thought, *is he back?* I quickened my pace. As I neared the apartment, I was relieved to see that the van was still gone.

I let out a sigh of relief then turned to enter my apartment building when out of the corner of my eye I spotted the tip of a hump behind a parked car across the street. It darted back and forth like some messed-up land shark.

I pulled out my iPhone, switched the camera to "video" then hit "record." Filming the scene live, I crossed the street, slipped between two parked cars and onto the sidewalk where I'd seen the hump. Through the screen of my iPhone, I could see the image of an old man hunched over, trying not to be seen. With his shopping caddy in tow, he moved quickly about, scattering handfuls of birdseed underneath the cars and onto the adjacent sidewalk, both of which—it suddenly dawned on me—were conveniently out of view from my apartment window.

"Giancarlo! What the hell?"

The pigeon man turned around and looked at me—right into the camera lens. His face said it all: Surprised. Guilty. *Busted.*

"How could you do this?!" I asked naively. A million thoughts raced through my head: *But we had a heart-to-heart . . . a real connection . . . I trusted you.*

I was about to ask the pigeon man how long he'd been doing this—sneaking around when I wasn't home and feeding the pigeons behind my back—when suddenly I figured out the answer all by myself:

"You son-of-a-bitch," I said. "You've been doing this the whole time, haven't you?"

The pigeon man revealed a big toothy grin and chuckled heartily, clearly getting a charge out of mocking me.

"Keep smiling, Giancarlo" I said, holding up my iPhone. "'Cause I got it all on video!"

At the mention of being filmed, the pigeon man's expression changed from mockery to rage. Just as he'd done to the old lady, he charged at me, growling. And just as he'd done to her and Julien, he fired a major loogie my way, which I dodged like Neo in *The Matrix*.

It took all my willpower not to charge back. Instead, I remembered what I'd been taught by a forest ranger in Yosemite if ever I was confronted by a bear: don't lie down and play dead; stand up on your tiptoes and make yourself appear as big as possible then yell as loud as you can. And that's exactly what I did.

"AYAYAHHHAYAA!"

The pigeon man stopped dead in his tracks. He looked scared as hell but held his ground. I did, too. Here we were, the old man and me, in a standoff in the middle of the sidewalk in the Marais. I could only imagine how crazy we looked.

I roared again, even louder. This time it worked. The old man backed away slowly, then turned around and trotted down the street with his shopping caddie trailing behind him. I held up my iPhone and yelled, "It's over, old man! You're going on YouTube!"

I burst through the front door of our apartment. "Julien, where are you? You won't believe what just happened!"

I looked around our studio apartment. It was empty.

Just then, I heard Julien's voice coming from the rooftop terrace. *"Oh, les salopards!"* (You little bastards!)

I climbed up the ladder and popped my head through the hole in the ceiling. Julien was standing beside the box gardens. Piles of dirt and torn up pieces of leafy vegetables were strewn about everywhere. The situation couldn't have been clearer: Giancarlo's pigeons had messed with Julien's kale. *Nobody* messes with Julien's kale.

With fire and fury in his eyes, Julien turned to me and said, "*C'est la guerre!*"

That was it! Let the battle begin: *The Pigeon Man vs. The Pancake Kid*. Like some warped, sorry-ass geek's superhero fantasy. French-style. Meaning . . .

It was *dossier* time!

The true Frenchman in Julien awakened at the mere mention of the word; "Did somebody say '*dossier*?!'"

It felt great to have the ire of a Frenchman on my side. Together Julien and I set about gathering as much documentation as possible to build our case. Along with the video I took of the pigeon man spitting at me, I filmed several more of him illegally feeding the pigeons in front of our apartment, being sure to note the date and time of each infraction. (The French love it when you bog down a dossier with tons of minute details.)

Next, I took pictures of all the damage done to my building as well as the surrounding buildings. I ended up taking more pictures of pigeon poop than I cared to imagine, employing my skills as a former filmmaker to create a kind of *montage de merde* that would have made Jean-Luc Godard proud.

Lastly, Julien and I supplied important facts and figures that gave our dossier weight. *Literally.* According to our calculations, the sheer volume of droppings produced by the pigeons came to a hefty 800–1,000 pounds a month. This figure was based on a case study of 200 birds (a low estimate) with a DPR (daily poop rate) of 30–50 times a day (a scientific fun fact). Now, that's a lotta *merde*.

As Julien and I prepared for our upcoming battle with the French authorities, all our energy was focused on one objective: ridding ourselves of the pigeon man. But seeing how obsessed we'd become, I suddenly felt a tinge of liberal guilt. Was I turning into the very person I once loathed? Was I becoming a NIMBY? No, it was much worse than that. I'd become a NOOGS (Not On Our Goddamn Sidewalk).

But, of course, the pigeon man had left me no choice. The day after our confrontation, he moved his van back to the exact same spot as before—as if he'd stayed up all night waiting for his spot to free up.

The next day, one thing became abundantly clear: the old man was digging in his heels, ready for a fight. Instead of limiting his feedings to two times a day—one at 8:00 A.M. and the other at 6:00 P.M.—he now started much earlier, at the crack of dawn, and continued all day long.

Same for the feeding area; like a mini tsunami, it spread out from under his van to every available inch of concrete in sight. Julien and I estimated that the quantity of birdfeed he was using must have increased by at least threefold—as did the pigeon population that, like fish in an aquarium, had no internal mechanism to stop them from eating themselves to death. Some pigeons were getting so fat they could barely lift off the ground when they tried to take flight.

"We better hurry up before the pigeons explode," I said to Julien as he put the final touches on our dossier, binding the pages together with a plastic spiral.

"Hmm, that's an idea," Julien said, holding up the dossier. "If we can't stop him with this, that'll be our plan B!"

"*Euuww.*" I cringed, unable to stop myself from grinning at the thought of exploding pigeons.

Our *dossier* complete, the next stop was the *commissariat* (police station) of the 4th *arrondissement*. Paris has so many beautiful buildings it's easy to overlook the ugly ones. Such was the case with the commissariat. Located near the Place de la Bastille, the building was a soulless block of crumbling concrete that contrasted sharply with the lovely Canal Saint-Martin flowing directly in front of it.

After a security check, Julien and I sat in the lobby, waiting for our rendezvous. Near the entrance, a potpourri of cops—male, female, black, white, and Arab—gathered in a circle, lost in animated conversation, their laughter echoing off the cold concrete walls.

I stared at them. "Aren't there, like, murders, robberies, and other important stuff the cops can be taking care of right now instead of chitchatting?"

"Ah, don't worry, *mon petit*," Julien said. "This is France. The robbers and murderers are probably gathered in a big circle right now themselves, doing exactly the same thing."

"Monsieur Carlson, Monsieur Chameroy," the receptionist interrupted us. "The officer will see you now."

The moment we entered the officer's cramped office, my first thought was we had to be in the wrong place. The walls were covered with posters of half-naked, muscular men in skimpy Speedos—some wearing even less. I knew we were in the Marais, but this was ridiculous. Sitting at his desk below the collection of ripped six-packs and bulging pecs was a potbellied, balding cop in his forties who did not want to be there.

"So," the officer said, never looking Julien or me in the eye. "You're here to file a complaint regarding a public nuisance, correct?"

"Oui, *Monsieur*," I said. "Just wait'll you see the *dossier* we've put together!" I smiled and looked over at Julien, waiting for him to hand it over. Instead, his eyes were glued to the bevy of beefcake adorning the walls.

"Uh, Julien?"

"Oh . . . right! *Dossier. Le voilà monsieur.*"

Julien handed the *dossier* over to the officer who flipped past the text, going straight to the pictures. The moment he saw the pigeon man, his shoulders slumped. "Giancarlo," he grumbled.

"You know him?" I asked. "Well, I'm not surprised. I knew there was no way we could possibly be the first ones to file a complaint."

"That is correct, *Monsieur*," the officer said.

"So there are other dossiers?" Julien asked.

"*Oui.*"

"How many?"

"Hmm . . . *une quarantaine.*" (forty-ish)

Julien and I stared at him in shock. "*Sérieusement?*"

"*Oui.*"

"Well, I'm sure none of the other dossiers are as strong as ours!" I proceeded to rattle off every grisly event that had happened to us since the pigeon man had entered our lives almost a year ago.

"*Bleck*, too many details," the officer said, fidgeting in his chair. Clearly he wanted our meeting to end so he could move on to other things. But at the rate he was going—using one finger at a time to type up our testimonial—our rendezvous was not going to wrap up anytime soon.

After what felt like an eternity, the officer finally finished the report. He printed up two copies and placed them in front of us. "Date and sign both, please." Once we did, the officer handed me our copy.

"What happens next?" I asked.

"Your *dossier* will be passed on to the police commissioner who will take over the case from here."

As we got up to leave, Julien shook the officer's hand and looked him straight in the eye, forcing him to do the same. "I trust we've provided you with enough information so that the appropriate action will be taken?"

"*Bien sûr, Monsieur*," the officer said in a tone that did not reassure me at all.

Outside the *commissariat*, I turned to Julien and said, "Can you believe that guy? So unprofessional! Posting pictures of naked men all over government property!"

"Yeah, I know," Julien said. "Those guys were so hot, I could barely concentrate on the *dossier*." I shot Julien a look. "Kidding, kiddo! Kidding."

"In all seriousness," I said, "what do you think the chances are the cops'll do something about the pigeon man?"

"Hmm, I'd say . . . one in *forty-ish*."

After our less than stellar meeting at the *commissariat*, I refused to let myself get discouraged thanks to two new strategies I had up my sleeve. First, I would phone the police commissioner's office every day if necessary and say something to the effect of: "*Bonjour*, I'm calling to check on the status of dossier #15-54811 to see what action points have been decided upon and when they will be implemented."

Next, as in any successful war, I decided to try my hand at utilizing "soft power"—or more precisely, psychological warfare. When the moment was right (and there were no witnesses around to claim I'd harassed him), I'd pay a visit to the pigeon man with the official police report in my hand. Then I'd wave it in front of his face and say, "See! Told you I meant business!" Then I'd sit back and watch him quiver in his boots.

D-Day arrived on a gray Sunday morning, the kind when Parisians preferred to sleep in late. I stood at my window, surveying the empty streets below (save the clusters of pigeons). It was time to make my move. I grabbed the official police report and raced down the six flights of stairs, too impatient to wait for the elevator.

Outside, I kicked at the mass of pigeons, clearing a path as I made my way toward the van. From several yards away, I could see that the side door was open. I circled around, getting ready to pounce, when suddenly I noticed that the pigeon man wasn't alone. A pretty Asian woman, no older than twenty-five, crouched down next to him. She held a microphone and a tape deck. I deduced that she must be a reporter.

Before they had a chance to see me, I tiptoed over to the other side of the street and watched from there. The woman was in the middle of asking the pigeon man a list of questions (in very bad French). As she did, Giancarlo seemed to transform into a completely different person—a natural media darling—as if he were being interviewed on the set of the *Today* show. Once the interview was over, the woman grabbed an expensive 35mm camera and started taking pictures.

Like a model during fashion week, Giancarlo smiled and struck a series of poses. At one point, he grabbed one of the shoeboxes, held it up in front of the woman and lifted the top off. Upon seeing the baby pigeons inside, the woman squealed, "*Kawaiiiii!*"

Since Julien spoke fluent Japanese, I'd picked up enough of the language to know that *kawaii* meant *cute!*

I couldn't help but guffaw. "Hah! *Kawaii* my ASS!"

Oops. Did I just say that out loud? The pigeon man and the Japanese woman turned and looked at me, their smiles dissolving into contempt, the look on their faces saying it all: *"Haters gonna hate."*

It's not true! I wanted to shout. I wished Julien were there so he could explain to the reporter in Japanese what the real story was. Instead, I slithered away, dodging the daggers that were shooting out of her eyes.

Over the next several weeks, any opportunity for me to confront the pigeon man with the police report seemed less and less likely. Journalists from all over the world were now lining up outside his van to interview him. Not only that, giddy tourists would stop by and ask to have their picture taken with him. The pigeon man was more than happy to oblige.

What the hell is going on? Where did all those people come from?

Right on cue, I received a call from Julien. "Come to the Hôtel de Ville right away!"

The immense city hall was just a short walk from our apartment. When I arrived, Julien was standing next to a photo exhibit that had been mounted on the iron gates surrounding the building. The exhibit was entitled: *Prises de rues: Paris vu par les habitants de ses rues.* (Street shots: Paris as seen by the inhabitants of its streets.)

It consisted of a series of photos taken by homeless people. The images had been blown up to the size of a Smart car and ran the length of the rue du Rivoli on one side, then wrapped around to the front of the city hall, by the entrance to the *métro*, on the other side. There were about a dozen photos in all. Julien stood by the last one.

"Take a look at this!" The photo had been taken behind the Pompidou Center—the northwest corner to be exact. In it, our old friend is hunched over, wearing a tattered trench coat, a shopping caddie by his side. He's surrounded by hundreds of excited pigeons, some blurry in the photo. The title contained just one word: Hitchcock.

"No freakin' way . . ." I said.

You didn't have to be a film buff like me to know what the picture's title was referring to: Hitchcock's classic 1963 film about a small California town terrorized by *Les Oiseaux—The Birds.*

Underneath the title was written in small letters: *1er Prix du public.* (First Prize—People's Choice Award)

Hitchcock
Par Bossu de Notre Dame
1ᵉʳ Prix du public

With the sound of cooing echoing from our rooftop, I stood at the window, gazing down at the crowds of people who were now lining up to meet the pigeon man. Next to the Buddha Bar and Café Georges, Giancarlo's van was fast becoming the hottest spot in town. The only thing missing was a bouncer and a rope line.

I held up my iPhone and hit redial. *"Bonjour,"* I said into the phone. "I'm calling to check on the status of dossier #15-54811 to see what action points have been decided upon and when they will be implemented."

"Oui, monsieur, c'est noté," the exasperated voice said on the other end of the line. The great thing about France is the police are obligated to take your call. Every single time. I hung up and hit redial.

"Bonjour, I'm calling to check on the status of dossier #15-54811 to see what action points have been decided upon and when they will be implemented."

What made me the most *fou*, though, was how cocky Giancarlo had become. Celebrity had definitely gone to his head. And why wouldn't it? He had groupies for Christ's sake! Groupies who gave him gifts—such as the brand-new pair of Reebok sneakers he was now wearing, which he showed off to his adoring fans.

"Oooh," the crowd swooned as they took his picture. Giancarlo waved back and smiled. *Yep, the pigeon man had definitely gone Hollywood.*

That night, I couldn't get the image of the pigeon man and his award-winning "Hitchcock" photo out of my mind. And just like a character in one of Hitch's films, I found myself imagining various macabre ways that Julien and I could get rid of Giancarlo—to make him disappear, *if you know what I mean.*

"We could always pour bleach on his pigeon feed," Julien said as we brainstormed over action points we could take since the *commissariat* was DOA on that front.

"Uh-uh, no way," I said. "I'm not murdering any of Giancarlo's pigeons!" I imagined the next day's headline on the front page of the French newspaper: "American Capitalist Pig—Enemy to the Down-trodden!" Plus, I couldn't shake my inner bird lover. It wasn't their fault they were being lured in by a madman!

"Don't worry," Julien countered back. "The smell of the bleach will disgust them. It won't kill them. But pushing the old man in front of oncoming traffic . . ."

I stared at Julien in shock, my mouth agape. "That's horrible!" I said. "Go on."

"Or . . ." Julien said, dialing it back a few notches. "We could always superglue the locks on his van. Or have it towed away to a junkyard while he's at the Pompidou Center."

I nodded, warming up to the idea. Just then, I heard voices coming from outside our window. I went over to take a look. Two guys in their thirties were standing next to Giancarlo's van. One seemed to be keeping a lookout, while the other pulled a screwdriver out of his pocket. He pressed it against the air valve of one of Giancarlo's tires.

"Hey!" I screamed. "What the hell are you doing?"

"We had to put up with the old man on our street for two years," one of the guys yelled back as he deflated the van's tires. "He's yours now!"

I turned to Julien. "This city's nuts."

Julien and I stayed up until the wee hours that night, plotting the pigeon man's demise, managing to spook ourselves with how gruesome we were willing to go. But of course, just like in a Hitchcock movie, it was only make-believe. Two guys talking tough. The hard truth was there was only one path left for me to take:

"*Bonjour*, I'm calling to check on the status of dossier #15-54811 to see what action points have been decided upon and when they will be implemented."

I hung up. Took a sip of my coffee. Did some of the *New York Times* crossword puzzle. Then hit redial.

"*Bonjour*, I'm calling to check on the status of dossier #15-548—"

"Okay, okay, Monsieur Carlson! *Ça suffit!*" (Enough is enough!), a female voice yelled through the phone. "Two officers are on their way right now!"

"*C'est vrai!*" I said excitedly. "*Oh, merci beaucoup, Madame!*" Right before she hung up, I could hear the woman mumble to her colleague, "*Les putains d'américains sont cinglés!*" ("Those f--king Americans are nuts!")

I skipped over to the window. *Oh boy, oh boy! They're finally coming!* I looked out the window. The pigeon man started rushing around, gathering his belongings. Just as a patrol car appeared at the opposite end of the street, Giancarlo grabbed his caddy and disappeared around the corner—his pigeons taking flight and following after him. *Was that a coincidence or did somebody tip off the pigeon man?* I wondered.

The patrol car pulled to a stop in front of my building, blocking traffic on the narrow street. Immediately car horns started blaring. Two cops exited the vehicle, ignoring the angry motorists and entering my building.

A second later my intercom buzzed. "Sixth floor," I said into the intercom.

"We know," a cold voice answered.

I opened the front door to the stairway just as the elevator arrived to my floor. Two cops stepped out. One was a tall, fit man in his thirties who looked like he hadn't had a good laugh in years. The other, a squat female cop with dark, cropped hair and a constant sneer.

"You just missed him!" I said.

"Who?" the tall cop asked.

"Giancarlo. The pigeon man." The tall cop let out a sigh. "It's okay, though," I gestured for the cops to join me at the window. "You can still see some of his pigeons, as well as the damage they've caused, from up here."

The tall cop came over to the window. I pointed to the 17th-century manor house to the left. Its restored rooftop and creamy tan façade were dripping with *merde*. "That's from the pigeon man," I said. "Ever since he moved here, he's made everybody's life hell."

"We're quite familiar with your *dossier*, Monsieur Carlson. What would you like us to do?"

"Well, for starters, isn't it against the law to feed pigeons in front of a residential building?" The cop nodded. "Then arrest him!"

"That's been done already. Many times. But do you know how long the prison sentence is for feeding birds?" I didn't have the answer. "Let me put it this way," the cop continued. "If the offender knows he'll be back on the street in a day or two, there's not much of a deterrent for him to change his ways, is there?"

I shook my head.

"And who's going to pay to keep locking him up? It's not cheap you know."

"But what about the health risk? What if someone comes down with pigeon disease?"

"You know why it's called *pigeon disease*, don't you? Because *pigeons* get it. Not humans."

An awkward silence ensued, save the car horns blaring outside. "We've taken enough of your time, Monsieur Carlson," the tall cop said, turning to leave. "Good day."

"Wait!" I said. "Can't you guys at least tow his van away?"

"You mean, his home. *Non, Monsieur.* You can't take away a man's right to live in his own home."

"So what you're saying is, I could pitch a tent on the sidewalk and live there if I wanted to?"

"No. You'd be arrested for illegal camping, because you already have a home."

I was quickly running out of arguments. I tried one last Hail Mary play, even though I feared it was for naught. "Take a look at this," I said, pulling out my iPhone. I played the video of the old man spitting on me. "Technically, that's assault, isn't it?"

The cop smiled. "Here's *you*, Monsieur Carlson," he said, holding his hand at the same level as my head, indicating my height. "And here's the old man," the cop lowered his hand way down, roughly to my waistline. "Uh, I don't think you were in any serious danger."

The female cop laughed. The tall cop cracked a smile for the first time, then motioned for his colleague to follow him to the door.

"Wait, wait, please! One last question: What if I make an appeal to City Hall?"

"Nothing will happen," the tall cop said, his patience running thin.

"Why not?"

"Because the mayor doesn't want to risk any more bad publicity."

"But—"

"You don't get it, Monsieur Carlson!" the tall cop said, losing his cool. "The pigeon man's *famous*! He's got over 50,000 Facebook followers!"

My jaw dropped. If someone were to walk into the room right now, it might look as if the sound of the blaring horns outside were coming out of my mouth.

The tall cop regained his composure, then turned toward the door. "Good day, *Monsieur*." With his partner in tow, the cop stepped out into the hallway then pushed the call button for the elevator.

"Oh, one last thing, Monsieur Carlson," the tall cop said as he stepped onto the elevator. "If I were you, I wouldn't waste my time calling the *commissariat* anymore. We've come once. We won't be coming back again."

The elevator doors closed. I stood there stunned, feeling paralyzed and helpless. After a moment, I shuffled over to the corner of the studio and plopped onto my sofa bed. Above me, the *click-click-click* of pigeon feet grew louder as the birds returned *en masse* to my zinc roof. I let out a sigh. I really was living a scene from Hitchcock's classic film—except my eyes hadn't been pecked out of their sockets by killer pigeons. *Yet.*

For the rest of the afternoon, I racked my brain, trying to think if there was anything else I could do. Slowly the harsh reality began to sink in: The war was over. The pigeon man had won.

Surrounded by boxes, I stood at the window of my apartment, waiting for the moving van to arrive. A SOLD sign hung on the balcony. It was a tough decision to make, but since it was obvious the pigeon man wasn't going anywhere, I had to learn to accept that, in France, *c'est comme ça.* (That's the way it is.)

"Look on the bright side," Julien said as he taped the last box shut. "At least we didn't lose any money on the place."

"*C'est vrai,*" I said, even though we hadn't made any money, either. We'd just barely broken even.

I looked down to the street below. The pigeon man was busy getting ready for his 8:00 A.M. feeding at the Pompidou. I then looked at the 17th-century manor homes dotting the Marais. They looked particularly lovely in the spring light, despite being covered with tons of *merde.* At that moment a thought occurred to me: *These elegant buildings have survived two World Wars, eight revolutions, and one* bobo *gentrification—but will they be able to survive the pigeon man?*

While our apartment was up for sale, Julien and I found a one-bedroom place to rent in a charming Art Deco building in the 5th *arrondissement*—or the "civilized *arrondissement*" as one of my French customers called it. It was almost twice the size of our last place. And although it didn't have a rooftop terrace, it did have something else going for it. On our first visit, Julien stood in the living room, while I stood in the bedroom.

"Look!" I yelled. "There's a wall between us!"

"Woo-hoo!" Julien yelled back.

The day before we moved in, I decided to familiarize myself with the neighborhood. Along with Julien's mom, Elisabeth, the three of us took a stroll to the nearby Jardin des Plantes, the beautiful botanical gardens founded in the 1600s. As I breathed in the fresh air from the stately syca-more trees, something caught my eye.

Along the fence near the zoo was another outdoor photo exhibit, this one sponsored by the nearby Natural History Museum. And featured among the photos was none other than . . . Giancarlo, the pigeon man. But this time, the picture was a medium shot of him holding a pigeon in each hand, looking angelic. If I squinted a little, I swore I could see a tiny halo photoshopped above his head.

"Incroyable," I said under my breath.

And at the bottom of the photo was written: *"Le prix nouveau regard."* Yet another award for the pigeon man. This time: "The New Vision Prize."

"Mais bien sûr," I said. *"Bien sûr . . ."*

The first night in our new apartment, I slept better than I had in years. I also awoke hungrier than usual, anxious to try out our local *boulangerie*. It had just been awarded the "Best Croissant in Paris," so of course, I had to make sure the judges hadn't awarded the prize in error.

As I headed up Boulevard Saint-Germain, I noticed a hefty woman sitting on the sidewalk across from the bakery. Her hair was up in a bun, and she wore sandals that were twice the size of her feet. Most curiously, something big and furry was waggling on top of her ample chest.

Upon closer inspection, I noticed there was a bowl on the sidewalk beside her. And the waggling creature? It turned out to be the biggest rabbit I'd ever seen, half tan, half white. It nibbled excitedly on a lettuce leaf.

The moment the woman saw me, she sprang to her feet, lifting the furry fellow off her chest and shoving it directly into my face.

"*Un euro, monsieur*! For my bunny! C'mon, he's hungry! *UN EURO! UN EURO!*"

Oh-la-la, I thought to myself. *What next?* Being the superstitious person I am, I dug into my pocket and pulled out a euro. *Best to start off on a good note*, I thought.

I didn't know it at the time, but from that day forward if ever I wanted to get my morning croissant, or needed to go grocery shopping, or had to take the *métro*, there was no way to avoid running into the woman. But the way I figured it, there was no way the Rabbit Lady of the Latin Quarter could be any worse than the Pigeon Man of Paris, could she?

I decided to start putting a *dossier* together, just in case.

PART TWO

WORKING IN FRANCE

FIVE

A Star Is Stuck

Back in the '90s, before I had the idea for Breakfast in America, my friends and I were in Jerry's Deli in Los Angeles when I experienced what was possibly *the* greatest celebrity sighting of all time. (Next to Cheryl Ladd on top of the Eiffel Tower, of course.) As a grad student at the University of Southern California, I'd just directed an award-winning short film and was overflowing with optimism, imagining the dizzying heights to which my future career in Hollywood would take me.

"Oh, my God," my pal Rod exclaimed. "Look who just walked in!"

"That's nice," I said, my eyes glued to the menu, my stomach grumbling from hunger.

I wouldn't say I'd gotten blasé, but honestly, you couldn't throw a script in LA without hitting a celebrity. After deciding what to order, I looked up. At that moment, just like in a movie, I saw her from across the room. Mesmerized by her silvery mane and glittering jewels, I was instantly hooked—like a trout to a lure.

Making her way across the deli with an entourage of college-aged kids was none other than Cleopatra herself, Liz Taylor. It was during the height of her perfume period, when White Diamonds had become the best-selling fragrance in the world. A true survivor of alcohol and drug addiction, Liz looked stunning.

Blasé begone, I was completely starstruck!

Unfortunately, it was *au contraire* for the waiter. He barely acknowledged Ms. Taylor as he grabbed some menus and led the star and her—what, grandchildren and their friends?—across the restaurant, seating them at a table smack in the middle of the room.

"What's that waiter doing?" I said to my friends. "Liz is Hollywood royalty! She should be seated in an area where she can have some privacy."

Sure enough, in a matter of minutes customers were ogling Ms. Taylor and whipping out their digital cameras. Just like that, one of the greatest actresses of all time was being treated like a fish in a fishbowl.

I felt so bad for her. But Liz remained classy the whole time. Without making a fuss or calling attention to herself, she set her menu down then whispered something to her entourage. They nodded and stood up, helping the Hollywood legend to her feet and accompanying her to the exit. By the time the waiter had come over to our table to take our order, Liz was gone. I looked at him, shocked by the way he'd treated her.

"Do you know who that was?" I asked.

"Who?" the waiter said.

I pointed to the table, which was now empty. "Elizabeth Taylor!"

"Oh, was that her?" The clueless waiter said as he held up his order pad and shrugged. "Whatever."

If Breakfast in America had existed back then and Liz had graced us with her presence, she would have been treated like a queen. An Egyptian queen to be exact.

They say a restaurant has really made it when it gets its first celebrity customer. Not long after I opened the first Breakfast in America (BIA) in 2003, a couple from New Jersey asked, "Has anyone famous eaten at your diner yet?"

"Depends," I said. "Does a celebrity's *mother* count?"

I first met Mme. P. one afternoon at the end of the lunch rush. An elegant woman in her sixties with layered brown hair that complemented her sleek equestrian boots, Mme. P. wore a heavy silk foulard that hung from her shoulders like drapery at the palace of Versailles. During the entire lunch service, I noticed that she'd been examining me from head to toe, as if I were a piece of *bavette* at the butcher shop. I was definitely getting a Mrs. Robinson vibe from her—although our age difference, thirty-nine vs. sixty-something, was admittedly not as shocking as the one in *The Graduate*.

"Young man," she motioned to me after the last clients had paid their bill. "May I speak with you for a moment?"

"*Bien sûr, Madame*," I said as I stepped over to her booth.

"*Asseyez-vous*," the *séductrice* patted the red cushioned seat next to her. "I have a proposition for you." I gulped slightly. Back then I still had a major problem with intimacy—no matter what form it came in.

As usual, my active imagination had gotten the better of me. Mme. P. was no Mme. Robinson. Rather, she was the mother/agent of one of the biggest comedians in France—Pierre Palmade. And her proposition? It concerned a *business* arrangement, not *l'amour*. She'd gotten the idea after reading the back of BIA's menu, which told the story of how I'd once been a Hollywood screenwriter. (Fortunately, I'd omitted the adjective, "washed-up.") Mme. P. said she'd like to hire me to adapt one of her son's stage shows into English.

"I have a strong feeling about you," she tapped my hand. "And my feelings are never wrong!"

Mme. P. couldn't have entered my life at a better time. That first year BIA was open, I didn't allow myself to receive a salary—despite my French accountant's recommendation to the contrary. "Let's wait until the business is fully up and running," I told her.

Not only was Mme. P. extremely generous (she paid me more in three months than I'd earned as a screenwriter in three years), we also became dear friends and confidants. Once I'd gained her trust, she invited me to see her son perform to a sold-out crowd. After the show, she took me backstage to meet him. I was a little nervous as I shook the French star's hand, saying, "You're lucky to have such a great agent . . . I mean *mother* . . . I mean . . ."

Mme. P. smiled at her son. "You hear that? I'm glad *somebody* around here appreciates me."

I certainly did. Mme. P. and I would end up collaborating one more time on another of her son's shows, which she planned to produce in English-speaking theaters around the world. As other gigs began to come my way, my film school friends back in LA joked, "How come your writing career's going better in Paris than it did over here?"

"Because in France, I'm *exotique*," I replied.

After Mme. P. the first real celebrity (and *not* a parent) to come by the diner was a French model from the '70s who'd made a modest leap from the catwalk to the stage and screen. Ironically, her last name translated into an alcoholic beverage, which was fitting because she would hang out at the counter several nights a week, taking advantage of the diner's full liquor license and get totally *merde*-faced. Fortunately, she was a happy drunk so hanging out with her was always entertaining.

By the time I opened the second location in the Marais in 2006, we had our first big wave of celebrity sightings. Most of the stars were from popular TV shows, but I didn't recognize any of them because Julien and I didn't own a TV. There were two reasons for this: Growing up with the boob tube as my babysitter, I would instantly turn into a couch potato the second the screen lit up; but more importantly, I was rebelling against France's "audiovisual" tax. I couldn't believe the government charged citizens 130€

a year ($150) just to own a TV set. *Isn't that what all those annoying commercials are for—so you can watch TV for free?*

Then in 2008, everything changed. After Obama's election, America was suddenly considered *hyper-cool*, especially with the young *français*. As a result, Breakfast in America received a ton of publicity from the French and international media, causing business to skyrocket. The ensuing eight years that Obama was president became BIA's golden era.

During this period even *I* recognized some of the celebrities who stopped by the diner, including a talented American superstar who has since become the highest paid actress in the world—*Mlle.* Scarlett Johansson. She came to the diner not once, but multiple times. (It helped that she'd been spending a lot of time in Paris after opening a gourmet popcorn shop a few blocks from BIA #2.)

As Breakfast in America became a kind of mini celebrity hangout, I began to worry about the stars' privacy, since both diners had no hidden corners for them to hide in. Fortunately that wasn't an issue in Paris, where asking for an autograph or a selfie showed that you were *mal élevé*. (poorly raised)

"Isn't it great how the French give famous people their privacy," I said to my manager one day as we watched a Grammy-winning duo polish off their French toast in *toute tranquillité*.

If Liz Taylor were still alive today, I thought, *she'd be in seventh heaven here!*

By the time one of the biggest French movie stars came to the diner, Breakfast in America was in the middle of a rough patch. The country was still reeling from the horrific *Charlie Hebdo* and Bataclan attacks of 2015, with nearly every business affected, especially the service industry. Tourism was down. People weren't going out as much and frequenting restaurants even less.

Furthermore, as protests grew more numerous and turbulent—often bringing the city to a standstill—it wasn't long before sales at the diners had plummeted by nearly 30%. The U.S. elections in 2016 didn't help, either. With Obama gone, BIA's golden era was replaced by a more orange-tinted one. Although still beloved by the French, America was no longer as *hyper-cool* as it used to be. (That said, by overwhelming demand, we left the popular Obama Milkshake on the menu.)

Taking all these factors into account, BIA seemed to be just barely treading water. One day, as I was struggling to make ends meet, I got a visit from a representative of the mayor's office from the 5th *arrondissement*. (Every district in Paris has its own mayor.) She was doing a PR tour around the neighborhood, introducing herself to all the local *commerçants*.

"*Bonjour* Monsieur Carlson," the chic and efficient *fonctionnaire* said, shaking my hand. "I'm here to express the mayor's support. Small businesses like yours breathe life into the community. Is there anything we can do to help?"

"Well, yes, actually," I said. "Could someone from your office please give me advance notice *before* workers start digging up the sidewalk right in front of my restaurant with jackhammers? And on a Saturday no less. All that dust and incessant pounding killed my busiest day."

"Oh, that would be the other mayor, Mayor Hildago at the *Hôtel de Ville*—in Paris's central office. She handles all the *travaux* in the city."

"That's good to know. Would she also be the person to speak to about the protestors?"

"*Pardon?*"

"Well, since demonstrations are considered a '*mouvement social*,' perhaps Mme. Hidalgo's socialist government can make *un petit effort* and cover some of the sales I've lost these past few months—ever since the protestors started smashing historic landmarks and setting vehicles on fire? As you can imagine, it hardly entices people to venture out for brunch."

The representative gave me a blank stare. Clearly, I was on my own.

With BIA's very survival at stake, I had to take action. But what? Given France's notoriously strict labor laws, it was extremely complicated to lay off employees—even during an economic slump. Nor did I want to even if I could. Revenue may have been down, but my staff at this point were all working hard and blessedly not stealing from me. Instead, I realized I'd have to come up with new and clever ways to bolster sales.

I knew potential customers were out there, but how to wrangle them in? Hardly a morning went by that I didn't see a tourist from some part of the world, usually America or England, enter one of the cafés in my neighborhood and ask the waiter in earnest, "Do you have eggs and bacon?"

"*Non*, but we have *omelets* after 12:00 P.M."

"With breakfast potatoes?"

"*Non*."

"Pancakes?"

"*Non plus*."

Seeing how disappointed the tourists were, I felt morally conflicted. I was friendly with the owners of all the cafés in my neighborhood, so it didn't seem appropriate to make a move on their clientele the moment the waiter stepped away.

"Psst, hey you," I'd imagine myself saying. "Over here." After I'd gotten their attention, I'd speak soft and conspiratorial-like. "Looking to hook up with a *real* breakfast?" I'd say as I slipped them BIA's business card. "Here. These guys'll take care of ya! Tell 'em Craigie 'Il Bambino' sent ya!"

Working with local hotels was even more of a challenge. They preferred gouging their guests with overpriced "continental" breakfasts. I can't count the number of times tourists staying at a nearby hotel would discover BIA on the *last* day of their vacation. "If we'd known you were here," they'd say, "we would have come every day for breakfast!"

In addition to attracting tourists, when it came to the local clientele I had to come up with new ways to bring in the bacon (so to speak). At first, coupons seemed like a good idea. As a starving screenwriter in LA, I used to jump at any opportunity to "clip and save." But the French couldn't be bothered. According to Julien, the whole concept was *très* gauche.

Next, BIA introduced fidelity cards. They helped, as long as the staff didn't fill the cards up with a bunch of stamps—and hence, free meals—then give them away to their friends and significant others.

Another revenue-generating idea: renting out the diner to films and fashion shoots that were looking for a classic American vibe from the '50s and '60s. However, most producers were too cheap to pay even the bare minimum, i.e., covering the loss of business from closing the diner down for the day.

Then there was the old standby: BIA's full liquor license. In the past we'd tried to promote cocktails during happy hour, but the only ones getting *heureux* were the staff who drank all the profits. Eventually I stopped serving hard liquor and began offering mimosas during Sunday brunch instead.

"Orange juice in champagne?!" Julien said in shock the first time I told him what a mimosa was. "That's *dégoutant!* Why would you ruin a perfectly good glass of bubbly like that?"

"You mean, like how you ruined a perfectly good stack of pancakes by smothering them with guacamole and black pepper?"

"That's when I thought a pancake was a blini, remember?"

"Anyway, you Frenchies have your own version of a mimosa, you know?"

"We do?"

"Yeah, what do you a call a *Kir Royale*?" (Champagne with black currant liquor.)

Julien nodded, but said nothing since the term "good point" didn't exist *en français*.

One last attempt at boosting sales: I tried to hook our wagon to the latest craze—food delivery. However, companies like Uber Eats and Deliveroo not only charged a delivery fee, they also took a whopping 30% commission off the top—which was, coincidentally, our profit margin, meaning for every to-go order, we were lucky to break even.

In the end, I could try all the promotions I wanted, but no matter how I cut it, the diner's survival depended on one basic thing: the weekends. Without them, we were goners.

Such was the state of affairs when one of the biggest movie stars in France came to BIA. It was a cool Sunday morning in November. I was on my way to work when I received a text from my manager, Bruce. "You'll never guess who's here!" After revealing the celebrity's identity, I texted back, "No way! Give her the royal treatment. Pamper her. Whatever it takes so she doesn't leave until I get there!"

When I entered the diner, the place was bustling with customers. And it wasn't even noon yet. I slipped behind the bar and whispered to Bruce, "Where is she?"

"Behind you. Table #17." I nodded and smiled. *Good move.* Of all the booths, that one was the most private, tucked into a corner of the room.

"How long's she been here?"

"Over an hour."

I was so glad I hadn't missed her. As discreetly as I could, I grabbed the coffee pot and starting making the rounds, going from table to table filling customers' mugs, eventually making my way to Table #17.

"*Encore de* coffee?" I asked the French movie star without making a fuss.

"*Oui, avec plaisir,*" she said.

I almost had to pinch myself. Never in a million years could I ever have imagined that one day I'd be serving fresh "sock juice" (as the French called American coffee) to *the*... Emmanuelle Béart. (The fact that she was willing to have American coffee put her even higher up on my list.)

As Ms. Béart held up her mug, I gazed into her deep blue eyes for the first time. At that instant, I was transported back to my film school days some thirty years earlier, when I'd first studied the star's work in my foreign film class. *Manon of the Spring*, based on Marcel Pagnol's acclaimed novel, had just been released and quickly became one of the top-grossing French films of all time, propelling the young actress into international stardom overnight.

In addition to winning the prestigious *César* Award (the French equivalent of the Oscars), Ms. Béart also made history in 2003 when her nude photo on the cover of *Elle* magazine sold out its entire run of 550,000 copies in just three days, making it the best-selling issue in the magazine's history. Legend had it that blowups of the risqué photo that were plastered on kiosks all over Paris literally stopped traffic.

Petit and buried in a sweater, Ms. Béart was tucked into the corner of the booth, *sans* makeup. Her hair was still golden, only now it wasn't nearly as big and puffy—nor sunlit from behind and constantly blowing in the wind as it had been in *Manon of the Spring*. (The movie was made in the '80s after all.)

As I served the star, I was reminded of my encounter with Liz Taylor years earlier. Like Liz, Ms. Béart was surrounded by an entourage of college-age kids and couldn't have been more down-to-earth. But unlike Liz, nobody bothered her. Except for a few starstruck glances, the patrons at BIA let Emmanuelle and her—what, kids and their friends?—enjoy their brunch in peace.

My first impulse was to give her extra attention. But then I remembered I was in France. During my recent trips back to the U.S., I'd been finding it harder and harder to relax in restaurants. I'd gotten accustomed to the French pace when it came to dining, meaning I took my time and breathed between bites and didn't need to be constantly "checked on."

"How's everything?!" a server in the U.S. would appear out of nowhere and shout, nearly giving me a heart attack.

"The same as it was five minutes ago," I'd say.

Even worse, whenever I'd take a pause, bussers in the States would rush over and try to take my plate away. "Easy fella," I'd say, staving him off with my fork. "I'm not done yet!" And don't get me started with *upselling*. By the end of the meal, I found myself longing for France, where I was free to *saucer* (sop up my gravy) for as long as I wanted, in *toute tranquillité*.

Back in the diner, I noticed that Ms. Béart and her gang still had a few morsels of pancakes left on their plate, so I left them alone. I then glanced up at the frying pan clock on the wall. The eggs read 1:15 P.M. Ms. Béart and her entourage had been in the diner for going on two hours now.

Just then, my attention was drawn outside. *Mon dieu*, I thought, *when did that happen?* BIA suddenly had the longest line I'd seen in years. Could it be that business was finally turning around?

Knowing we had a short window to turn the tables—roughly between noon and 3:00 P.M.—I laser-focused on one thing: turning the tables. Complicating matters, most of the people waiting in line were groups of three or more, which meant I'd have to start clearing out some booths. (BIA only had six. Unlike the States, space was very limited in France.)

I did a quick survey of the room. Customers at every booth were still in the middle of their meals—except for one: Table #17.

I felt so guilty. Just a moment ago, I'd been thrilled to have the beloved French icon grace my diner with her presence. Now, I wanted her to settle up lickety-split so I could have her booth.

I took a deep breath then stepped up to Table #17.

"How was everything?" I smiled as I cleared away their plates. *Hint hint.*

"*Très bon*," the actress said.

"Can I get you anything else?" *Hint hint hint.*

"*Oui,*" Ms. Béart said as four empty mugs rose into the air. "More American coffee, please."

I nodded and scurried off. Once again, I was faced with a difficult cultural dilemma. In France, whether it be a café or a restaurant, if a customer purchased something (no matter how big or small), it was understood that they were effectively "renting a seat" for as long as they wanted. Hence it was considered *très* rude to bring a customer their check before they asked for it.

However, at BIA, we'd tried to find a happy medium. Or course, when it came to American customers, they were used to restaurants in the States giving them the bill without having to ask for it. But sometimes we'd forget and Americans tourists, who weren't familiar with the French custom, would sit there suffering in silence, itching to run off to the Louvre, but waiting for us to bring them their bill.

As for French customers, we had to tread much more lightly. As a general rule, we'd wait a half hour after they'd finished their last bite before setting the check on the table. "No hurry," we'd say. "Whenever you're ready."

Most of the time, the customer would get the hint and move on. But when they didn't, I'd point to the long line outside and evoke *La Révolution* (the big one from 1789). "I need your help," I'd say with a knowing smile. "Those folks out there are starving and are about to storm the diner!"

The best was when there was a family in line with a screaming baby. I'd point to the child, then give the squatting customer a sad look. How could anyone refuse to feed *un enfant* who was *très faim*? (very hungry)

In rare cases, some French customers would become extremely irate after I'd dropped the check, whipping out the ultimate insult: "All you Americans care about is making money!"

I had to admit, there was some truth to the stereotype. However, what they failed to take into account was if *les euros* weren't coming in, how would I be able to pay the high employee charges, high overhead costs, high taxes, five weeks paid vacation, and the rest? Ask any restaurant owner: it's a fine line between boon and bankrupt.

I surveyed the diner. An Aretha Franklin playlist blasted from the sound system. "*R-E-S-P-E-C-T/Find out what it means to me!*" Before I knew it, the Queen of Soul had gotten the clientele up and dancing in their seats, including Ms. Béart and her entourage. Customers were having such a ball, *nobody* was leaving now.

As the line outside grew longer, I was overcome with anxiety. It didn't help that just a couple months earlier, the diner had gotten a surprise visit from URSSAF—the labor office. I was shocked to learn that if I lost my job (i.e., the diner went out of business), I would *not* be eligible for any unemployment benefits, even though I was a salaried employee—and even though I'd paid 47% of everything I'd ever earned to the French government.

"*C'est pas juste!*" (It's not fair!), I said to my accountant after the inspection was over. "How come there's a generous safety net for everyone in France *except* entrepreneurs?"

"Because the government thinks, you're the boss, you'll figure things out," she said.

After I got home and vented to Julien, he said I'd be amazed how much financial aid there was in France—especially if it involved iconic images that were on French tourism posters.

"Did you know there's a subsidy for baguettes?" Julien said. "Well, for bakeries, anyway. That's why a baguette barely costs a euro."

"That one makes sense," I said, "since 'let them eat cake' didn't go over so well with the starving masses."

"You know what else?" Julien continued. "Certain millionaires get subsidies, too. For the upkeep of their 'historic' *chateaux*, since they're considered part of *le patrimoine français*."

"You're kidding me. Next thing you'll tell me *mimes* get extra benefits, too."

"Actually, they do. There's a special category for performers and stage technicians called, '*intermittent de spectacle*.' After you've acquired enough 'performance points,' the government pays you to stay at home, developing your craft."

"Is it too late for me to become a mime?"

"Uh . . . Earth to Craig," my manager Bruce said, jolting me out of what had become a mild anxiety attack. "Are you all right?" I didn't realize I'd been standing there like a deer in the headlights, panting and sweating.

"Yeah, yeah, I'm fine," I said. Then I looked outside. Oh, *merde* . . .

At that moment, the clouds opened up and a downpour ensued. Within seconds, half the customers waiting in line fled, while the other half stood there staring through the window, giving the evil eye to customers so they'd hurry up and finish their meals. But those inside didn't budge, preferring to stay put where it was warm and dry.

Right on cue, Ms. Béart waved her empty mug in the air, "*S'il vous plaît?*" she said, looking at me with her deep blue eyes. "More American coffee, pleeease!"

I smiled at the star and grabbed the coffee pot. As I filled up her mug, the Frenchman in me tried to accept the fact that she wasn't going anywhere. *C'est comme ça*, I said to myself. *She bought her seat. Guess that means she can stay as long as she wants.*

As if to rub it in, the voice of Aretha Franklin blasted through the diner, echoing in my ears: "*Sock it to me! Sock it to me! Sock it to me! Sock it to me!*"

Photo by Meredith Mullins

SIX

Follow That Customer!

I should've known from his pinstriped suit, perfectly contoured facial stubble, and slick air of entitlement that the customer was trouble.

"How would you like to pay?" I asked in French as I handed the man his bill. "Cash or credit?"

"Neither," he said.

"*Tickets restaurants* then?"

"*Non plus.*" (Not that, either.)

I felt a familiar pang in the pit of my stomach. Something was up. One thing I'd learned as a business owner in Paris was that the "customer" in front of you might very well be an undercover *contrôleur* (inspector) from the French government, ready to bust you for the slightest infraction. Such was the case two weeks earlier when a priggish-looking fellow tried to trap me as he was paying for his brunch.

"Do you accept *tickets restaurants* on Sundays?" he asked.

Tickets restaurants were a perk most French workers received from their employer. They varied in denominations from 3.02€ to 10.48€, the odd amounts a result of, I supposed, the conversion from the franc to the euro in 2001. Employees could redeem them at restaurants during their lunch breaks—or at a grocery store for food purchases—but no more than *three* of them at a time.

"I'm sorry, we *don't*," I lied, covering my ass just in case the man really was a government mole who was there to bust me for breaking some obscure law I didn't even know existed.

"Good," the man said. "Because as you can see here," he turned the restaurant ticket over and pointed to the fine print on the back, "you're only allowed to accept these Monday through Saturday. Not on Sundays."

I had no idea there was such a restriction. (Interpreting French legalese was never taught in my French classes.) Still, I found it odd, the assumption being that nobody worked on Sundays. Except, of course, those of us who labored in restaurants and cafés, museums and monuments, *métros*, buses, and trains . . . pretty much any job that allowed nine-to-fivers like Secret Agent Man to enjoy his (ample) time off.

But I shut my mouth, happy that I hadn't fallen for his ruse. The *contrôleur*, like most government workers, was not a very good actor.

Back in the present, I stared at the slick man in the pinstripe suit, wondering how he intended to pay for his burger now that we'd covered all the payment options. After a moment, he reached into his attaché case and pulled out a large leather bound checkbook.

"Oh, I'm sorry, *Monsieur*," I said. "But we do not accept personal checks."

"*Tant pis.* You don't have the right to refuse them."

"Oh, I certainly do," I said, puffing out my chest, confident that after all these years in business, I was finally getting a handle on the complexities of French law. "Look," I pointed at the menu. "It's written right here: *La maison n'accepte pas les chèques . . .*"

"You can write whatever you want, but in France *commerçants* must accept all forms of payment. And personal checks are a legitimate form of payment."

The customer made his case with such conviction, I began to doubt myself. Maybe he was right; maybe I was breaking the law. But I decided to press on, having recently been the victim of one too many *chèques en bois,* or "wooden checks," which are the equivalent to the "rubber" kind in the States.

"If what you say is true," I said to the man, "how come the Franprix across the street—and virtually every other shop in Paris—has a sign posted by their register saying they don't accept checks?"

The man ignored me and pulled out a Mont Blanc pen from his vest pocket and started writing out a check for 10.95€, the amount of our fixed-priced lunch menu.

Oh, come on. Sérieusement? I thought. "*Monsieur,* please, there's an ATM right across the street if—"

"Look, if you truly believe you have the *right* to refuse my check, let's take a walk over to the *commissariat* and see what the police have to say about it, shall we?"

At this point I was pretty sure the man wasn't a *contrôleur,* just a pompous ass. And at the risk of being redundant, he was probably a lawyer, too, judging from the way he spoke. As it turned out, I was half right; the man was a professor at the nearby *Faculté de Droit,* literally the Law Faculty at the Sorbonne.

"Well . . . ?" the man said, holding up his check. "Are you going to take this, or shall we go to the *commissariat?*"

Uh uh. No way. I was *not* going back to the police station, especially after the way they treated me the last time I was there.

I surveyed the diner. With the lunch rush over, a bunch of customers stood up at the same time to pay. There was no way I could leave now. The man noticed and grinned, knowing he had won. "*Et . . . voilà,*" he said, ripping the check out of his checkbook and handing it to me.

Espèce de con, I thought. (A not-so-polite term that's best left untranslated.)

On the way home that night, I thought about what had happened—and in particular how the concept of one's rights in France differed sharply from that in the States. As if to hammer the point home, when I entered the *métro*, I watched in astonishment as a bunch of teenagers hopped the turnstile, one after the other, without paying—right under the nose of an employee in the information booth who couldn't have cared less. He was too busy chatting on his cell phone, occasionally taking a drag from his cigarette, which he half-hid under the counter, flagrantly violating the "No Smoking" sign on the wall behind him.

"So tell me," I asked Julien when I got home that night. "Did that customer really have the right to pay with a check?"

"Who knows?" Julien shrugged. "I'll have to look it up. But you know what they say: In France, when it comes to one's rights, *'Ma liberté s'arrête où commence celle des autres.'*"

I'd never heard that expression before. Although I understood each word individually—"My freedom ends where that of others begins"—the deeper meaning escaped me. I asked Julien to clarify.

"Okay, let's take our favorite annoyance: second-hand smoke," said Julien, the former-smoker-turned-ultra-intolerant-*anti*-smoker. "A person's right to smoke ends where my right to breathe begins."

That made sense—in theory. Try as I might, I couldn't remember the last time I'd been able to enjoy a café at an outdoor terrace in Paris without choking. This made me think about an article I'd recently read about a waiter from France who was working at a restaurant in Toronto. He'd been fired because of his bad attitude, in particular his "combative and aggressive" tone with his coworkers. The axed waiter sued the restaurant, essentially saying that, as a Frenchman, it was his *right* to be rude.

I sympathized with my fellow restaurateur in Toronto. Nothing was more complicated than workers' rights in France. Maybe it had something to do with the fact that, in French, the word for rights (*droits*) is the same as it is for law, as in the Faculté du *Droit*. In fact, since I'd opened my diner, the French government had been pumping out so many new laws/rights, I joked with Julien that instead of calling it "The Law Faculty," they should call it "The Law *Factory*."

Not surprisingly, based on my personal experience, 90% of those new laws tended to favor the worker, never the employer. Especially now, in the age of *les gilets jaunes*, who were in full protest.

"You know what really gets my goat?" Julien fumed one Saturday morning as the smell of tear gas wafted through our apartment window. (Yes, we lived *that* close to a major protest route.) "The French are *never* happy. Always complaining and demanding more. Let them go to America for a year. Then they'd realize how good they've got it here!"

"You say 'they' as if you come from somewhere else," I teased the *Frenchman*.

"Alas," Julien let out a long, exaggerated sigh. "I'm a man without a country."

"Or," I smiled. "You can be a man of *all* countries—like me!" I pulled out my passport and pointed to the cover I'd just purchased at a (slightly pretentious) boutique in our neighborhood. Etched on it were four elegantly written (and slightly pretentious) words in gold leaf:

Citizen of the World.

"Nice try, kiddo," Julien said, knowing full well it was impossible to ever completely *un*French himself.

Of course, I knew Julien was right. From the perspective of an American living abroad, the French did have it pretty damn good. To illustrate this, I put together a short list of what every French citizen is entitled to by law: universal health care, paid vacation (A minimum of five weeks, but many government employees, such as Julien's brother-in-law, a landscape architect, can get twice as much. And that's *not* counting paid public holidays.), paid sick leave, paid maternity and paternity leave, free job training, generous unemployment benefits (that can last up to two years), and last but not least, strict *permanent* contracts (called CDIs), that virtually give employees lifelong job security.

On the other end of the spectrum, I was amazed to learn that in the U.S. not a single item on my list has ever been mandated by the federal government as a right for *all* its citizens. Sure, depending on the size of a company or what state you live in, there are certain requirements that must be met (such as minimal health coverage). But overall, the very things that are considered *rights* in France are cheerfully rebranded in America as *benefits* or *perks* or my favorite, a *compensation package*. And who gets to determine what benefits and perks go into said compensation package? Why, business owners and CEOs at private board meetings, of course.

Digging deeper, I had to laugh when I saw how certain American companies were touting their "generosity" via popular business sites I'd found on line. In-N-Out Burger, for example, was quite proud of their policy of offering employees a "Double-Double burger and fries" with each shift. Compare this to France where not only were *all* restaurants required to feed their staff at least one free meal a day (two if they worked an eight-hour shift), we also had the honor (benefit?) of being taxed on the very same meals we lost money on.

How can a company be taxed on a negative amount? you may wonder. I'm not sure, but the French government has figured out a way.

But perhaps my favorite corporate backslap had to be at Gap Inc. Employees at their corporate headquarters in San Francisco were given the perk of free access to the San Francisco Museum of Modern Art where they had the privilege of appreciating the "Prominent Private Collection" of the Gap Inc. founders. *Sure, we* could *afford to pay you a livable wage with* beaucoup de *benefits, but we prefer to splurge on overpriced art, then get a tax break for putting it on display—all so that you can revel in what great taste we have!*

Now if that wasn't the kind of thing that would get your head chopped off in France, I don't know what was.

I have a confession to make: I'm actually glad the French government forces me to give employees five weeks paid vacation, health care, and the rest. As a business owner, if the choice were left to me, I don't think I'd voluntarily take on the huge expense. But by forcing me to do so, I get to complain about it—just like a true Frenchman does—while at the same time, secretly appreciating it. (Ironically, the things that drove me crazy about France were the very same things that contributed greatly to what I *loved* about France.)

I know it may not be the tenor of our times, but I get great satisfaction knowing that, even though my diner can't afford to pay high wages like bigger companies, my employees can still have a decent quality of life, thanks to the benefits . . . er . . . *rights* built into the French system.

Of course, I know this kind of thinking would get me laughed out of the Wharton School of business or kicked off cut-throat, entrepreneurial shows like *Shark Tank*—or heaven help us—*The Apprentice*. But I'm fine with that.

Ultimately, for me, it comes down to one question: who should determine what constitutes a worker's inalienable rights?

    a)   the laws of a nation upheld by democratically elected officials or;

    b)   the generosity/goodwill of an Amazon or Walmart, where the corporate motto is: *"You should be thankful to have a job!"* or;

    c)   a schmuck like me, the Pancake Kid?

In honor of my dad, Fast Eddie, who never knew what it was to have job security; who never could afford to take his kids to a doctor when they had a 103°F fever; and who believed that higher education and taking long vacations were a privilege reserved for the rich, I think I know which option I'd choose.

All this—and more—was churning around in my head the day the anarchist stepped into the diner. Unfortunately, that week we'd been creatively screwed twice: first, by customers who had left a 50€ bill on the table, next to their check, before heading for the door, smiling and pointing at it so the busy server could see they'd paid. The 50€ turned out to be nothing more than a color Xerox copy—and on one side only!

The second time, on another busy day, a group of customers paid their bill at the table in front of the server, counting out a pile of *tickets restaurants*—ten in all—at 9.68€ a pop. Later that night, as my manager was scanning the tickets into the computer, he discovered that only the top one was valid; the other nine had long since expired.

So, yeah, I was in no mood for the anarchist, an angry-looking customer who seemed to have been wearing the same tattered T-shirt with the Ⓐ symbol on it ever since the Ramones first hit the airwaves back in the late '70s. After finishing his bacon and eggs, he squatted in a booth for hours, polishing off two pots of sock juice. When I brought him the bill, he mumbled something under his breath.

"*Pardon?*" I asked, unable to decipher what he was saying.

Avoiding eye contact, the anarchist mumbled again, but this time more loudly and clearly, *en français*. "I said: I don't have to pay if I don't want to. *C'est mon droit.*"

I rattled my head like a baby's toy, not believing what I'd just heard. This wasn't a kid I was talking to. The customer had to be at least forty-five, his thinning hair stretched back into a knobby ponytail.

I wanted to say: *Let me guess: you're getting bored smashing storefront windows and have decided to move on to stiffing Mom & Pop shops?* Instead I said, "That's a good one, *Monsieur!* 11.50€, *s'il vous plaît!*"

But the guy wasn't joking. He got up and headed for the door. "Uh, where do you think you're going, *Monsieur?*" The lanky man mumbled a slew of expletives as he exited the diner. I turned to my waitress and said, "Hold the fort! I'm going after the anarchist!" A look of panic crossed the young American's face; she'd never seen a real anarchist before.

A slow-speed chase ensued. Two angry, middle-aged, out-of-breath white guys. Somehow the anarchist managed to always stay a couple steps ahead of me—just out of reach—as we made our way across several *arrondissement*s: past the *Sainte-Chapelle* church, past *la Consiergerie*, past *la Tour Saint-Jacques*. At one point, I got close enough to grab him, when suddenly he made a sharp left turn and crossed the busy rue de Rivoli—without using the crosswalk. I stopped dead in my tracks, thinking: *Wait. Does he have the right to do that?*

As I watched him disappear around the corner on the other side of the street, I knew I had no choice but to follow suit. The moment I put my foot onto the busy boulevard, I suddenly understood the appeal of anarchy. What a thrill it was to break the rules, to do whatever the hell I wanted!

Making a mad dash across the street, I weaved in and out of the traffic as drivers honked their horns and yelled at me. "Out of the road, jackass!"

"Hey, I'm jaywalking here!" I yelled back like some crazed Ratso Rizzo from *Midnight Cowboy*. "It's my freakin' *right*!"

As soon as I made it to the other side, I rounded the corner where I'd last seen the anarchist, afraid that he'd be long gone. Instead, he was just a couple blocks away, hunched over and panting.

At this point, I was panting, too. "Don't . . . you . . . move . . ." I wheezed. The anarchist looked up, startled. I took a deep breath, then broke into a sprint when suddenly:

Cramp! My legs knotted up like a coil. *Pain! Incredible pain!*

The anarchist grinned. Reached into his pocket and pulled out a stubby little cigarette which he'd rolled himself with his tobacco-stained hands. In between pants, he lit it up. Took a few puffs then trotted off.

I hobbled after him, massaging my legs as I dodged the clouds of smoke popping out of his mouth.

After a few blocks, I finally caught up to him—right at the entrance to his apartment building, which, coincidentally, happened to be just a block away from BIA #2. Before he had a chance to enter, I leapt in front of the doorway. A slew of profanities—many of which I never even knew I knew—spewed out of my gutter mouth like a French sailor.

"Putain d'e*cu!é de !s&!#ud de m^rd*!!"

Before you knew it, a crowd of beaming Parisians had gathered around us, egging us on. I was this close to slugging the errant customer when a voice from behind the crowd said, "What's going on here?"

I turned to see a husky French cop standing there. *Surely, I must be dreaming,* I thought. There's *never* a cop around when you need one.

With all eyes on me, I noticed for the first time that I was still wearing my waiter's apron. All the better, I thought, to give my story street cred.

"Officer," I said, pointing at the anarchist. "This gentleman had a full meal—and bottomless beverage—at my restaurant, then tried to . . ." (*Hmm, how do you say "dine and dash" en français?* I wondered.) "Uh . . . he *refused* to pay, saying it was his *droit*."

"Is that true?" The cop looked at the anarchist who said nothing. "Where's your wallet?"

The anarchist jerked his head upward. "Fourth floor."

"Then go upstairs. Get your wallet. And pay the man."

The anarchist grumbled like a spoiled child then entered his apartment building. A few minutes later, he returned and handed me 11.50€, all in small change.

"Now that wasn't so hard, was it?" the cop said.

"Thank you, officer," I said, shaking his hand. "I really appreciate it!"

Filled with immense joy and feeling lighter than air, I skipped back to the diner, content in the knowledge that a large portion of the money that was now jingling in my apron pocket would eventually go to the French government, so that *all* citizens—*contrôleurs*, lawyers and anarchists alike—could have a better quality of life.

SEVEN
Flâneur O'Connor

I always looked forward to meeting with my French banker because she never failed to give me chocolate. And an espresso. Or rather, a fancy Nespresso—with a choice of four fabulous flavors. (No sock juice here!)

Wearing a chic leather skirt and tall, clog-like boots that accentuated her petit frame, Mme. Zaël handled all of my banking needs with the upmost professionalism: from business and personal loans to insurance and retirement accounts, and on this occasion, the yearly wiring of dividends to BIA's investors back in the States. And she did it all by herself, without an assistant.

"Can I get you anything else, Monsieur Carlson?" Mme. Zaël asked as she rummaged through a large bag full of complimentary swag emblazoned with the bank's logo. "Pens? Lollipops? A wall calendar?"

"Well," I hesitated, sipping my Nespresso. "I could use some more deposit bags."

Mme. Zaël looked up from her swag bag. For the first time I noticed dark circles under her eyes, which she'd been unable to hide with her makeup. She gave me a weary smile and said, "Fortunately, we have someone who can assist you with that." There was a long pause, both of us knowing what that meant: I'd have to deal with the receptionist downstairs. Mme. Zael looked me square in the eye. "Call me if there's any trouble."

As I descended the narrow staircase from Mme. Zaël's office, I took a deep breath, slowly approaching the "gatekeeper" of the bank. Sitting behind the receptionist's desk, which was ironically marked *"Accueil"* (Welcome), was Mme. Zaël's polar opposite, an aloof woman with poof-permed hair and enormous, plastic-framed glasses that, chances were, she'd been wearing since the '80s—the last time she'd given a hoot.

The receptionist glanced up from her magazine. *"Vous partez* (you leaving), Monsieur Carlson?" she asked.

"Oui, mais—"

"So am I!" she said, cutting me off. "In eighteen months, three weeks, and four days!"

Of course, I knew what the receptionist was referring to. Ever since I'd first met her, she'd been literally counting down the days until her retirement. After giving out the latest tally, she topped it off with her favorite expression: "I can't wait to do *absolument rien*! (absolutely nothing!)"

And how's that any different from what you do now? I thought.

In France, they had a name for someone whose main ambition in life was to do *absolument rien*. A *flâneur*. (Or *flâneuse* for a female.) Although technically a true *flâneur(se)* was someone who dawdled about town doing nothing, usually in cool hangouts like a café—*not* at their actual workplace. That was just *lazy*.

CRAIG CARLSON

But no matter. Mme. Flâneuse, as I came to call her, fit the bill to a tee. However, she seemed a bit young to be retiring. My guess was that she was part of the generation born before July 1, 1951, which meant she'd be eligible to receive her full French pension at the age of sixty. (By law, anyone born after that date could retire at sixty-two, but if they wanted to receive their *full* retirement benefits, they'd have to add an additional five years.)

"I'm jealous," I said to Mme. Flâneuse, knowing full well that the only chance I had of getting what I wanted was to flatter her. "Me, I have to wait until I'm at least sixty-seven before I get to retire. But before then, may I please have some deposit bags: twenty for bills and ten for change?"

Mme. Flâneuse shook her head. "Sorry, we're all out."

"Would you mind taking a look please?"

"Why? It changes absolutely nothing."

Please, Madame, I wanted to say. *Un petit effort,* which, incidentally, was one of my favorite French expressions. So simple, yet means so much. In this case: *Get off your lazy butt and take a look!*

Mme. Flâneuse returned to her magazine.

"Excuse me one moment," I said as I stepped down the hallway. Out of the receptionist's view, I pulled out my iPhone. "Mme. Zaël?" I whispered into the receiver. "She won't give me any deposit bags."

Mme. Zaël's voice pierced through my phone's earhole. *"Oh-la-la! C'est pas vrai!"*

Clomp, clomp, clomp. The sound of Mme. Zael's heavy, clog-like boots echoed through the bank as she made her way down the stairs from her office above.

Given the same situation, most workers in America would be *merding* in their pants, afraid that their boss would be showing them the door. Not Mme. Flâneuse. She had job security *à la française.* Which meant instead of licking her boss's boots, she licked her fingertip before flipping a page in her magazine.

Mme. Zaël went into the bank's safe and popped out a few seconds later holding a pile of deposit bags. "Eléonore," she said in exasperation as she waved them in front of Mme. Flâneuse. "What is this *cinéma*? We received a new batch of bags yesterday!"

"I wasn't here yesterday." *Lick. Page flip.*

Turns out Mme. Flâneuse's absence the previous day—a Wednesday—had not been due to illness. Nor had she taken a vacation day. Instead she had benefitted from a job perk in France known as the *RTT* (*La réduction du temps de travail*). In a nutshell, when the infamous thirty-five-hour workweek was enacted into law in February 2000, one of the main arguments was that with employees working fewer hours, companies would have to hire more, thus bringing down the record-high unemployment rate at the time.

Then there was *reality.*

Since many businesses were open forty hours a week, that left a gap of five hours to fill, certainly not enough to hire a whole new employee. For those who worked "behind the scenes," such as administrators or bureaucrats, it wasn't that difficult to adapt to the new law. But for positions in the service industry, which dealt directly with clients, it was definitely a challenge.

To solve the problem, the French government came up with the *RTT.* Using Mme. Flâneuse as an example, in order to cover the bank's opening hours, she would work a full forty-hour week—sometimes two in a row. Then all the time she'd worked *above* thirty-five hours would be added up and converted into "get-out-of-work-free" credits that could be used to take a day (or a half-day) off.

And who ended up filling in those gaps? Why, serious and conscientious middle management employees like Mme. Zaël, who were too busy working to count their hours. With her own workload piling up, Mme. Zaël would have to sit at the front desk while Mme. Flâneuse stayed at home doing *absolument rien.*

I felt bad for Mme. Zaël. For a system that was meant to create equality, it somehow didn't seem fair.

"Another thing I noticed," I said to Julien when I got home later that night. "Mme. Flâneuse acts as if she's doing everyone a favor by just *being* there."

"In a way she is," Julien said. "At least in her mind. And certainly in France."

Julien went on to explain that it's not uncommon for an employee who's a year or two away from retirement to ask their doctor for an *arrêt de travail* (work stoppage). From there, it's surprisingly easy to renew the *arrêt* over and over again, right up to one's retirement date, effectively running out the clock. Not only is it against the law to fire an employee when they're on sick leave, depending on factors such as seniority and pay grade, many can receive 90% of their salary for up to three years. And the cherry on top: the employee continues to *accumulate* vacation days, even while they're sitting at home watching Netflix.

"Not a bad deal, right?" Julien said. "And the best part is: you don't even have to be sick to get sick leave!"

"For real?"

Julien nodded then told the story of a young man who worked at a famous museum in Paris with a friend of his. For the past two years, the guy had been on indefinite sick leave for "psychological stress."

"You've gotta be kiddin'," I said. "It's a *museum*. With paintings and sculptures. Please tell me how that's stressful?"

I imagined the worker standing in the main hall, surrounded by art lovers. "Everybody's looking at me!" he says, paranoid. "No, they're not," his colleague reassures him, "They're looking at the *tableaux*." "No," he responds. "They're looking at *me*!"

"Don't laugh," Julien said. "But that's not as far-fetched as you might think."

Turns out, a social worker met with the guy every month or so and actually *coached* him on how to behave so he could prolong his sick leave until he felt "comfortable" enough to go back to work.

"Everybody at the museum knew he was just hanging out at home, getting stoned," Julien said.

"How?"

"'Cause everybody went to his place and got stoned with him. Apparently, he had the best weed."

As I thought about Mme. Flâneuse and the stoner guy from the museum, I found it hard to believe all the studies that consistently showed France being one of the most productive countries in the world. In the Top Ten actually, ahead of Germany and the U.K.

Comment est-ce possible? I wondered. As an exhausted, overworked businessman, if there was a way to do nothing *and* be productive, I wanted in on the secret!

Experts had many theories to explain why France was so high on the list. First, unlike in other countries, French workers were less likely to hang out and socialize with their coworkers, which gave them the opportunity to get more done in a shorter space of time. (I assumed that didn't include French salespeople, who often huddled together in a circle while at work, chitchatting and getting annoyed if you interrupted them to ask for help.)

Another reason for the high productivity level in France: job security. According to researchers, since French employees stuck around longer and got to know their jobs better, they tended to be more efficient. Or so the theory goes. (Mme. Flâneuse exempted, of course.)

But perhaps the most difficult statistic to wrap my head around: France's high unemployment rate may actually *help* productivity. Experts say productivity levels are higher when the *least* productive members of society aren't being calculated into the equation.

So much for the so-called experts. I came up with a couple theories of my own to explain France's high output. First, vacations. It's amazing how much work gets done the week or two before an employee goes away on holiday. Speaking for myself, nothing motivates me to clear out my in-box faster than knowing I'm about to board a plane to a destination where I'd rather not have to worry about work. And in a country where, on average, every six weeks there's some form of vacation (such as school breaks), before you know it, *boom*—France is propelled into the Top Ten!

My other theory on why France has such a high productivity rate has never been mentioned in a single study I've come across. Pride. Despite their nonchalant, *laissez-faire* veneer on the outside, on the inside the French really care about the quality of their work. How else to explain the exquisite detail in everything from the beautifully sculpted façades of Parisian architecture to the delicacy of French pastries like the *millefeuilles*. (It takes a lot of work to pack "a thousand layers" into a single dessert.)

Of course, critics are quick to point out that, despite the evidence, France should be much lower on the list. *Why?* Because the math is wrong, they claim. Or more precisely, researchers have been using a faulty denominator. For those who were never good at math, I'll keep it simple: most studies determine a country's productivity by dividing their gross domestic product per capita by the average number of hours worked. But what if the number of "hours worked" used to calculate productivity is actually *not* the number of hours worked in the real world?

As my banker Mme. Zaël showed, countless numbers of employees in France work far more than the thirty-five hours they're technically paid for. Sometimes it's because an employee has negotiated a contract based on a *salary* amount (not an hourly amount), where it's understood that, *wink-wink*, the thirty-five hours listed on your pay stub is just a technicality.

Then there were cash businesses, like restaurants, where the calculation was even more skewed. I wished I had a euro for every time a potential employee asked me if I'd be willing to declare only half their hours—and pay the rest in cash. (This was especially common with cooks, since many of them were refugees from foreign countries who would, quite absurdly, lose their government benefits if they worked full time.) This was the main reason why I had so much trouble finding—and holding on to—cooks. When I told them that BIA didn't pay anything under the table, they'd say, "but *every* other restaurant does!"

As they'd head toward the door and on to a place that paid them in cash, I'd try to convince them to stay. "But think of the future," I'd say. "The more *declared* hours you work now, the more you'll get when you retire!" But instead of waiting patiently until they were sixty-seven (when God only knew if there'd be anything left in the public coffers to pay for retirement), today's cooks preferred to get all their benefits *now*.

The more I thought about it, the more I had a newfound appreciation for Mme. Flâneuse. Not only did she never miss a day of work, she played by the rules. Having paid fully into the system, she waited her turn (albeit impatiently) until the big day arrived. Ironically, as she continued to do nothing, somehow the countdown clock seemed to accelerate. Soon six months turned into six weeks, then six days and finally—just like that—she was gone. With her absence, I imagined France's productivity level ticking up an infinitesimal notch or two.

Not so. The bank had *beaucoup de* trouble finding her replacement. For the next several months, whenever I passed by, there was always a new receptionist, each more dour and less motivated than the last. None made it past their two-month trial period, the only time an employer can safely get rid of an employee.

One day while I was meeting with Mme. Zaël, I noticed a young woman with pink hair and multiple piercings sitting in the office across the hall with a gray-haired administrator. Through the office window, I could see that the young woman was sobbing. I could only make out snippets of their conversation—the gist being that she couldn't handle "all the pressure."

"Is that the newest receptionist?" I asked Mme. Zaël.

She let out a long sigh. "God, I hope not."

"Let me guess," I said, having dealt with my share of millennials at the diner. "Her boss is trying to give her some constructive criticism."

"*Non*," Mme. Zaël shook her head. "He's just going over her *job description*."

Turns out, it was the young woman's first—and Mme. Zaël hoped—*last* day on the job.

After our meeting, Mme. Zaël accompanied me to the exit, stopping in front of the empty receptionist desk. "That reminds me," she said. "Wait here a second." She disappeared into the safe and came out a moment later holding a stack of deposit bags. "Don't forget these," she smiled.

As I left the Les Halles district where my bank was located, I cut across the Marais to my next, *très* important rendezvous: *le Centre des Finances Publiques*. There'd been an error on my tax return, which I hoped to have corrected before forking over 47% of my gross adjusted income to the French government. (I'd even brought along my checkbook.)

It was easy to find the tax bureau. Like most government buildings, it stuck out like a sore thumb, a big ugly block of crumbling concrete that was exempt from the strict codes requiring all new construction in Paris to harmoniously blend in with the ancient architecture of the surrounding neighborhood.

Stepping up to the building, the first thing I noticed was that all the lights were off inside, the place deserted. A simple, handwritten note taped to the inside of the glass door proclaimed: On Strike! There was no indication of when the office would open again, or even why they were on strike in the first place. No surprise since most of the time French people didn't know what their fellow citizens were protesting about, either. Often times it was just a way for workers to flex their muscles, to remind the powers that be not to mess around with them. I was all for "power to the people" and all that, but with the government offices shut down, it begged the question: *If I can't pay my taxes, who's going to pay for French bureaucrats to go on strike?*

I also wondered why French people didn't get more worked up by the constant *mouvements sociaux*. Everyone seemed to take it in stride. Then I learned that for them, there was an upside: When the city shut down, Parisians did too, often using it as an excuse to skip out on work—(*Hey, what could I do? The métro was closed!*)—and instead, head straight to a café to have a drink and a smoke.

As I left the tax office, I could hear the chants from the striking workers off in the distance, at the Place de la République. As sometimes happens at the end of a march, protestors gathered together to party, often with their families joining in. They'd light up a barbecue, grill some chicken and merguez sausages, then dance the afternoon away to techno music. It was like the French version of a tailgate party in the States—only minus the football and pickup trucks. (Turns out, the researchers got it wrong; French workers *did* socialize with each other. But *outside* of work, while they were on strike.)

With the din of the distant *fête* echoing down the narrow Marais streets, I thought about my recent visit to my doctor and how she'd been monitoring my heart ever since I'd collapsed while jogging on the Seine three years earlier.

"When was the last time you had a day off, Monsieur Carlson?" she'd asked during my checkup. I couldn't recall.

Perhaps the tax office being on strike was a sign from the universe, I thought. Maybe I needed to chill out, to shut down like my fellow Parisians did.

There was no doubt about it. All the signs were pointing in the same direction: It was time to get my *flâneur* on.

Half a block from the tax office I found *the* most picture-perfect French café to try my hand at doing *absolument rien*. With its dark green awnings and enormous open-air terrace, the café was tucked into a small square beside a medieval water fountain whose lion head sculpture had been continuously spitting out potable water since the 17th century.

I was relieved to see that the café was facing north, in the shade. It was late September and Paris was in the middle of an unusual heat wave, with temperatures rocketing up to the low 40s (100°+F). Even with climate change and the record-breaking heat that came with it, it was still rare to find air conditioning in Paris—the exceptions being certain office buildings and department stores like Galeries Lafayette and the nearby BHV.

I stood in front of the café and checked out the place. The accordion façade had been folded wide open so that the outside terrace seemed to blend into the café itself. With the terrace half full, I tried to find a spot outside the circumference of cigarette smoke. No such luck. I ended up sitting inside the café, but right on the terrace's edge. With any luck, the slight breeze outside would not shift direction.

After ordering a *kir à la mûre* (white wine with blackberry liquor), I sat back and tried to be idle. It wasn't easy. The last time I'd attempted to be a true *flâneur* was back in the summer of 1985. It was the end of my junior year abroad. All the other students had rushed back to the U.S. to be with their families. Fortunately, since I had no home to rush back to, I ended up staying in Paris, where I'd found a cheap studio to sublet and a job that paid under the table at an English-language bookstore.

Being penniless, I borrowed books from my job, then sat in a café, ordered a single espresso and read for hours on end. By the end of the summer, I'd almost finished John Steinbeck's entire body of work, nurturing my desire to one day become a writer.

And now here I was, some thirty years later, rusty at doing nothing. I needed practice. I surveyed the café, looking for *flâneurial* inspiration. Most of the clientele were fashionable young men (it was the Marais after all), who wore pants so tight it was impossible for them to wedge two of life's most basic necessities into their pockets—a cell phone and cigarettes—forcing them to carry both by hand.

As I stared at the svelte, stubbled hipsters, I suddenly felt frumpy and self-conscious. They seemed to enjoy being on public display. Some seemed especially proud to show off their brand-new designer shoes, their pant legs rolled up high, revealing their bare ankles. *What, are socks on strike now, too?*

What was my problem? Why couldn't I just relax? I felt so guilty sitting there doing *absolument rien*. All I could think about was work—and the dripping faucet in BIA's kitchen that needed fixing. (*Note to self: After being idle, swing by BHV and pick up some washers.*)

I was reminded of an ad I'd seen in the American Airlines magazine on my last flight to the States. A handsome young businessman wades in a pool in the middle of a tropical island paradise à la Club Med. With one hand, he holds an umbrella drink. And with the other, he taps away at his laptop, which sits on the edge of the pool in front of him—the epitome of the perfect American oxymoron: the "working vacation."

That's how it was in the coffee shops I used to frequent back in LA, too. Nobody could just sit there and relax. Instead, everyone was glued to their computer screens, writing the Great American Screenplay. (I should know. I was one of them.)

Back at the café in Paris, it was just the opposite. French people sat there perfectly still, gazing ahead, needing nothing to distract them—save the occasional sip of their drink or a drag off their cigarette. As I stared at the puffy white clouds that rose up from the terrace like geysers at Yellowstone, I tried not to be judgmental. But smoking was the one thing I had trouble tolerating in France. I just couldn't understand how seemingly smart, well-educated, and refined people could *voluntarily* put noxious fumes into their system. Wasn't there enough pollution in the air already?

I cut some slack for older smokers, though, since chances were they'd grown up in an era when magazine ads used to boast: *"More doctors smoke Camels than any other cigarette!"* But times had changed. Hadn't people read the latest science? Or at the very least, taken a moment to look at the graphic pictures of cancerous lungs and esophagi that were now required by law to be wrapped around every pack of cigarettes sold in France?

I had a theory why people smoked so much, which I shared with Julien over breakfast one morning. "I think, for the French, smoking is a fashion accessory. Like a handbag or an ascot."

"It's more than that," Julien, the former smoker, said. "It's about freedom. And the social interaction that goes with cigarette breaks."

Julien had a point. I had to admit, the smokers on the terrace seemed much more stress-free than me. Like a deep breathing exercise in yoga class, they would take a long drag on their cigarette until their lungs were full. Hold it. Then let out a long exhale. Over and over again. Deep breathing and deep *being*. As if mastering the "power of now."

I began to wonder, *Maybe the French were onto something*. With more and more studies showing a strong link between stress and disease, I wondered if there'd been any counter-studies suggesting the *benefits* resulting from the calming effect of smoking—not to mention the weight loss.

Hmm, I thought. *All things being relative, perhaps smoking wasn't so bad after all*.

But then the wind shifted. Literally. Suddenly, I was engulfed by a suffocating, copper-colored haze, which emanated from a hipster's e-cigarette directly in front of me. It wouldn't have been so bad if the flavor was something like, I don't know, blueberry and white chocolate chip pancakes. Instead it was closer to "unwashed manly musk." *Ack*.

Since I'd arrived at the café, I'd watched the hipster go from smoking a cigarette to vaping—then back and forth, over and over again, never once stopping to pause in between. I wanted to shout, *Don't you want to breathe regular air for, like, five minutes?*

So much for relaxing. After fifteen minutes at the café, I was all *flâneur*-ed out.

Time to get back to work. There was a drippy faucet at the diner that needed fixing.

On my way to the BHV department store, I thought about Fast Eddie and all the ways he would've made a great *flâneur*. First, when it came to doing nothing, he was a Zen master. I remembered hanging out with him at the Rustic Bar & Grill, a dive bar with wall-to-wall paneling and shuttered windows to keep out the light. Because I was only eight years old and legally not allowed to be around alcohol yet, I was relegated to a booth in the "grill" section of the Rustic, whereas my dad got to sit in the "bar" section.

Back then, before moving to Frenchtown, I lived with my Grandma Mary and sometimes my mom, when she wasn't in the asylum. To give them a break, my dad agreed to pick me up every other Sunday. But instead of taking me to play catch or go fishing, Fast Eddie would let me accompany him to his favorite watering hole.

I would sit in the booth, watching him nurse his beer. He would sit there for what felt like hours, completely still, looking off into space, as if in deep thought—much like the French—puffing on his cigarette. I wanted him to hurry up so we could get the hell out of there. But Fast Eddie would drag out that one beer for as long as he could.

Then, mercifully, he would get to the last bit and gulp it down. I would spring up from my seat, ready to leave, only to see Fast Eddie motion to the bartender for another round. My dad must have seen me sink in my seat because the next thing I knew, a bag of chips flew through the air and landed on the table in front of me. "Eat up, son," he said, as if it were giving me a year's worth of allowance.

And, of course, another reason Fast Eddie would have made a great *flâneur* was that he loved to smoke. Up to three packs a day. He would have been thrilled that, in 2020, there was still no stigma in France regarding his favorite pastime. How different from the States, where as far back as the 1980s my dad was already feeling the social pressure to kick the habit. He'd been working at McDonald's as a janitor (or "custodial engineer" as he preferred to be called) when one day, his boss told him he could no longer smoke in front of customers, even when he was outside sweeping or collecting garbage. Instead, he had to go behind the dumpster to light up.

"Isn't that a kick in the pants?!" Fast Eddie would say. I could only imagine how humiliating it was for him, a grown man, to have to hide behind a dumpster like a teenager. That never would have happened to him here in France.

And lastly, like Mme. Flâneuse, Fast Eddie was a master at doing *absolument rien*. He thought ambition was a total waste of time and energy, and would often sleep on the job. On the plus side, I never felt any pressure from him to succeed.

"It doesn't matter what job you do," Fast Eddie said. "As long as there's air conditioning."

Since I lived in a country where there was virtually no AC anywhere, including my diners, I wondered if my dad were still alive today, would he consider me to be a failure?

I couldn't shake this thought as I entered the BHV department store, with all its AC and *successful* people. The sales clerks were so successful, in fact, they couldn't be bothered to assist me. I was on my own. *No problem.* I'd mastered that.

As I made my way toward the escalator to go down to the hardware department, I noticed someone familiar coming in the opposite direction, from the book section. It was none other than Mme. Flâneuse, her hands full of future reading. The moment she saw me, she smiled.

"Ah, Monsieur Carlson! *Comment ça va?*" I was amazed she remembered my name. It had been over a year since I'd last seen her.

"How's retirement been treating you?" I asked.

"Oh, it's been heaven! Pure heaven!"

"What have you been doing with all your free time?"

"*Rien! Absolument rien!*"

Just then, my phone began to vibrate—not once, but several times. "Excuse me a moment," I said as I quickly read the slew of incoming messages.

The first one: *The blender just broke! Can you pick up a new one?* (There'd been a spike in milkshake sales thanks to the heat wave.)

The second message: *The ice machine broke, too! But the repairman said he's too busy right now and can't come until next week!*

And finally the last message, the reason why I was at BHV in the first place: *The drip in the kitchen sink has become a torrent. Hurry!*

I shoved my phone back into my pocket. "I'm sorry, Madame," I said. "I need to take care of a *petit* emergency."

"Of course," Mme. Flâneuse smiled warmly. "You do that. *Au revoir,* Monsieur Carlson."

Mme. Flâneuse looked into my eyes, and for the first time I noticed how genuinely happy the former bank receptionist looked. And how, generally, she'd always been happy—now that I thought about it.

As I watched Mme. Flâneuse turn around and fade into the crowd of shoppers, carefree and free, I vowed to one day find a balance in my life. To subscribe to the old adage that had so impressed me the first time I'd heard it: *The French don't live to work; they work to live.*

But as my phone began to vibrate again, nonstop, I knew that day would have to wait.

Le Palais de Justice (The Paris Courthouse). Photo by Meredith Mullins.

EIGHT

The Trial Period

It's hard to find a French cook in France. In all my years at Breakfast in America, I've never received a single CV from one. At first, I thought it had to be because BIA served American grub, and that no self-respecting, classically trained French chef would be caught dead flipping burgers and flapjacks. But after speaking to some of my fellow Parisian restaurateurs, I learned that perhaps the problem ran much deeper.

"Times have changed," Franck, a hard-edged, third generation French owner of a restaurant in my neighborhood told me. "Most French people don't want to work in *any* restaurant nowadays."

The reasons according to Franck: The long hours. The grueling, back-breaking work. The hot, uncomfortable kitchen environment. "Young people prefer *les start-ups*!" he lamented.

After my conversation with Franck, I felt a sense of relief. At least the reason there were no French chefs at my diner wasn't *personal.*

But it hadn't always been that way. Ironically, one of the first chefs I ever hired happened to be French—although he never actually applied for the job.

I first met Tito, a talented young sous-chef from the Ivory Coast, when I was working at a French restaurant in Paris the summer before I opened BIA. (I was there to get some much needed restaurant experience before opening a place of my own.) After being insulted one too many times by his prima donna boss, Tito asked if I needed a chef at BIA.

"No," I said. "But we could definitely use a *cook*."

It was important to make the distinction. Being a short-order cook was a completely different *métier* (profession) than what Tito had been trained to do at the *restaurant gastronomique* where we'd worked together. After I explained what those differences were, mainly organization and speed, Tito said, "*Pas de problème!*" He was up for the challenge.

Unfortunately, from his first day on the job, Tito couldn't keep up. Orders would pile up on the spinning wheel above the grill as Tito—in the fine tradition of *haute cuisine*—carefully prepared each dish one at a time. As the weeks went by, he seemed unable—or perhaps unwilling—to adapt to the needs of a diner. No matter how hard I tried, I couldn't get him to organize multiple orders into groups so that he could get them out faster.

"Okay, Tito," I'd say as hungry customers waited impatiently. "I need you to throw ten burgers on the grill, eighteen slices of bacon, five sunny-side up eggs, and three orders of onion rings!" Tito would give me a blank stare then continue preparing one order at a time.

In addition to being interminably slow, Tito shared another trait that was very common among French chefs: he considered himself to be an *artiste*, meaning he would often take it as a personal affront if a customer wanted to change one of his creations.

As a lover of French cuisine, I totally respected this. But my friends visiting from the States were often perplexed. When I'd take them to a traditional French restaurant, they'd ask, "Why won't the chef cook my steak well done?" Or, "How come they won't substitute the Roquefort sauce on my duck with the pepper sauce? They already have the sauce. Why can't they just pour some on my duck?"

"Because the chef truly believes he knows better than you," I'd say. "And from my own experience, more often than not, he does." (Although at times, I would secretly *kill* for the pepper sauce.)

Of course, this kind of capriciousness was deadly for an American diner. One morning, an American tourist who had been backpacking across Europe for months, came in dying for a hearty breakfast. After ordering bacon and eggs, she asked if we could mix some cheddar cheese into her scrambled eggs.

"You betcha!" I said.

"Absolument pas!" Tito huffed when he saw the order. "That is *not* on the menu."

For the umpteenth time, I had to remind Tito that BIA was an American joint, which meant that, like it or not, the customer was always right. After much hemming and hawing, Tito grabbed a ramekin and shoved some grated cheese in it.

"Et voilà!"

"Uh, Tito, she wants the cheese *inside* her eggs, not on the side."

"Well, then, she can mix it in herself!"

After six months at BIA, Tito kindly agreed to move on. (It was a mutual decision.) I'd end up hiring only one more French cook after him.

Ludo found us through a government program that placed older workers in job positions by offering a slight tax incentive to companies that hired them. I was happy to give an "old guy" a chance to get back into the workforce. (Although technically—shockingly—Ludo, at fifty-two, was only a couple of years older than me.) With decades of restaurant experience, Ludo got off to a promising start. But then one afternoon, he suddenly disappeared. He didn't answer his phone or text messages. No one knew if he was dead or alive.

Weeks passed then suddenly Ludo reappeared on Facebook where, like a tragic figure in a French romance novel, he took to writing long, melancholy missives about the heartache of "*le grand amour.*" (I later learned it was just one of a long string of breakups with his on-again, off-again ex-wife.)

So, yeah, I didn't have much luck with French cooks. And my track record with French waitstaff wasn't much better, either.

To be a server at BIA, only two things were required from applicants: they had to have a minimal amount of restaurant experience (although in many cases, we were willing to train newbies); and second, because of our international clientele, they had to be conversant in both French and English.

Almost all the CVs we received for waitstaff came from international students. Very few were French. At first, I thought it might have something to do with the language requirement. But then I figured out a more likely reason, summed up in two words you *never* hear in France: "student loans." Unlike in America, public universities in France were virtually tuition free. My French friends were shocked when I told them I'd graduated in the U.S. with $64,000 in student loan debt, a mere fraction of the amount many American students were burdened with nowadays.

In addition to free college, students in France were also entitled to numerous stipends, including one for rent and another for transportation to visit their families *en province*. Not only was there very little incentive for them to work, it was actually frowned upon.

"Students should study, *c'est tout!*" the argument went. As a result, young people in France often didn't have their first job until they were twenty-five or twenty-six.

Compare this to the States, where a large percentage of Americans start working straight out of high school and never stop until they're dead.

Although I'd love for there to be more French students working at BIA, the few who applied rarely made it past their first interview. The reason: right out of the gate, they'd declare, "I don't work weekends!"

"Why not?"

"Because *nobody* works on weekends."

"Really? Have you ever been to a restaurant on the weekend?"

"Yeah. So. What's your point . . . ?"

French students also tended to wait until the end of the school year, usually in May, to send out their CVs. Then they'd come to their interview with a long list of demands, even if they'd never worked a day in their life.

"Okay, so after finals, I'm going away for two weeks in June to 'decompress.' When I'm back, I can start work the second week of July, but then I'm gone on vacation for the whole month of August. For the *rentrée*, I can maybe work the week I'm back (if I'm not too tired), but then school starts up again in October so after that I'm *un*available."

When I mentioned to them that usually an employee has to accumulate vacation days *before* taking them, the young French student would get ornery and say, "But vacations are my *right*!"

Which brings me to the biggest challenge I've faced with certain French employees at my diner. They can be . . . how to put it gently, a tad *difficile*. Take Giselle. Right in the middle of service, when the diner was at its busiest and the staff was in "the weeds," she would grab her cell phone and florescent Bic lighter and head toward the door.

"Uh, where are you going, Giselle?"

"Cigarette break. It's my *right*. Five a shift."

After coming back, Giselle would sit at the counter, ignoring the line of customers outside, and order her staff meal.

"Uh, sorry, Giselle. Meal breaks are either before or after the rush."

"But it's my *right* to eat when I'm hungry."

Another French server, Chloé, was a philosophy student who was a hard worker, but for some reason, had great difficulty smiling. She reminded me of when I worked as a temp at Miss Universe, Inc. in LA, where I was hired to answer the phone in my deep male voice: "Miss Universe, may I help you?"

As if adhering to the clichés of their respective countries, the ever-cheery Miss USA listed her favorite actor as Kevin Costner. And her favorite book: *The Bridges of Madison County*. (This was the '90s after all.) And Miss France? Actor: Gérard Depardieu. And book: Albert Camus' *The Plague*.

I imagined Miss France standing backstage, glum in her evening gown, sucking on a filterless Gitane, saying in her hoarse smoker's voice, "What's the point? Really, why bother?"

That was Chloé. I knew it wasn't fair to ask her to be fake, or to change her nature. But customers—even French ones—expected an American diner to be cheerful. As Chloé would bring food to the tables, accompanied by her ever-present dark cloud, I would get her attention from across the room, put my fingers up to my lips and remind her to smile. She'd do her gallant best, but instead her face would get all contorted, as if she were seriously constipated. *Never mind!* I'd think. *Don't smile.*

Lastly, there was Philippe. Like Giselle, he would take his meal break whenever he wanted. Even more flagrantly, he'd order a *pavé de bœuf* (an expensive, profit-killing steak) for his staff meal, which was against company policy.

"Um, Philippe, that's not part of the employee menu," I'd say.

"*Ecoute* (listen). I work hard. You have no *right* to deprive me of a thick, juicy steak!"

Of course, back then, I was just starting to learn the ropes, so I didn't know if Philippe was within his rights or was just taking advantage of my naïveté.

"Gee, workers' rights sure are complicated in France, aren't they?" I said to Franck, my French restaurateur friend.

"You got that right, *mon ami!*" Franck said. "My staff knows the *Code de Travail* better than me—or my lawyer!" The *Code de Travail* was the behemoth 3,300-page "rule book" detailing France's insanely complex and contradictory labor laws, which seemed to change on a daily basis.

"I don't know how they keep up with it," I said to Franck. "It's like every French person takes the *Code de Travail* with them to bed at night and uses it as a pillow."

"It's worse than that," Franck said, lowering his voice. "Did you know there are actually *fonctionnaires* working for the government whose sole job is to coach employees on how to screw their bosses?"

"Hah, that's a good one, Franck!" I chuckled. "You almost had me there!" From the dark circles under his eyes and his punchy, manic nature, I convinced myself that the old man was just another sleep-deprived restaurateur cooking up a crazy conspiracy theory.

Franck stared at me long and hard, his eyes so lucid and free of crazy it sent a chill down my spine—a harbinger of things to come. *God, I was so naïve back then.*

French employee problems were the last thing on my mind the day Maurice, my French neighbor, contacted me about getting together for a coffee. He said he had a proposition for me.

Maurice lived two doors down from BIA #1 in the Latin Quarter, and was one of its first customers. We had a lot in common, particularly our passion for *le cinéma*. But unlike me, Maurice had eschewed film school and went straight to knocking on doors until he convinced a producer to hire him as a production assistant. With no contacts or family in the business, Maurice climbed his way up the ladder until he became an assistant director.

Seeing a lot of similarities between the different paths we'd taken, Maurice said he admired my "entrepreneurial spirit" and how I had started out with nothing—no restaurant or business experience, no rich relative to foot the bill—and created two successful diners. He particularly liked my mantra, which I repeated every time the business became too much to bear: "I'm living my dream. I'm living my dream . . ." According to Maurice, my mantra ended up saving his ass.

He was working on a film shoot in Croatia—a period piece in the vein of *The Count of Monte Cristo*. It was the dead of winter and the crew was knee-deep in mud, shivering in the cold, miserable. From their grumblings, he sensed there might be a revolt. Thinking quickly, he grabbed a megaphone and turned it up to the max, shouting, "Remember, everyone: 'You're living your dream!'"

The crew broke out into laughter, averting a most certain mutiny.

After years of working as an assistant director, Maurice was itching to make his own films. He'd stop by the diner with scripts he'd written and ask me to critique them. Soon he was inviting me to his screenings.

I really enjoyed his earlier work. But as time went on, his films became very self-absorbed, particularly his last one. It had no story—just two hours of a wealthy, badly shaven Frenchman having kinky sex with his much younger, Eastern European girlfriend, moving from room to room inside his cold and empty chateau, which, judging from the film's stark black and white imagery, was meant to mirror the rich man's soul.

"Who'd you make this film for exactly?" I asked.

"I don't understand the question."

"You know, who's your audience?"

"Audience?"

Unable to find a distributor for his film, Maurice's days as a director came to an abrupt end. At forty-six, he enrolled in pastry school. After finishing an internship at a local bakery, he decided he wanted to take a stab at starting his own business. That's where BIA came in.

"I'm thinking of opening a little coffee shop where I can serve my pastries," he said one day over espressos. "But I need experience—to learn the ins and outs of running a business."

"That's exciting, Maurice," I said. "I'd be happy to offer any advice I can."

"Actually, I was hoping for more than that . . . I'd like to work at BIA."

I was a little taken aback by his request. Not only did Maurice have no restaurant experience, more importantly, he was a neighbor, a customer, and an acquaintance. I had to be careful. *What if it didn't work out?* I thought, recalling the old adage: "Don't shit where you sleep."

"Right now there are no openings," I said (which was the truth). "But let me think about it."

"Okay, I'm in no hurry," Maurice said. "But if anything opens up, let me know."

Over the next several weeks, Maurice sent me emails from time to time, asking if any spots had freed up. He never put any pressure on me, and in fact, became more convincing with each email. He said he preferred to start off working only a few hours a week. Then if I was okay with it, he'd like to stay at the diner on his own time, learning every job—from dishwasher, to server, to cook, to manager.

"It's a win-win situation," he said. *You'll* save money and *I'll* learn everything I need to know to open my pastry shop."

"Sounds too good to be true," Franck said when I told him about Maurice's offer. "Plus he's French. Do you really want to hire *un français*—after what happened with the last ones?"

"Yes, because *everyone* deserves a chance." I said. "And why would you say such a thing? *You're* French."

"Exactement!"

When a server at BIA suddenly left without notice, taking off to Australia with her French fling, I sent Maurice a text: "Are you still interested in working at BIA?"

"Bien sûr!" he texted back.

I still had some reservations about hiring Maurice. But when we met later that week, he put my fears to rest. Having worked his whole career in the film world, he said he had been *dégouté* (disgusted) by his first "real job" at the bakery.

"I couldn't believe how much the workers complained about everything," he said. "I felt like saying, 'You haven't seen anything! Come work on a film set, where sixteen-hour days are the norm!'"

I smiled, recalling my own experiences making films. However, a few months after I'd opened BIA, I found myself lying on a ratty mattress in the cellar, exhausted to the point of semiconsciousness. That's when I realized that the restaurant business was even *harder* than the film business.

"What disgusted me the most, though," Maurice continued, "was how one of the employees at the bakery totally screwed over the owner, taking her to court on a bunch of bogus, trumped-up charges. It killed me because the owner had been so nice to all of us. She didn't deserve that."

I was floored by what Maurice was saying; the similarities to what I had gone through with my last cook were striking. However, when Maurice started to say that *all* French people were "lazy and spoiled," I had to defend them.

"That's not true, Maurice," I said. "Since moving to France, I've come across some of the hardest-working people I've ever seen." My banker Mme. Zaël immediately came to mind.

"Don't get me wrong," Maurice said. "I'm proud to be French. But look how many times you've been sued."

"Yeah, but, Maurice, none of them were French."

"Okay, but did any of them have French spouses or partners?"

I didn't have to think too long about that one. "Yeah." I said. "Everyone but one."

"Hah!" Maurice smiled. "What'd I say? The baker that sued my *patronne* wasn't French either, but his girlfriend was. And she pushed him to do it."

Once again, the similarities to my own experience were striking. Maurice looked me deep in the eyes; he really seemed to understand my pain.

That did it. He got the job.

Any remaining doubts I had about Maurice were assuaged by three of my favorite words in the French language: *La période d'essai*, aka "the Trial Period." It was the one and only saving grace when it came to hiring someone in France.

The Trial Period worked like this: I started Maurice off with a temporary contract (CDD) at twenty hours a week. During his first two months if I felt it wasn't working out for whatever reason, I could let him go. However, if I was on the fence and needed more time to decide, I could extend his trial period for another two months—but only once. After that, his CDD (*contrat à durée déterminée*) would turn into a CDI (*contrat à durée indéter-minée*), meaning he'd now have a *permanent* lifetime contract, which would be extremely difficult and costly to break.

Of course, during those first months, an employer had to be extra careful the new hire wasn't pretending to be on their best behavior until the trial period ended. That's what had happened to me with my very first full-time employee, Stewart. The day after his trial period was over he completely changed his behavior. He came in late and stopped giving a *merde*. One day during the lunch rush, he became super aggressive, so I fired him after his shift. Stewart took me to court. The case dragged on for two years and, of course, he won. Although he'd barely worked two months, Stewart was awarded thousands of euros.

But that was then. Now I wasn't so green. After all these years, I was becoming an old pro at navigating France's complicated labor laws. And with the Trial Period on my side, what could possibly go wrong?

I met with my manager, Bruce, a reserved Welshman in his forties, to fill him in on the newest member of the BIA Team. Of course, since Maurice was our neighbor, Bruce knew who he was, but didn't seem very enthusiastic about hiring him. "Don't worry," I said. "He'll only be with us temporarily. Until he picks up enough experience to open up his own pastry shop."

"But do you think he'll be able to fit in?" Bruce asked. "He's twice as old as most of the staff."

"Yeah, I know," I said. "But I figure it might be nice to have a mature presence around." No sooner were the words out of my mouth when I suddenly recalled the kinky, sex-filled film Maurice had made. "Uh, by the way," I said to Bruce. "Just so you know: I warned Maurice that if he tries to hit on any of the waitresses, he's out of here."

"Okay, got it," Bruce nodded.

After Maurice's first day of training, I checked in with Bruce to see how it went. "Not bad," he said. "He's friendly enough. But since he doesn't have any restaurant experience, it might take him some time to learn the job."

"Okay, but if he doesn't pick it up quickly, let me know. Remember, we can always let him go at any point during his trial period."

After his second shift Maurice had just one more training day left before the weekend, which all the staff knew were BIA's most important days; they paid the rent and most of the salaries. "Do you think he'll be ready for this Saturday?" I asked Bruce.

"Yeah, I think so," he said, not very convincingly. "But since I don't get in until 4:00 P.M., you might want to swing by and check on him."

That Saturday morning, I got to the diner early. Maurice was wearing a grandpa sweater that made him look much older than his forty-six years. Short and chubby, he had a Mr. Rogers quality to him as he shuffled about the room, smiling at customers and chatting them up. Although I wished he'd move faster, he seemed comfortable in his surroundings.

As business picked up, I noticed Maurice was forgetting a lot of things, such as making sure all egg dishes came with toast, which was one of my pet peeves. I pulled him aside and discretely told him, "Right after taking the order, drop the toast. Also, don't forget to go around from time to time and fill up customers' coffees."

Maurice nodded, but didn't say anything. Over the next couple of hours, he made a lot of the same mistakes most new hires make, so I cut him some slack. But one thing I wouldn't let slide were fidelity cards. I watched Maurice as he joked with a group of pretty English girls, putting multiple stamps on each of their cards.

After he was done, I motioned for him to meet me behind the bar. I reminded him of our rule: *one stamp per customer per card.* "Otherwise, each time you put an extra stamp, it's like giving a fifteen-euro meal away for free."

Maurice shrugged indifferently and said, "Okay." I made him issue new cards with the correct number of stamps on them. When he brought them over to the table he said, "Sa-ri, girlz-er, ma boss eez mah-kin' mi mah-ke you new cardz-a!"

I stared at Maurice, realizing that, except for a few words, all my conversations with him had been in French. Furthermore, since he'd directed a short film in California (with an all American cast and crew), I had no reason to doubt him when he said he spoke English fluently.

As I listened to him converse with a family of American customers, part of me thought he had to be faking it; his accent was just too clichéd. He sounded exactly like Pepé Le Pew, the lovemaking skunk from the old Warner Bros. cartoons. Fitting, since Maurice considered himself to be quite the ladies' man.

Whether he was faking his French accent or not, most of our customers seemed to like it, so I figured, *tant mieux* (all the better). However, before I left the diner, I reminded Maurice how crucial weekends were and that I needed him to pick up the pace. I then pointed to the other waitresses and said, "Remember, the team is here to support you. Don't be afraid to ask them questions if you're unsure about anything, okay?"

Maurice nodded, but the way the wheels seemed to be spinning around in his head, I didn't get a good feeling. On the way out the door, I turned to Savannah, our waitress from Mississippi, and said. "Please keep an eye on him, will you?"

"You got it, honey-bun!" she replied with her deep Southern drawl.

For the next several days, I got bogged down with administrative work and had almost completely forgotten about Maurice. Then the following Saturday, I got a panicked call from Bruce at the end of lunch service.

"Maurice has got to go!" he said. It was the first time I'd heard the normally reserved Welshman get so worked up.

I hopped on my bike and raced across town to meet Bruce at a café across from the diner. "What's going on?" I asked, still winded from my bike ride.

Bruce pulled out a folder from his attaché case and handed it to me. "Take a look at this," he said. "I had a bad feeling about Maurice right from the start, so I decided to write down everything that's happened over the past two weeks."

"But . . . why didn't you tell me this before?"

"I don't know . . . He's your friend, and . . . I thought I could handle him on my own."

I wanted to remind Bruce that he'd never been obligated to keep Maurice on, friend or not. But instead, I thanked him for his foresight—and for starting the ever-important French *dossier*.

"No problem," Bruce said. "After all that's happened at BIA, it's better to err on the side of caution, right?"

I nodded. I could feel my heart racing as I opened up Bruce's file and began to read his daily log. It ran several pages and was chock full of details, which I narrowed down to the highlights:

Day 1—Thursday, 2nd March

At the end of Maurice's first shift, Katie (a waitress who worked at BIA for two years), asked Maurice how his first day went. "I don't want to work weekends!" he said. Katie reminded him that at BIA, everyone works weekends.

Day 2—Friday, 3rd March

On his second shift, Maurice was trained by Tessa (a young waitress from Russia). Maurice complained that he wasn't happy with all the side work, like cleaning and refilling ketchups. He also made a fuss about his meal break, saying he didn't want to wait to eat until after the rush. When Katie arrived at 4pm, she asked, "How'd it go?" Maurice gave Tessa a dirty look then turned to Katie, "I preferred working with you.*" Afterward, Maurice told me he was exhausted and that "it was impossible to do everything this job requires!" I started to suspect that perhaps he didn't like taking orders from women younger than him. He said he didn't mind. "As long as they are pretty!"*

Day 3—Saturday 4th March

When I arrived at 4pm, none of the staff looked happy. I met with Maurice in my office. He said the job was a "nightmare!" That his colleagues were the rudest people he'd ever met. That they kept telling him what to do during the service. And that Savannah had called him "hon," which he found very "disrespectful."

Day 4—Wednesday 8th March

I arrived at 4pm. Savannah said Maurice still refused to follow instructions. Since it was becoming a pattern to have a 30-minute conversation with him at the end of every shift, I chose not to meet with him that day.

Day 5—Friday 10th March

During the entire service, Maurice undermined everything Tessa did, shouting at her in front of customers and calling her "my dear" in a very sarcastic manner. When she poured a demi *(beer), he said she was doing it all wrong. "I know French people, and they would not be happy with your* demi!*"*

Day 6—Saturday 11th March

Maurice tried to take his meal break in the middle of the rush—again. "I know French law and it's my right to eat whenever I want." He also said it was against the law to make him refill ketchups or do other side work. He then asked to see the Code de Travail, *saying it was*

*a "legal requirement that all employees get two days off in a row!" I
told him that would not be a problem since he only worked three days
a week!*

*Later, Katie told me she had been alone with Maurice when he
took his meal break and that she felt very uncomfortable. "He told
me he lived 'just two doors down from the diner' and that he
would like to 'show me his apartment,' but I'd have to wait until
his girlfriend was gone because she'd probably get upset. Then he
said, 'In fact I have three girlfriends, all your age, and one of them
is studying the same subject as you.'" Katie said she felt totally
"grossed out." That's when I called Craig and told him Maurice
had to go.*

I closed the *dossier. Incroyable.* The very same behavior that Maurice said
he loathed about the French, he was now copying down to a tee.

"I'm sorry you went through all that," I said to Bruce. "But the good
news is, you don't have to anymore—thanks to the Trial Period."

"Uh, yeah, about that . . ." Bruce fidgeted in his seat. "Maurice still
hasn't signed his contract."

"What?!"

"He took it home with him last week. Said he wanted to 'study' it first."

"Oh, *merde.*"

I grabbed my phone to call my lawyer. But with all the excitement, I'd
forgotten it was Saturday and that her office was closed. After an interminably long Sunday, (fortunately, Maurice wasn't on the schedule until
Wednesday), I reached my lawyer bright and early Monday morning. I told
her that Maurice hadn't signed his contract yet.

"Not good," she said. "If there's no signed contract, there's no trial
period."

My heart sank. "What does that mean exactly?"

"The temporary contract defaults to a *permanent* one, meaning if Maurice were to take you to court, you'd be subject to the same damages and
penalties as a long-term employee."

"But he's only been with us for two weeks! *Six shifts*, to be exact!"

"Doesn't matter. You've got to get him to sign his contract."

"But . . . what if he refuses? I thought you said I can't force employees to sign anything."

"No, you can't. But at the same time, a judge can throw the book at you if you don't get him to sign."

"That's absurd," I said.

"*Et oui*," my lawyer said. "*C'est la France!*"

As soon as I hung up the phone, I called Bruce. "See if you can get Maurice to swing by the diner and sign his contract."

"How?"

"I don't know . . . Tell him you're doing the schedule for next week and can't put him on until he signs."

"Okay," Bruce said.

A couple hours later, my phone vibrated with a text message: *"He didn't want to . . . but he signed it!"*

Yes! I let out a big sigh of relief. Just then, my phone vibrated again with another message: *"p.s. I locked the contract in the safe."*

I couldn't wait to tell my lawyer the good news. "Excellent!" she said. "I'll draft up an 'end-of-trial-period' letter and send it to you right away. Make two copies: one for Maurice and one for you, making sure he writes, '*remise en mains propres*' (delivered by hand) on your copy."

Before his shift on Wednesday, Bruce sent Maurice a text message asking him to come in a little early so they could "go over some things." When Maurice arrived, Bruce handed him his end-of-trial-period letter. Maurice went ballistic, refusing to sign for it.

"I told him he might as well," Bruce said. "Otherwise, I was just going to walk across the street to the post office and send it to him by *lettre recommandée*." (certified mail)

"Yeah, and then the postman will walk right back across the street and hand it to him. Absurd."

The next day, I called my lawyer and ran through the list. Contract signed: *check*. End-of-trial-period letter sent by *lettre recommandée*: *check*. Exit interview telling him why we were ending his trial period: *check*.

"Wait, wait! Back up," my lawyer said. "Did you just say your manager told Maurice the reasons why you were ending his trial period?"

"Yeah, so? I thought that was the point of *dossiers* and all that—to justify an employee's dismissal."

"*Not* during a trial period!" she said. "That's the *one* time you're not supposed to say anything."

"Even if the employee asks why they're being let go?"

"*Especially* if they ask why they're being let go. They can use it to trap you."

I could feel my head starting to throb. "I'm sorry, you've lost me."

"Let me put it another way: if you give an employee something to argue against—such as the grounds for their dismissal—then they have the *right* to defend themselves. But if you say nothing, *voilà*! There's no argument. Case closed!"

After fifteen years in business, I still had a *lot* to learn about French labor laws.

Back at the diner, the spirit of Maurice continued to haunt the place. A couple days after he'd gone, a group of six pretty Scandinavian women stepped up to the register and tried to use six fully stamped fidelity cards to pay for their meals. Bruce examined them then asked the women to hold on a moment. He stepped over to the counter where I was nursing a mug of joe and handed me the cards.

"Take a look at these." All of them were stamped in perfect rows, clearly in one go—and by the same person.

"Are you thinking what I'm thinking?" Bruce asked. I closed my eyes and nodded.

Bruce returned to the Scandinavian women. "Excuse me. May I ask you who stamped these cards?"

"Oh, one of your waiters. The short, balding one. He asked for our telephone numbers too, but we said no. Luckily, he gave us back our fidelity cards first!"

Just then, the tall woman in the group pointed to the front of the diner. "Speaking of which . . . there he is now!" I turned to see Maurice standing there, leering through the window. The moment he saw everyone staring at him, he turned and scurried off down the sidewalk, disappearing into his apartment building two doors down.

At that moment, I truly understood the old adage, "Don't *merde* where you sleep." Or in this case, don't hire friends, neighbors, or frustrated filmmakers. The thought of having to go through this kind of thing with Maurice day after day—crossing the street to avoid each other, watching him stare into the diner and make everyone feel uncomfortable—was way too stressful. Although my lawyer strongly advised me against it, I realized that if I wanted any peace of mind, I'd have to have a conversation with Maurice in person.

Through text messages, Maurice and I made a rendezvous to meet at a café around the corner from BIA. When I arrived, Maurice was standing outside, wearing his grandpa sweater, his hands in his pockets. He seemed calm. Too calm.

Once we'd sat down and ordered our espressos, I turned to him and said, "Look, I wanted to meet today because you and I are neighbors, which means we have to find a way to live together, right?"

Maurice shrugged. "I don't see what that has to do with anything."

"As you may recall, you're the one who came to me asking for a job, *n'est-ce pas?* And I did you a favor." Maurice just sat there, silent. "What if it were the other way around? What if *you* got *me* a job on one of your films? What if I went around complaining about everything—bringing down the morale of the crew and accusing you of breaking the law?"

"I would expect you to do that," Maurice said. "Nobody should get away with breaking the law. Not BIA, not anybody!"

"But we weren't breaking any laws!"

"Hah! We'll see about that."

"Is that a threat?"

Maurice shrugged again. *Why was he being so coy?*

I had no choice but to play hardball. "Remember when I first hired you?" I said. "Remember the one thing I told you I would *not* tolerate at BIA when it came to the waitresses?"

"Oh, so that's what this is about, huh?!" Maurice said, losing his cool for the first time. "I knew Katie was behind this! Well, she's lying! Everyone knows Bruce is the one who's having *une aventure* (a liaison) with all the waitresses!"

"Yeah, well, since I haven't received a single complaint from any of them about Bruce, how about we focus on you, huh?"

Maurice smirked, then changed his tone. "My brother's a lawyer, you know. I told him *everything*. You're in deep trouble."

"Really? How?"

I was sure Maurice had to be bluffing. I had his signed contract, plus the confirmation card from the post office that he'd received his end-of-trial-period letter.

Maurice leaned in close. Real close. "I know what your biggest fear is, Craig," he grinned. "Getting sued! Well, guess what? You're going to get sued again—by me!"

"Yeah, on what grounds?"

"The grounds that this isn't America!" Maurice stood up and pounded the table. "You can't just go around firing people. You're NO Donald Trump!!"

I could feel a smile slowly crossing my face. *Why. . . that's the* nicest *thing any French person has ever said to me,* I thought.

"Go ahead and smile all you want!" Maurice said. "But you're going down." He then pointed to himself. "You know what my name is . . . ?" He paused for maximum dramatic effect: "NIGHT-*MARRRRE*!" Maurice then pulled out his iPhone from his sweater pocket and shoved it in my face. "I've been recording this conversation the whole time!"

"Why, you son-of-a-bitch," I said, losing *my* cool for the first time. *That's why he'd been so coy.*

Maurice chortled like a movie villain as he headed toward the door. "Wait!" I said, following after him. "I'm not paying for your goddamn espresso!"

I chased Maurice outside, but he was too fast. He sprinted down rue Monge, then disappeared around the corner.

Great. Now *he's fast.*

The next day, I received a long email from Maurice, which included a cc to his brother/lawyer. In it, he falsely claimed all the ways the diner and I had broken the *Code du Travail*. He also threatened to take me to labor court (*les Prud'hommes*)—unless, he suggested, I preferred to make a settlement for several thousand euros. (He didn't specify exactly how many thousands.) The next day, a signed copy of the exact same letter arrived by *lettre recommandée*.

I forwarded a copy to my lawyer, then gave her a call. "Did you read his letter?" I said. "It's so convoluted. What exactly is he threatening to sue me for?"

"From what I can tell: an *abusive* end-of-trial-period," she said.

"Does that even exist?"

"It's the first time I've heard of it. But if an employee is clever enough to come up with something—no matter how outlandish—then it sets a precedent; therefore it exists."

"Do we answer his letter?" I asked.

"No. We wait. Call his bluff. See if he summons you to *les Prud'hommes*."

"If he does, then what?"

"It's his word against yours."

I could feel my blood pressure rising. "What about the recording he made of our conversation on his iPhone?"

"Did he ask for your permission first?"

"No, of course not."

"Then it's not admissible."

Whew! That was a relief.

I had one last question: ever since Président Macron's election, there'd been talk about putting a cap on labor lawsuits—and in particular, ones involving new employees. "Do you think it's going to pass?" I asked.

"Probably. Let's hope it does *before* the *Prud'hommes* contacts you. That is, *if* they contact you."

"How long could that take?"

"Up to two years. That's how long Maurice had to file his claim."

After I hung up with my lawyer, I suddenly had a huge craving for BIA's signature dish, the aptly named CC'S Big Mess, a breakfast scramble with everything in it but the kitchen sink. After pouring myself a mug of joe, I crawled into a booth with my comfort food. I was just about to take a bite when I noticed Maurice passing by the diner. He spotted me through the window. Stopped and scowled at me. Then continued on his way.

It was going to be a *long* two years. But I was okay with that. In France, *c'est comme ça.*

I settled into my booth then scooped a forkful of breakfast bliss into my mouth, savoring each and every delicious morsel. *Yum.*

Thank God for my Big Mess.

PART THREE

EATING IN FRANCE

A special delivery to 15, Quai de la Tournelle.

NINE

The Silver Tower

The longer I live in Paris, the harder it is to not become a snob. This is rather ironic, considering I've been battling snobs my whole life.

The first time I realized there might be some kind of social hierarchy occurred when I was a kid growing up in Frenchtown. With my ripped clothes that I would hold together with masking tape (but discreetly on the *inside*), it was already hard enough to make friends at school. But the moment their parents found out where I came from, they would turn their noses up in the air, then swiftly forbid their children from coming to my part of town to play—just because there'd been a murder or two recently. I couldn't say I blamed them; I didn't want to be in Frenchtown, either.

My brushes with snobbism reached a whole new level after coming to France as an exchange student. The day before classes started, the *université* made all the students fill out an application form, *en français*, which included a section marked: *Profession du père* (father's profession). I was a little taken aback by the question, having never been asked anything like it by the schools I attended in the U.S. I just couldn't see how what my dad did for a living had anything to do with me.

I looked around to see what the other students were writing down: *médecin, avocat, financier, ingénieur* (doctor, lawyer, financier, engineer). Not knowing the term for what my dad did, I pulled out my pocket English-French dictionary. The term wasn't there, so I decided to do a French *non-non*: writing down the word-for-word translation.

"*Excusez-moi*, Madame," I said to an administrator from the *université*, "Is this correct?" I held up my form and pointed to what I'd written: "*Travailleur du jour.*" (Literally: "Worker of the day.")

"Oh, you must mean, *jour-naliste?*" she said.

"Uh, no, actually . . ." I said, suddenly becoming self-conscious. In my best Pidgin French, I tried to explain that my dad worked a series of odd jobs, most not lasting more than a week or two: sandblaster, housepainter, barman, mall cop. "He was even a Tupperware lady once," I said, my face turning red as I recalled the image of Fast Eddie showing a group of women from the neighborhood how to properly "burp" a plastic food container. "To keep the freshness in!" he'd say, flashing a devilish grin at "the ladies." With any luck, Fast Eddie would be letting the freshness out later that night.

Back at the *université*, the administrator looked at me and said flatly, "Oh . . . the word you're looking for is *ouvrier* (blue collar worker)." Her contempt dripped all over the word.

By the time I'd moved to France to open my diner, I'd already become an old pro when it came to dealing with *les snobs*. "You want to open an American restaurant in Paris?" French people would guffaw. "What are you going to serve—"

"'*amburg-errrs?*" I'd say in unison with them, having heard it a thousand times before. "I'll have you know," I continued, unabashed, "there's a lot more to American cuisine than 'amburg-errrs."

"*Mais oui*," they'd say sarcastically. "Cheeseburg-errrs."

"And *bacon*-cheeseburgers, *et* le Big Mac *et* . . ." I smiled, actually enjoying playing along with the stereotypes French people had about Americans. By the time I'd rattled off every cliché in the book, they'd be putting their arms around me, making me feel like an honorary member of their "*Les-Américains*-have-no-culture" Club.

But it wasn't just the French who were looking down their noses at me. Many Americans, especially expats, were quite happy to let me know that they would never be caught dead in Breakfast in America. "Why in the world would I want *American* food when I'm in France?" they'd say. Of course, I got that. Back when I was an exchange student, you couldn't have found a bigger Francophile than me. I wanted to be 100% *français* so badly, sometimes if a tourist stopped to ask me for directions, I'd pretend I didn't speak any English. *That's* how badly I wanted to be French.

As for "*les 'amburgers*," ironically, I was never a big fan of them. Even as a kid. I'm guessing it might have had something to do with a story my mom used to tell me. Back in the late '50s, before I was born, my mom did what was expected of most women at the time and gave up her job (as a grammar school teacher) to become a housewife. Determined to be a better cook than her mom—my Polish Grandma Mary, whose specialty was boiling chicken until any trace of taste was gone ("Bullshit taste!" she'd say.)—my mom found a recipe in *Good Housekeeping* magazine, slaving away all day in the kitchen until it was perfect.

"I was so excited for your father to come home so he could try my creation," she said.

The moment Fast Eddie walked in the door and saw his meal, he squinted his eyes and said, "Louise . . . what the hell is that?"

"Chicken Cordon Bleu!"

"Now why'd you go and waste your time making that? Just fry me up a burger, will ya?"

My parents divorced shortly thereafter.

Looking back now, I suppose that one of the reasons I'd never been very fond of burgers was because subconsciously I've associated them with the breakup of my family. *Well, at least my parents didn't split up over pancakes*, I reasoned. Otherwise, there might never have been a Breakfast in America.

From the first day I opened BIA, I knew that for the diner to succeed, I'd have to wean my future French customers off their snobby stereotypes about Americans. "Not only do we enjoy *lots* of other dishes besides 'amburgers," I said to Jean-Philippe, a French customer who was fast becoming a regular. "We're also quite capable of appreciating fine French cuisine, too!"

As if on cue, an American woman in her early forties walked into the diner, followed by her twelve-year-old daughter. Both were wearing matching Disneyland sweatshirts and mouse ears. The mother, let's call her Carol, looked at a table of customers eating burgers, then proclaimed as loudly as she could for the whole room to hear:

"Oh, thank God! Finally! *Real* food!"

Jean-Phillipe laughed. I gave him a look, then greeted the mother and daughter with a smile, although inside I felt a little embarrassed. It wasn't because of the decibel-breaking volume at which Carol spoke. I was used to that. Some would even say that that was part of her charm as an American. But the remark about "*real* food." As if it didn't exist in France—the culinary capital of the world? For me, that bordered on sacrilegious.

Of course, because I loved French *and* American cuisine equally, if someone put a gun to my head and said I had to choose one meal to eat for the rest of my life—either *confit du canard* (caramelized duck) with roasted garlic potatoes, for example—or ham steak and eggs with hash browns and fresh blueberry pancakes smothered in 100% maple syrup, I'd have to say, "Screw it! Just shoot me!"

Fortunately, most Parisians don't own a gun, so I get to eat *both*.

After seating Carol and her daughter in a booth, I went to hand them their menus, but Carol waved them away. "We know what we want already. Two cokes and two cheeseburgers—very, very, *very* well-done."

By now, I'd been working at the diner long enough to develop a kind of second sense of what made certain American customers happy. "Would you like ice in your cokes?"

"Oh, my God! Yes!" Carol squealed. "You're the first person in this city who's asked us that. What's up with the French? Why won't they give you ice?"

"Same reason they don't give you free refills. It's a different culture here."

"Boy, I'll say! It's *nothing* like America, right honey?" Carol's daughter nodded and adjusted her Mickey Mouse ears.

As I headed over to the register to tap in the order, I mumbled a little mantra I'd come up with for situations like these: *Don't be a snob, Craig. Don't be a snob.*

Back in the kitchen, once all the flavor and color had been cooked out of Carol's burgers per her request, I brought them over to her table. The moment her daughter saw the lettuce, tomato, onions, and pickles on top of her bun, she jerked her hands up into the air and shrieked. "Off! Off! Off!"

Carol slid the vegetables from her daughter's burger and dumped them onto her plate. Turns out, the young girl did not eat anything that grew naturally from the Earth. "It's okay, honey," Carol said as she put her arm around her sobbing child. "The nice man didn't mean to frighten you, did he?" She looked at me.

"No, of course not," I said. *But I may want to strangle you. Don't be a snob, Craig. Don't be a snob.*

For the rest of the meal, the young girl picked at her food, leaving half of it on her plate to be thrown away. If Julien had been there, he would have been furious; nothing gets him more upset than people wasting food. As I scraped the veggies from the burger tops into the trash bin, I made a mental note that, should Carol and her daughter come back to the diner again, I'd make sure their burgers were served plain.

Sure enough, the next morning, the two were back for breakfast. Before I had a chance to suggest the *pancake du jour*, Carol ordered the exact same thing as the night before—two cheeseburgers—extra well done. My French cook Tito was working that day, which always meant trouble. When the order was done, he pinged the bell harder than usual. I went over to grab the plates, then stopped in my tracks; Tito had put *double* the amount of lettuce, tomato, onions and pickles on top of the cheeseburgers.

"Uh . . . Tito, what are you doing?" I asked in French. "The customers specifically asked for plain burgers, no top."

"But they are fat! They need to eat more vegetables!"

"*Ecoute*, that's not your decision to make."

"Why not?"

"Because in America the rule is: 'The customer is always right.'"

"But we're not in America!" I gave Tito a stern look, having gone over this with him a thousand times. After a moment, Tito harrumphed, then grabbed a spatula and slapped the organic matter off the burgers and into the trash bin.

For the rest of their trip, Carol and her daughter came to the diner every day—sometimes three times a day. (I eventually learned that they'd flown directly from Disneyland in Florida to try out their annual passes at Disneyland in Paris, its *faux chateau* being the only castle they'd see while in France.)

Of course, I appreciated Carol's business. But at the same time, the Frenchman in me wanted her and her daughter to *profiter* from their experience, to have the courage to try something new. But, of course, I knew that was easier said than done. A few months earlier, Matt, a childhood friend of mine from Frenchtown (one of the only kids who hadn't been afraid to cross the tracks and be my pal), stopped in Paris for a couple days with his family on their way to Ireland. After Julien and I joined them on a Bateaux Mouches river tour, it was time for dinner.

"Where would you guys like to eat?" I asked.

"Anywhere. As long as it's fun," my friend's wife, Deedee, said.

"Fun?"

"Yeah, you know. Fun. For the kids." Deedee gestured toward her eleven-year-old son, Tyler, and eight-year-old daughter, Zoey, both of whom were glued to the video games on their cell phones.

Since Julien and I had no children, it took me a moment to understand the question. When choosing a restaurant, we never stopped to consider whether the place offered a sufficient amount of distractions to hold the short attention spans of post-millennials.

"Do you mean a restaurant with clowns and balloons and face-painting?" I asked.

"Yes, exactly!"

"Nope. Restaurants in Paris aren't fun that way. You gotta go to Disneyland for that."

Deedee looked crestfallen.

Don't be a snob, Craig. Don't be a snob.

"Hold on," I said, determined to please my friend's wife. "There's a Greek restaurant over in the Latin Quarter, by Saint-Michel, where they dance the *Horos* and smash plates on the floor. Does that count as fun?"

"Heavens, no," the nurse in Deedee said. "That sounds *dangerous*. What if a shard from one of those broken plates goes into somebody's eye?"

By this point, Julien couldn't stop himself. "I am sorry, but I have to say something. Here in France we do not play with food. We *respect* it. Gathering with your family at the dinner table is an opportunity to teach your child manners: how to sit up straight; eat properly with a knife and fork—not a fork and a finger; partake in engaging conversation. It's how we evaluate a child's education. A way to show that you are master of yourself, not some animal running around wild."

Deedee stared at Julien, her mouth agape, not accustomed to such Franco-directness. I looked over at my old friend, pleading with him with my eyes to do something, to take charge. Never much for words, Matt, who had been a lithe, long-distance runner in high school, had since settled contently into his dad-belly ("beer gut"). After a moment, he nodded, rubbed his belly and said, "All righty, then. It's decided! We're going to a French restaurant!"

With that hurdle over, it was on to the next challenge: the food itself. I specifically chose a French restaurant that did not serve burgers, hot dogs, or chicken nuggets. *Would there be anything on the menu that the kids would eat?* I wondered. On the plus side, the restaurant was located off rue Mouffetard, one of the oldest streets in Paris. The décor was straight out of *Game of Thrones*, the closest to fun I could find.

"Look around kids," I said, pointing at the 16th-century stone walls, vaulted wood-beamed ceilings, and ancient lead glass windows. "This place is *real* medieval. Almost five hundred years old. Not *make-believe* medieval, like you-know-where."

"Cool!" Tyler said. "Is there a dungeon?"

"Only for kids who don't finish their supper," Matt teased.

Now that I had Tyler's attention, I said, "You know what would be the most cool? If you go back to your school and tell all your friends you ate snails."

"Tyler won't eat snails," Deedee interjected.

"Yes I will, Mom."

"No, you won't."

"I will, too! Watch me!"

Matt turned to me and whispered, "Order them!"

All eyes were on Tyler as the waiter placed six, garlic butter–drenched *escargots* in front of him. Julien picked up the de-snailing tools and showed Tyler how to pull out a soggy mollusk from its shell. With determination in his eyes, Tyler shoved the snail into his mouth. After a second, he gagged, as if he were about to spit it out. Then to everyone's shocked expression, he smiled and said, "Just kidding! It's delicious!"

This caught Zoey's attention, who was now determined to impress her big brother. "I wanna try one, too!"

Zoey bit on the snail, doing her gallant best to eat it. But after a couple chews, she removed it from her mouth and tried to stick it on the underside of the table, like chewing gum at a desk in school.

"Zoey!" Deedee said. "On your plate if you're not going to eat it."

Wanting to make Zoey feel like she'd triumphed, I grabbed a piece of baguette and started sopping up the melted garlic butter. "Here, try this." Zoey took a bite. The moment she tasted the buttery goodness, her eyes lit up. She wolfed the baguette down in one gulp, then grabbed another piece and started sopping up all of Tyler's garlic butter.

"Hey! Get your own."

I nodded at the waiter. *"Encore six escargots, s'il vous plaît."*

Zoey was in seventh heaven, sopping away. At just eight years old, she'd already figured out what had taken me years to learn: when it comes to *escargots,* it's all about the garlic butter.

Deedee stared at her kids, hardly believing her eyes. "Well, what do you know . . ." she said softly. I wasn't a parent, and could only imagine how difficult it was for Matt and Deedee, but it seemed to me that most kids will rise up to the expectations you have for them. No matter how low or how high. And strangely, mysteriously, some of us thrive simply because their parents have no expectations at all.

I thought about this back at the diner, when Carol and her daughter came in on their last day. "It's been so wonderful having you here," I said in all sincerity. "But since it's your last day in Paris, may I make a suggestion: there are so many delicious French restaurants in this neighborhood, perhaps you'd like to try one before you head back to the States?"

"But there's nothing for us to eat at a French restaurant," Carol said.

"Sure there is!" Of course, I knew they'd never go near an escargot. So I suggested something a little less . . . scary.

"Have you ever tried duck? It's a lot like chicken, only way better."

"*Ewww*, gross," the daughter said as she stuck out her tongue.

"Okay . . . How about beef stew? Here they call it *bœuf bourguignon*. It's kinda like a burger, only the meat's all chopped up and served in a rich, yummy gravy."

An even bigger look of disgust crossed the girl's face.

"Wait, I got it!" I said as the obvious answer hit me. "You guys love cheese, right? How about cheese *fondue?*"

"What's that?" the daughter asked, the door opening slightly.

"Well," I said, describing the French specialty with great gusto, "it's super *fun!* Each person gets a sharp poker with which to stab a stale piece of bread. Then you dip the bread into a pot full of hot, melted cheese, which sits atop an open flame. After you swirl the bread around until it absorbs the cheese into a big clump, then pop it into your mouth, making sure to blow on it first so you don't burn your tongue off. *Et voila! Fondue!*"

"Oh, my," Carol said. "Sounds *dangerous*." She looked at her daughter who smiled and nodded back. "Two cheeseburgers, please!"

Of course, mine is not to judge. Yet at the same time, I couldn't help but think of all the amazing experiences people miss out on because they let fear get in their way. I can only speak for myself, but if I hadn't been willing to get out of my comfort zone—especially where food is concerned—I never would have had what turned out to be one of the best culinary experiences in my life.

My second diner had been open for less than a year when I received some unsettling news: our head chef, Lindsay, the best we'd ever had, was returning to the States along with her newly wedded French husband. "So, I was thinking . . ." Lindsay said, "Instead of giving me a bonus, would you be willing to take me to La Tour d'Argent?" (The Silver Tower)

Wow, how did she know I was planning on giving her a bonus? I thought. (Yep, Lindsay was *that* good.)

Of course, I'd known about the world-famous restaurant long before my foodie friends had raved about it. I also happened to pass by it almost every day, en route between the two diners whenever one of them had run out of bagels, bacon, or maple syrup. But given that La Tour d'Argent had been awarded two stars at the time by the much-coveted *Guide Michelin*, I never imagined that I'd ever be able to afford to eat there.

Yet the more I thought about Lindsay's proposal, the more it appealed to me. Before I could say yes, there was one *petit* detail I needed to check on first. "Is it fiscally legal in France to take an employee to a fancy restaurant instead of giving them a bonus?" I asked my accountant.

"Hmm . . . I'm not sure," she said, unable to keep up with the ever-changing laws in France. "I suppose we can give it a shot."

That was good enough for me.

Dressed to the nines, Lindsay and I stepped into the lobby of La Tour d'Argent and instantly felt as if we had entered a page in history. Not only did the restaurant date back to 1582, but judging from the vintage pictures adorning the walls, nearly every dignitary and celebrity had once dined there, from Richelieu to Roosevelt, from JFK to Marilyn Monroe.

After going up the private elevator to the top floor, we were led to one of the best tables in the house. At least for Lindsay; her seat faced the enormous bay windows that afforded a panoramic view of the Seine, replete with Notre-Dame lit up in the background. Mine faced a wall. But a big, beautiful *gilded* wall.

Once my eyes had adjusted to all the glimmer, the first thing I noticed was that there seemed to be more waitstaff than customers, ready to tend to our every need. If we so much as reached for the bottle of Evian on our table, a server would appear out of nowhere and gently remove it from our hand. "I'll take care of that, *Monsieur*," he'd say.

After handing out menus, the first of a long line of waiters stepped up to our table. "Shall we start you off with a bottle of champagne?" Lindsay must have seen the panic in my eyes, (just one bottle of the right bubbly could easily have disrupted the cash flow of my diners for months to come). "*Non, merci*," she said. I let out a sigh of relief as Lindsay continued. "But we *will* take two *coupes* (glasses), *s'il vous plaît*."

Good move, I thought. As waiter #2 poured champagne into two long-stemmed glasses, I noticed that our menus had come in two versions: *His* and *Hers*. His (mine) had all the prices on it. Hers (Lindsay's) had only the good stuff—descriptions of the scrumptious dishes—but without the eyesore of numbers and euro signs getting in the way. *Hmm, that seems awful sexist*, I thought. But I let it slide; I didn't want to spoil Lindsay's special evening.

"Do you know what you'd like for your starters?" a third waiter asked.

"Oh, everything looks so delicious," Lindsay said as she brushed back her long red hair. "Especially the white truffle soup."

By this point, I wished they'd given me the *Hers* menu instead. It would have been a lot less stressful to *not* know the prices, especially for the truffle soup, which cost well into the three digits. "Yes, the soup does sound heavenly . . ." I said, trying in vain not to stare at the items on the menu that cost a third of the price, ". . . but the endive salad with bleu cheese crumbles sounds like the perfect spring dish!" (It was January.)

"I'll take the white truffle soup, *s'il vous plaît*!" Lindsay beamed.

"*Moi aussi*," I said, taking a big gulp of my champagne. *Screw it*. I thought. *I was going to enjoy this night, even if it killed me*!

For the rest of the meal as the red wine soothed my nerves, I sat back and let myself go with the flow. Perhaps the greatest pleasure was watching how happy Lindsay was. She'd come from a working-class family, like me, and had found her passion in France, attending one of the most prestigious culinary schools in the country, where she was the top student—and only woman—in her class.

I felt so fortunate to have her working at Breakfast in America. Immensely overqualified, not once did Lindsay act as if she were above working at a diner. *Au contraire*, she put the same amount of love and attention into making pancakes as she did appreciating La Tour d'Argent's specialty, pressed duck, which she ordered as her main course.

"Do you know how much skill it takes to make a duck this perfect?" she said, savoring every morsel. "I mean look at this skin, how exquisite the color is, the crispness . . . and the meat, cooked evenly throughout. And, oh, that juice . . . just waiting to burst out with every slice."

Sharing a meal of this caliber with a pro like Lindsay gave me a whole new appreciation for the art of fine cuisine, including the importance of the setting and décor. For the first time, I noticed that each table in the dining room was adorned with a small crystal duck.

"Did you know that every duck served here is numbered?" Lindsay continued.

"Really? Why's that?"

"So they can trace each bird back to its origin and ensure its quality."

"Wow, they definitely don't fool around with their fowl, do they?"

Lindsay smiled. And she continued to smile throughout the cheese course, (which arrived on a traditional wooden cart), throughout dessert, (a cherry *clafoutis* and *Baba au Rhum*) and finally through the coffees and Calvados, an apple brandy from Normandy that's designed to help you digest the monumental feast you've just indulged in.

As the *digestif* worked its magic, Lindsay and I sat there completely content, staring out the window at the view. After the lights illuminating Notre-Dame went out, I realized it was already midnight. I turned around to see that we were the last customers in the place.

Oh, right. We have to pay for this, I thought.

I raised my hand as if holding an invisible pen and scribbling a note—the international sign for requesting the bill. After a moment, waiter #23 came over and placed what looked like our check in front of Lindsay. When I went to grab it, the waiter said, "*Voilà, Madame.* Your certificate." Lindsay held up a rectangular card on which was a 19th-century oil painting of a bearded man carving a plump duck resting on a silver platter. Above it was written: *Le numéro de votre canard: 1,053,019.*

"Wow, that's a helluva lotta ducks!" I said.

"Yes," Lindsay said. "But there's only *one* I'll never forget."

Sated and satisfied, I drank in the view one last time as I handed the waiter my credit card. *If it didn't cost the equivalent of two months' rent,* I thought to myself, *I could definitely get used to this place.*

But the good news was, I didn't have to go to fancy places like the Silver Tower to live the life of Riley. I had Paris—and all of France—where I'd learned you don't have to be wealthy to eat well. From a *cassoulet* in the countryside to a freshly baked *baguette* at your corner *boulangerie*, one's quality of life did not depend on money. It was about much more than that.

There was no better example of this than a man I'd seen on TV years earlier when I was visiting the States. He had just won the Super Lotto jackpot—we're talking more than a $100,000,000—*after* taxes. (Fun fact: in France no matter how much you win in the lottery—or on a game show—*none* of it is taxed.) I don't recall where he was from, but the man had a deep Southern accent and wore a baseball cap, rumpled T-shirt, and baggy shorts that reminded me a lot of Fast Eddie.

"Now that you're richer than your wildest dreams . . ." a reporter shouted during the press conference, finally getting to *the* question they always ask: "How's your life going to change?"

The big winner paused a moment to ponder the question, then said, "Not much, I reckon. It's not like all a sudden I'm gonna start eating filet mignons."

Yes! Start eating filet mignons! I wanted to scream at the TV. *Expand your horizons! Try new things! Otherwise you'll* never *get out of Frenchtown!*

Feeling myself getting carried away I quickly repeated my mantra: *Don't be a snob, Craig. Don't be a snob.*

In all fairness, though, wasn't that lotto winner being a bit of a snob himself? A redneck snob. Convinced that his way of life was better than them fancy city folk, something I'd heard my whole life growing up. How was his attitude any different than those who refused to dine at a restaurant unless it had a star attached?

That's when a revelation hit me: being a snob was just an excuse to keep your mind closed. From that day forward, I vowed to keep my mind as wide open as possible.

Nearly ten years to the day after that unforgettable dinner with Lindsay, I was bussing tables at my diner when my manager Bruce held up the phone. "It's La Tour d'Argent," he shouted across the room. "They want to speak to a 'Monsieur Carlson,'" Bruce smiled, exaggerating the pronunciation of my name *en français*.

My curiosity piqued, I held the phone up to my ear. It was the maître d' from the restaurant. "Monsieur Carlson, I am calling in regards to a special event we're organizing for our staff. Apparently, your *daïneur* has a lot of fans *chez nous*, because in lieu of a traditional meal, they've voted overwhelmingly to have cheeseburgers and chicken wings served instead. Would your establishment be willing to cater the event for us?"

Ooh, *establishment*. I let the word sink in for a moment.

"*Mais bien sûr, Monsieur!*" I exclaimed. "I'd be honored."

I couldn't wait to tell Julien the news! Here I was, a scrappy kid from Connecticut who couldn't even cook, and now I was about to cater for one of the most famous restaurants in the world. I grabbed a notepad and wrote down their order: forty cheeseburgers, twenty California chicken wraps, twenty veggie wraps, fifty chicken wings, thirty portions of fries, five bottles of *sauce ketchup Heinz*, and three bottles of *sauce moutarde French* (French's Mustard).

On the big day, the kitchen scrambled to get the order done in time for a 10:55 A.M. delivery. Fortunately, Julien was there to lend a hand as we crammed fifty to-go boxes into delivery bags. We then made the five-block trek on foot to the Tower just in time.

Monsieur Terrail himself, the young and handsome fifth-generation owner of La Tour, was there to greet us. He graciously let me take a photo of us standing in front of the piles of boxes full of burgers and wraps.

"Ten years ago, your team served me," I told Monsieur Terrail. "And now I have the honor of serving yours. *C'est pas magnifique ça?*" (Isn't that grand?)

Over the next several months, my little diner would go on to cater La Tour d'Argent not once, but *four* times.

As Julien and I made our way back to BIA, I looked up at the top floor of the Silver Tower, imagining the staff wolfing down their 'amburgers.

"How does it feel to corrupt the French?" Julien asked.

"*Pas mal*," I smiled.

As I gazed at the huge bay windows of La Tour above, I was sure there had to be at least one holdout inside, one disgruntled employee who had voted against having American grub served at such a distinguished venue. I imagined him standing there with his arms crossed as the maître d' holds a cheeseburger in front of him.

"Oh, don't be such a snob, Henri," the maître d' says. "Man cannot live on numbered duck alone."

TEN

Madame Hubert Eats a Burger

The median age of my customers was getting older, but that was no surprise because I was getting older, too. Restaurant owners age with their clientele.

When Breakfast in America first opened in 2003, most customers were students in their twenties—and of those 70% were American. Within a couple years, it had completely flipped and 70% were *français*. And thanks to "regulars" who'd been frequenting the diner for nearly two decades, the average age was now thirty to thirty-five.

That said, it was rare to get anyone over sixty, unless they were dining with their extended family or babysitting their grandkids. And seniors over seventy—almost unheard of. That's why I was so excited when our eighty-six-year-old neighbor said she'd never been to an American restaurant and wanted to try mine.

I first met Mme. Hubert on the fifth floor of her apartment building while the two of us were waiting for the elevator. It was 2005—a full year before I'd met Julien and five years before the apartment with the pigeon man. I'd just purchased my very first property, a 9.22-square-meter *pied à terre* (roughly one hundred square feet—or about half the size of a standard room at a *Motel 6*). Although too small to live in full-time, the tiny space was meant to guarantee that, should Breakfast in America fail, I'd never be homeless. Fortunately, business was doing well enough for us to open a second location in the Marais. And since the *pied à terre* was only a couple blocks away from BIA #1, I decided to convert it into an office.

Mme. Hubert lived at the opposite end of the hallway from my *bureau/* safety net. Built in the 1930s as a "workers hotel," all the apartments in the eight-story building (unusual for Paris, where most topped off at six floors) were the same tiny size as mine—except for "double units" at the end of each floor, which included Mme. Hubert's place.

Adding to the building's "old world charm," most residents didn't have an indoor toilet. Instead, there were two "shared WCs" on each floor, which Mme. Hubert unabashedly used. (I, on the other hand, would wait until the hallway was empty—then sneak in.)

After the customary exchange of *bonjours,* Mme. Hubert and I squeezed into the tight, phone booth–sized elevator so common in Paris's older buildings. Slightly hunched over and supported by a cane, Madame wore her silver hair pulled back into a chic ponytail that spilled onto her iconic Burberry trench coat and matching cashmere scarf. I'd first become aware of this stylish ensemble as an exchange student in Rouen, where bourgeois women seemed particularly fond of wearing it.

Mme. Hubert looked at me through her thick black-framed glasses (also stylish, *bien sûr*) and launched into a fascinating analysis of the president at the time, Jacques Chirac and his likely successor, Nicolas Sarkozy. She spoke very quickly and passionately—and in the most eloquent French I'd ever heard—incorporating a deep knowledge of history, psychology, and culture into every subject she approached. Although I could barely keep up, I was thoroughly enthralled.

A former university professor, Mme. Hubert reminded me of Simone de Beauvoir. They were both French intellectuals of the highest order—a time-honored tradition in France that was becoming more and more rare. Until meeting Mme. Hubert, I didn't realize how much I'd missed such sophisticated, witty repartee and verbal sparring. But that wasn't the only thing I missed.

Mme. Hubert was a member of the last generation often referred to as *la Vieille France*, the kind of older woman I used to see riding on the *métro* back in the '80s. Fearless and principled, these matriarchs weren't shy about telling young people to take their feet off the seats. Or to turn down their boom boxes because, *"Just who do you think you are, disrupting the tranquility of others?"*

Nowadays, though, I rarely saw *any* older women riding on the *métro*. And when I did, they never lectured anyone, but rather stared ahead, clutching their purses tightly.

Since Mme. Hubert was a direct link to a nostalgic time long since gone, I soon found myself looking forward to our elevator rides together. However, one interesting thing about the *Vieille France* generation: they could paradoxically be awfully reserved. Despite our fascinating discussions on a myriad of topics, it took Mme. Hubert years before she dared to broach a subject that was considered highly personal in France.

"I can't help but notice your charming American accent," she said one day on the elevator ride up to the fifth floor. "At the risk of being rude, may I ask what you do for a living?"

"Je vous en prie, Madame" (please do), I said. "I own a couple of traditional American restaurants."

"Ah, bon! And where may I have the opportunity to see these restaurants?"

"Actually there's one just two blocks down the hill, on rue des Écoles. Right next door to the piano shop."

"Hmm, I'm familiar with that shop, but I've never noticed yours. I will have to make a point of investigating it the next time I'm down that way."

A few months later, as I was serving customers inside the diner, I noticed Mme. Hubert standing outside wearing her Burberry ensemble. I stepped out to join her.

"*Bonjour Madame*," I smiled. "I see you found us."

"*Effectivement*" (indeed), she said. Balancing herself with one hand on her cane, she gestured with the other toward the red neon DINER sign hanging above the striped awning. "What is this, '*dee-nay, dee-nay?*'"

By now, I was used to French people pronouncing *diner* like the word "*diner*" *en français*, which of course meant, "to dine or eat dinner."

"It's a type of American restaurant," I explained to Mme. Hubert. "But we pronounce it '*daïneur*.'"

"*Ah, bon!*" she said, intrigued. "And what do you serve at this *daïneur*? 'Amburgers, I suppose."

"Among other things," I grinned. "I'd love to invite you so you can see for yourself. My treat!"

Mme. Hubert looked at her watch. It was a little after 4:00 P.M. Too late for lunch and too early for diner. "I would like that," she said. "*A la prochaine.*" (Until next time.)

With great care, Madame pivoted around on her cane and made her way toward the crosswalk. My first instinct was to assist her, but every time I'd offered to accompany her in the past, she'd refused my help, saying she was fine. "I'm in no hurry."

Sure enough, it took Mme. Hubert three cycles of red lights to cross the street. The whole time she stayed calm and focused—even as she stopped traffic and certain impatient *imbéciles* started blaring their horns at her.

Ironically, as time seemed to slow down for Mme. Hubert, it had the opposite effect for me. Months flew by but somehow Madame and I never managed to set a time for her to come have a meal at my diner. I began to worry that it might never happen.

One day, the elevator in our building was "*en panne*" (out of order). As I headed down the stairwell, I came across Mme. Hubert just below the fourth floor. She was making her way up the stairs one slow and excruciating step at a time, her face bright red, sweating profusely.

"Are you okay, *Madame*?" I said, worried that she was going to have a heart attack.

As usual, Mme. Hubert never complained. "*Oui, oui, ça va!*" she said between pants, slowly catching her breath. She looked at me through her thick glasses, her eyes more lucid than I'd ever seen. "Nature's got it right!" she said, thumping her cane for emphasis. "The body starts to give out at just about the same time as one's desire to live. I used to love playing tennis. Now I can't. But I no longer *want* to, either. See how perfect that is?"

"*Allez, madame,*" I said. "Don't go anywhere just yet. I still have to treat you to my *daïneur.*"

"*Et oui! Effectivement!*" she chuckled, her shoulders bobbing up and down.

Mme. Hubert and I knew each other well enough now, I felt comfortable telling her an off-color joke as I helped her up the stairs. "You see, Madame, the way it usually works is: People have a heart attack *after* eating greasy American food. Not *before.*"

Mme. Hubert let out a deep guttural laugh that echoed through the stairwell. "*Quel fripouille vous êtes!*" (What a scoundrel you are!)

Once we'd reached the fourth floor, Mme. Hubert let go of my arm. "*Merci,* but I can take over from here," she said. "I'm in no hurry."

After the scare in the stairwell, I saw less and less of Mme. Hubert. Each time I went by my office, I would glance at her door, hoping to see her come out. But for weeks on end, she never did. I found some solace whenever I'd hear her favorite radio station—France Inter (similar to NPR)—blasting through her door, the volume set to the max.

It reminded me of when I was a paperboy and used to deliver the daily news to an "independent living" retirement community on the outskirts of Frenchtown. Most of the residents back then were World War II vets and hard of hearing. Their radios would always be cranked up really loud, tuned into twenty-four-hour news programs.

Decades later and a half a world away, I wondered if any of those vets from my paper route had ever crossed paths with Mme. Hubert. Turns out, she'd grown up in Normandy and had witnessed D-Day firsthand.

"It was the scariest time of my life," she told me.

After hiding in bomb shelters for days, her family emerged to find most of their village in ruins. As allied forces rolled through town, a tank stopped in front of her and her siblings. The portal opened and out popped an African American soldier. For Mme. Hubert, who was a little girl at the time and had never ventured further than twenty kilometers from her home, the GI was the first person of color she'd ever seen.

"He and his fellow troops were so kind to us children," she smiled. "They gave us candy and bubble gum!"

"That's an amazing story," I said. "I wonder if those soldiers were part of the 320th Brigade!" I was referring to the famous African American contingent, which was still fresh on my mind since I'd recently read the bestseller, *Forgotten*. It told the story of how these courageous men had been left out of so many history books.

To think: Mme. Hubert had been there. And now she was my friend, a direct link to the past. *History at my doorstep*, I thought, feeling grateful as I left my office and headed toward the elevator. Just as I pushed the down button, Mme. Hubert's door opened. It was dark inside as Madame's in-home nurse stepped out. She took care of Mme. Hubert several days a week, thanks to the humane and generous health care system in France.

"Is Madame all right?" I asked the nurse.

"*Oui, oui*," she answered. "*Elle est juste un peu fatiguée.*" (She's just a little tired.)

"Please tell her that her American neighbor said '*bonjour*'—and that I'm counting on her to get back *en forme* soon so we can have lunch together."

The nurse nodded. Then the two of us squeezed into the elevator and rode the whole way down in silence.

As I anxiously waited for Mme. Hubert to get her mojo back, a strange coincidence happened. I received an email from a young French filmmaker, Joël. He was directing a documentary about his grandmother, Liliane, who was in her nineties and came from the same generation as Mme. Hubert. According to Joël, his grandmother had lived an incredible life. Most notably, she'd fought in the Resistance against the Nazis during World War II and later was a pioneering crusader for women's rights.

"My grandmother has lived her whole life in the service of others," Joël wrote. "But now it's time to take care of her." Ever the adventurer, Liliane wanted to spend her remaining years doing things she hadn't had the chance to do before. As she and her grandson were putting together a kind of "bucket list," they discovered that in her ninety-plus years, Liliane had never tried a hamburger. That's where BIA came in.

"For the sequence in the film where my grandmother eats the first hamburger of her life," Joël wrote, "I'm looking for a landmark location that represents American culture. I visited your establishment and was won over by it. I'd like to see if it would be possible to shoot this touching scene *chez vous*."

I was flattered. Of all the words that could be used to describe the scene of somebody eating their first hamburger, "touching" had never crossed my mind.

Of course, Mme. Hubert would have had a field day with this. Ever the intellectual, she had no patience for gauzy sentiment, especially when it came to the biggie: *amour*.

"Love is so overrated!" she said one day as we waited for the elevator. "I was married for fifty years and neither my husband nor I had the patience for such nonsense. *'Je t'aime chéri, je t'aime!'*" she said mockingly. *"Bon sang!* We're *reasoning* adults—not impetuous children!"

Of course, I was much more sentimental than Mme. Hubert, convinced that it was quite possible to film a scene of somebody having their first burger that was so touching, it would move an audience to tears.

"Bien sûr, you can shoot in my diner," I wrote back to the young filmmaker. "But only during the slow times, between 3:00 P.M. and 7:00 P.M., Tuesday through Thursday. And *only* if you promise to not disturb any of my customers."

I may have been an old sap, but I was also a *ruthless* businessman.

On the day of the shoot, Joël arrived at the diner with a surprisingly large crew in tow. As a former filmmaker, I could tell right away from his fancy equipment and three-camera setup that he had deep pockets. *All that footage for just one scene?* I thought as I looked at the three cameras. *At that rate it'll take him* forever *to edit his film.*

Photo by Alex Berthier

After Liliane settled into a booth, I went over to introduce myself. She was quite spry for someone in her nineties, having no need for glasses or a cane. "It's an honor to meet you, *Madame*," I said offering my hand. Like most true heroes, the former Resistance fighter gave me a humble look, as if to say, "Why? What did I do?"

I hung around the diner for over an hour, hoping to witness the big moment. But Joël and his crew were still busy doing sound checks and futzing with the cameras.

"Do you have a rough idea when your grandmother's going to eat her hamburger?" I asked Joël.

"Actually, she's not hungry right now," he said. "But it's okay, she's used to hanging around on the set."

That was my cue to *scram-ez*. (I'd forgotten how tedious film shoots could be.) On my way out the door, I turned to my newly promoted assistant manager and said, "As soon as the nice lady starts eating her burger, please take a bunch of pictures. I want to post the historic moment on our social media."

"You got it!"

A couple hours later, I called the diner back. "Well, how did it go?"

"They're still rehearsing."

"For a documentary?"

"I guess so. They're just sitting around chitchatting."

"Okay, but remind them that if the place starts to fill up with customers, they'll have to wrap it up and come back another day."

"You got it!"

By ten o'clock, I still hadn't heard back from the assistant manager. I figured it must have gotten busy, so I decided to swing by. *Au contraire*, the diner was mostly empty, the film crew long gone.

"Well?" I said excitedly. "Can I see the pictures?!"

"I didn't take any."

"Why not?"

"The old lady chickened out and ordered an omelet instead."

As it turned out, Liliane could fight Nazis and champion women's rights—but to eat a hamburger? That was just *crazy*!

Although I was a little disappointed, I still longed to see Joël's documentary, especially the climactic moment when Liliane decided to forego her burger, concluding that perhaps her bucket list wasn't so important after all—and that, really, what did she have to prove? (Four years hence, I asked Joël if I could see the scene, but he said they still hadn't finished filming yet. On the plus side, that meant Liliane was still alive and kicking.)

I hoped to say as much for Mme. Hubert. "You never know how much longer she'll be around," Julien said over lunch. "You should go see her and set up a date. You don't want to have any regrets, *n'est-ce pas?*"

That night, I hopped on my bike and raced over to Mme. Hubert's apartment. Just as I was locking up my bike, I heard a familiar voice from behind. "Can you believe Président Macron and his four-hour-long speeches?" I turned around to see Mme. Hubert standing there in all her Burberry glory, a baguette tucked under her arm. "*Oh-la-la, sérieusement!* The human brain can only handle so much!"

"Mme. Hubert, am I glad to see you! When can we do lunch?"

She shrugged. "*Vendredi?*"

"*Vendredi* it is! I'll come by and pick you up."

That Friday, it felt so good to ride the elevator with Mme. Hubert again. And this time, she let me hold her arm as we made the three-block trip down the hill from her apartment to the diner. Although she was psychologically back *en forme*—and sharp as a tack—her body had trouble keeping up.

After seating Mme. Hubert in my favorite booth, I handed her a menu. Recalling what had happened with Liliane, I pointed out all the different dishes available. "As you can see, we serve a lot more than just hamburgers here, so order whatever you want."

"*Non, non, non, allez!*" she said. "We're in an American *daïneur*, so let's go all the way! Bring me a 'amburger!"

"Which kind?"

Mme. Hubert looked stumped. "You mean, there's more than one?"

"*Ah, oui!*" I smiled. "There's like, fifteen."

"*D'accord,*" Mme. Hubert said, pointing to the first burger on the menu that caught her eye. "How about this one?"

"The 'chili con carne' burger?" I asked. "Hmm, I'm not sure; that one's kind of *spicy*."

Usually when I say the word "spicy," French people recoil, since they generally have a very low tolerance for fiery food. But not Mme. Hubert. She was ready to try it all. (Except for her side; she ordered a "sensible salad" instead of French fries.) I, of course, ordered breakfast—a "lumberjack breakfast" to be precise.

As we waited for our food to arrive, Mme. Hubert unfolded her bright red napkin and tucked it into her yellow velour shirt, turning the napkin into a bib. *What a contrast to how she'd grown up*, I thought, recalling the stories Mme. Hubert had told me of dinners with her bourgeois family in Normandy. Not only did everyone have to dress up every night, there were so many utensils laid out on the table in front of them—different ones for each course—it was hard to know which one to use when.

But at Breakfast in America there were just two utensils: a knife and a fork. Mme. Hubert subsequently used them to attack her chili burger—a classic cheeseburger with a mound of chili on top—doing so with the same gusto she'd seized life with for the past eighty-six years. Before you knew it, kidney beans and chili sauce was flying everywhere. At one point, an errant bean ricocheted off her bib, knocking it off. Unfazed, Mme. Hubert kept going until she'd completely polished off her plate.

As I proudly watched Mme. Hubert take her last bite, I could feel a tear bubbling up in the corner of my eye. *How touching*, I thought. *Where's a film crew when you need one?*

"How was it?" I asked.

"*Pas mal. Pas mal de tout.*" (Not bad. Not bad at all.)—which I'd learned after all these years was French for "*fan-f*ckin'-tastic!*"

"Any room for dessert?" I asked.

"*Non, non, non! Juste un café.*"

Of course, I couldn't resist taunting Mme. Hubert, to see if she really was willing to go all the way. "Do you mean an *American* coffee?"

"Hah, you must be joking! *Jus de chaussettes?! Sérieusement?!*"

After letting out a hearty chuckle, the former professor broke into an in-depth dissertation about the origins of the term, "sock juice." According to her, some historians speculate that the French thought American coffee tasted so bad, it was like drinking the liquid squeezed out of wet socks. But most believe that soldiers during wartime didn't have filters to make their coffee, so they had to use their socks instead.

I held up the pot of sock juice and waved it temptingly in front of Mme. Hubert. "Well . . . ?" I smiled. "Are you ready for '*le total*?'" (the works)

Mme. Hubert shook her head. "World War II is over," she said. "Give me an espresso!"

ELEVEN

Turkey Day at BIA

T hanksgiving was six months away, but I was already starting to stress out. I'd just received an email from a customer asking if she could make a reservation. In *May*. Thanksgiving was in November. But since Breakfast in America was one of only a handful of places in Paris to celebrate the holiday, people were intent on reserving a table earlier every year. Only problem was, this year I didn't have a cook to make the special holiday meal.

My head chef, Quentin, an American, had been promoted to manager five years earlier and was enjoying life without kitchen burns, cuts, and *hallux rigidus* (chef's foot). Luckily for us, every year he reluctantly agreed to put his apron back on and cook for that one day in November. However, this year, he had decided to make a career change and move on from the diner.

"Relax," Julien said. "You have plenty of time to find someone."

"Oh, yeah? Where do we find a cook in Paris who not only knows how to prepare an authentic Thanksgiving dinner for 150 people, but can do so in the walk-in closet that *is* BIA's kitchen?"

"Worst-case scenario: You do it."

I stared at Julien, stone-faced. He knew I could barely boil an egg. "That would *definitely* be the worst-case scenario."

Complicating matters, since Thanksgiving didn't exist in India, Sri Lanka, or Ethiopia, none of my cooks knew how to make the traditional holiday meal, either. Quentin had tried to show them, but while often delicious, each cook's turkey plate would inevitably be influenced by their own country's cuisine, i.e., a curry sauce instead of gravy, or spicy, dried turkey instead of moist.

Of course, it didn't help that Julien, like most French people, didn't get what all the hoopla was about surrounding Thanksgiving. "We don't need an excuse to have a big, delicious meal," he smirked.

Other French people were even more perplexed by the holiday. "Let me get this straight," they'd say. "On one of the few days you Americans get off from work, you're supposed to sit around being thankful? For what? Not having any vacations?"

Undaunted, I did my best to explain to Julien what made the holiday so special—and why cancelling it was out of the question. First, homesick American expats and tourists were depending on us. They needed a place to satisfy their cravings for stuffing and cranberry sauce. Next, Thanksgiving had become part of our brand. Every year, BIA was featured in magazines and social media as one of *the* places in the world where Americans could celebrate Turkey Day abroad.

Last but not least, Thanksgiving was *my* favorite holiday. Unlike Christmas and Halloween, the fourth Thursday of November still hadn't been overly commercialized yet. (Although Black Friday was desperately trying to change that.) For me, what I loved most about the holiday was its simplicity; just dining and drinking with loved ones for hours on end. Of course, as Julien had happily pointed out, this was the centerpiece of French life—and one of the main things that had attracted me to the country in the first place.

So, *oui*, for all these reasons Thanksgiving had to go on. Even if Julien had no idea what all the fuss was about. "Maybe it'll help if you tell me what Thanksgiving was like in your family," he said.

"You sure?" I said. "'Cause chances are it ain't gonna be pretty!"

"I know. That's why I want to hear it!"

Like a deck of playing cards, my mind flipped through the years, struggling to think of a Thanksgiving that wasn't marred by family drama—or heated arguments over politics and religion.

"Okay," I said. "I've got two that are pretty tough to top."

Julien listened intently as I began to tell the story of my first Thanksgiving in California, after I'd come to study cinema at USC. I'd been invited to the home of a relative who'd married into a family of 100%, bone fide Okies. Like the Joads in Steinbeck's classic novel, *The Grapes of Wrath*, the family had made the trek from the Dust Bowl of their native Oklahoma to seek their fortune in California during the Great Depression. According to the relative, their family had not one, but *two* mattresses strapped to their Ford pickup truck, which meant, compared to the other refugees, they were a family of "standing."

Even though the family had made the journey sixty-plus years earlier, they still hadn't lost their accent. And their children, one of whom had married my relative, had all inherited the same Southern twang. The matriarch of the family, let's call her Ma Kettle, was as kind and sweet as molasses. With her towering bouffant hairdo, Ma Kettle referred to me—and anyone who was so much as a year younger than her—as a "young 'un."

"I hope you're hungry, young 'un," she'd say to me. "'Cause I made enough vittles to last till the cows come home."

Ma's Thanksgiving meal was the closest to Norman Rockwell Americana that I'd ever seen—albeit with a few modern touches. Glowing in the center of the dining room table was her signature green Jell-O mixed with canned fruit—the cherries, grapes, and peach wedges floating in the emerald-colored pectin like galaxies in the universe.

But by far the most popular dish was Ma's sweet potatoes, covered with toasted marshmallows. The Kettle family lapped them up so quickly, there was none left for me, which was a *good* thing. When I was a child living in the orphanage, I had a bad experience with sweet potatoes, forever associating the starchy vegetable with one of the most difficult periods of my life. Since then, I've never touched the stuff.

With a dozen members of the Kettle family vying for a place at the dinner table, I happily gave up my spot. I ended up eating my holiday feast on a TV tray in the living room, directly in front of a vintage RCA console (with stereophonic sound). On the tube was a preacher man. He lifted his hands up in prayer, then pressed them against the TV screen so hard it looked like they might pop out and steal my turkey leg. Tears streamed down his face as he repeated the telephone number flashing at the bottom of the screen, making sure viewers knew exactly where they could send in their tax-free donations.

"Cash, check, or credit card! God accepts all!"

"You enjoyin' yourself?" a voice behind me said. I turned to see Pa Kettle, Ma's other half. Dressed in loose jeans and a tight T-shirt, he was remarkably fit for a man in his seventies. "Ma's a great cook, ain't she?"

"I'll say!" I looked back to the slick-haired charlatan on the boob tube. For some reason, I couldn't take my eyes off him.

"Your kinfolk tells me you're a fill-um maker," Pa Kettle said, giving the word "film" two syllables.

"Well, not quite," I said. "I'm a film *student*." *At the greatest film school in the world!* I wanted to add, but modesty held me back.

Pa Kettle pointed at the TV set. "See that fella? When you're done with your schoolin', you oughta contact him. His ministry's looking for full-time fill-um makers such as yourself to spread the word. In Jesus's name! Amen!"

I stared at the sobbing preacher man, wondering if, like on a film set, the prop man had rigged tubes to his eyes so that the tears could flow without end.

"So what'd'ya think, son?" Pa Kettle smiled. "You ready to work for Jesus Christ and have eternal life? Halleluiah! Praise the Lord!"

For the first time, I noticed a framed picture of Jesus hanging on the living room wall. The tableau was from the early Kmart period, when the Son of God was at his most Caucasian and most buff. How ironic to think that back then I had no idea that one day I'd be attracted to lean and handsome men, much like the Savior.

"Well . . . ?" Pa Kettle said, jerking his head toward the TV screen.

I looked at the sobbing preacher man, then back at *GQ* Jesus who peered down at me from the wall with his big blue eyes. *What would buff Jesus do?* I thought.

Julien stared at me as I finished the story. "Now I see why you moved to France."

"Shush," I said. "I'm not done yet."

My very last Thanksgiving in the U.S. took place in a Public Storage facility. It was the early 2000s, and America had gradually become a nation of hoarders, many of whom were willing to fork over a healthy chunk of their paycheck in order to rent a tiny, overpriced box in a warehouse to store all their crap. (That's exactly what I'd done before moving to France.)

With the storage business booming, my brother's sister-in-law Rowena and her husband Bob managed a facility two hours outside of Los Angeles—in a veritable ghost town in the high desert with more Joshua trees than people. The pay wasn't much, but the couple got to live in an apartment for free above the company's office. Protruding from the backside of their place was a small wooden deck where I, along with eight other guests, gathered around Bob's newest prized possession—a huge vat filled with cooking oil.

Bob grinned through his bushy moustache. "Ain't she a beauty?"

The vat sat atop an open flame, which was fed by a propane gas tank dangerously close to the fire.

"What's that?" I whispered to my brother.

"Oh, c'mon, bro, where've you been livin'—under a rock?" he chided me. "It's a deep fryer. *Everybody's* cooking their Thanksgiving turkey this way now!"

But of course. In a country that deep-fried everything, why not a twenty-five-pound bird? I surveyed the scene. Boiling oil. A wooden deck. A rusty gas tank. It looked more like a recipe for disaster than a Thanksgiving feast,

I mused as I slowly backed away from the makeshift fryer and took cover behind a lounge chair.

Sure enough, with the deep-fried turkey craze sweeping the country, it wasn't long before YouTube was inundated with videos of exploding birds, many of which ignited deck fires, burned down houses, and sent bumpkins diving to the ground, their baseball caps and tank tops ablaze, as they tucked and rolled to snuff out the flames.

Back on the wooden deck, I peeked over the top of the lounge chair as Bob held a long metal pole from which a humungous turkey hung by heavy-duty fishing line, straining from the weight. I winced as Bob slowly lowered our *plat principal* into the boiling oil.

How did I end up with this family? I wondered. *Oh, right. My brother married into it.* I was relieved by this thought because, technically, that meant these folks were kin, which gave me license to make fun of them. Not that I needed to worry about that, since they happily made fun of themselves. Unlike me, they were quite comfortable in their own skin—proud to be rednecks. How do I know this? Because I read it on Bob's T-shirt: PROUD TO BE A REDNECK.

And if ever I wanted to know where Bob and his kin stood on some of the most important issues of the day, all I had to do was look at the bumper stickers on their monster vehicles, which often posed deep, philosophical questions like: IF GUNS KILL PEOPLE, DO PENCILS MISSPELL WORDS? Or: HOW 'BOUT I PUT MY CARBON FOOTPRINT UP YOUR LIBERAL ASS? You know, the kinds of questions that make you go, *Hmm . . .*before you go, *Huh?*!

As it turns out, most of the people I dined with that Thanksgiving day would—just fifteen years hence—proudly don bright red MAGA caps and replace their PROUD TO BE REDNECK T-shirts with new ones that said: PROUD TO BE DEPLORABLE. Or my favorite, ADORABLE DEPLORABLE, which seemed more apt for Bob, who had graciously invited me into his home.

Whenever French people ask me how the 2016 election could have turned out the way it did, I think about that Thanksgiving at Bob's place and realize it hadn't been a fluke; supporters of *Monsieur* Trump didn't just suddenly appear out of the woodwork. They'd been there the whole time, right under our noses. An oasis of red in the bluest of states. Including California.

That said, regardless of red state, blue state, or purple state, I longed for the days my Grandma Lizzy used to tell me about, when people knew the wisdom of the old adage: *Never discuss politics or religion*—especially during the holidays. Of course, the Thanksgiving at Ma & Pa Kettle's had centered around religion. I only hoped that Bob and his guests would express their politics chiefly through their T-shirts and bumper stickers and not at the table.

Then there was my mom—bless her heart—who somehow managed to mix both. "There's a war on Christmas!" she exclaimed in panic the last time I'd visited her at her retirement home in Florida, months before the holiday. Like Christmas itself, the battle cry coming from Fox News and right wing radio, both of which my mom and her husband Dick tuned into religiously, seemed to be taking over the airwaves earlier each year.

"Mom, there's no war on Christmas. They're just trying to get you all worked up so you'll tune in and increase their ratings."

"Easy for you to say. You live in a *Socialist* country."

"Yeah, that's full of *atheists*!" Dick chimed in. "I hear it's gotten so bad in France, you can't even say 'Merry Christmas!'"

"It's true," I said. "You gotta say '*Joyeux Noël*.'"

One day my mom and I were in the post office when a young gentleman smiled at her and said, "Happy Holidays!"

My mom's face turned bright red. "Damn liberal!" she growled.

From her reaction, it was hard to believe that my mom had once been the president of her local chapter of the feminist organization NOW (National Organization for Women). I literally had to hold her back as she yelled at the poor guy, who was now running for the door. "Don't let them stop you from calling it what it is: *Christmas*! *He's* the reason for the season, you know!"

Mercifully, Bob and the rest of the in-laws didn't bring up politics during our Thanksgiving meal. Or if they did, I couldn't hear them, thanks to the big-screen TV, which was just a few inches from the dinner table, set to maximum volume. It allowed me to feel every bone-crushing, helmet-banging sound from not one but *three* back-to-back football games. By the sixth hour, I found myself missing the sobbing preacher man from the Kettles' Thanksgiving celebration.

On the plus side, the turkey did *not* explode. (Bob had the good sense to thaw it out first.) Furthermore, I was pleasantly surprised by how plump and juicy it was, one of the best turkeys I'd ever tasted.

But the real *coup de grâce* came after dessert.

After rousing everyone up from their food comas, Bob led us outside where we followed him to the far end of the storage facility. "You're in for a real treat," my brother smiled, apparently the only one who was in on the secret.

Bob stopped in front of what looked like a garage, but was actually the largest storage unit on site. "Y'all ready?" Bob grinned as he lifted up the garage door as slowly as possible, for maximum dramatic effect. The light from the setting sun poured inside, revealing a huge room filled with boxes and boxes overflowing with tons of stuff.

"This here's the belongin's left behind by folks who ain't paid their rent—or just plum disappeared," Bob said.

I stared at the boxes, imagining dead bodies chopped up inside, buried deep beneath piles of Styrofoam peanuts.

"Take whatever you want!" Bob beamed.

The in-laws rushed in, tearing boxes open and rummaging through them like a bunch of mad shoppers at a fire sale for Deplorables 'R' Us. There were black velvet paintings of wolves. Unicorns. Elvis. Chipped and broken furniture, including a leaky beanbag chair. Neon signs for down-home beers like Schlitz and Coors. So many Big Gulp cups I lost count. Plus baseball caps of all sorts. And most unsettling, an arsenal of arms: pistols, machine guns, and other automatic weapons, but in *plastic*, kids toys. To get them off to an early start. And to go with it all: Camouflage *everything*. Shirts, jackets, hats, and boots.

"*C'est pas vrai!*" (You're making this shit up!) Julien stared at me wide-eyed as I finished telling him my story. "What did you take?"

"Nothing."

"Why not?"

"I didn't want to commercialize Thanksgiving."

By the time September rolled around, I still hadn't found a cook for BIA's Thanksgiving. Making matters worse, Julien and I had just arrived in the States, where we were about to begin the West Coast leg of my book tour, which ran from LA to Vancouver. Here I was, thousands of miles from Paris, starting to seriously contemplate the unthinkable: cancelling Thanksgiving at Breakfast in America.

I was reminded of the classic Christmas special *Rudolph the Red-Nosed Reindeer*, with its iconic stop-motion animation. As the big day approaches, Mrs. Claus hounds her husband to "Eat, papa, eat!" because "nobody wants a skinny Santa!"

Eventually Santa works through his eating disorder, only to be forced to cancel Christmas after a blizzard unexpectedly hits. (Because, you know, that kind of weather pattern is so rare in the North Pole.) Of course, everybody knows what happens next, and I was hoping for the same thing: that an underappreciated individual (preferably a cook *without* a glowing nose, although if he could cook turkey, glow away!) would appear out of nowhere and save the day.

It looked as if my wish might come true when, on the second to last stop of my book tour—in Lake Forest, just outside of Seattle—something wonderful happened: my former head chef, Lindsay, with whom I'd had one of the greatest meals of my life a decade earlier, showed up for my book presentation.

I was so excited to see my old friend and coworker again, and thrilled to hear how well her life was going. She was now the executive chef at an upscale retirement community for influential society women, many of whom were generous supporters of important nonprofit organizations and foundations. These women also had exquisite taste, which suited Lindsay and her classical culinary training perfectly.

"Remember our dinner at La Tour d'Argent?" I asked Lindsay after I'd finished my book presentation.

"Are you kidding," she glowed, her face matching her naturally red hair. "I still talk about that duck to anyone who'll listen."

"Yeah, and customers still talk about that Thanksgiving dinner you made at BIA ten years ago!" This was the perfect opportunity for me to segue to a thought I'd had the moment Lindsay stepped into the bookstore. "I know it's a long shot, but . . . would you be willing to come to Paris and do our Thanksgiving dinner again this year?"

"Oh, I'd love to," Lindsay said. "But right now, I'm in charge of over one hundred employees. Plus you know how hard it is for us Americans to take time off from work?" Lindsay smiled, looking heavenward. "God, I miss my five weeks of paid vacation in France!"

"You don't have to," I said. "If ever you want to come back to work at BIA, the door is always open!" Lindsay seemed genuinely flattered, vowing to let me know ASAP if she were able to figure out a way to make it happen for Turkey Day.

When Julien and I returned to Paris at the beginning of October, my generally reserved manager Bruce looked frazzled. "All three seatings for Thanksgiving are completely full," he said. "I had to start a waiting list already!"

Adding to the stress, Bruce said a customer, Noah from New York, had started stalking the place from the other side of the Atlantic, calling and emailing the diner every day, trying to bypass the waiting list and grab a spot for his large family. From the tone of his emails, I did not get a good vibe from him. ("I want a table for five!" he wrote. "And there better be a lot of dark meat!") I wrote him back and politely recommended that he check out the two other restaurants in Paris that offered a traditional (but much pricier) Thanksgiving meal. That only made Noah call and email more.

I was reminded why we only took reservations once a year; it was an extremely complicated process. For example, what to do when homesick Americans like Noah were dying to get a spot, while at the same time French people wanted to reserve—but mainly out of curiosity's sake? Since they didn't have a cultural connection to the holiday, nine times out of ten French customers would end up being disappointed with the whole "Thanksgiving thing." Like Julien, their reaction would be, "What's the big deal? It's just a turkey dinner. Who needs a special day for that?"

I soon learned that, except for the occasional salad or sandwich, the French rarely ate turkey. In all my years living in France, I've never once seen it served as a main course. The reason, according to Julien, is that turkey is associated with being on a diet, much like cottage cheese is for Americans. So not exactly "comfort food" for the French.

And if you're craving a whole turkey à la Butterball, you won't find one in the freezer section of your favorite French grocery store. You have to specially order one from the right butcher. Some places, such as the USC alumni association in Paris (of which I'm a member), go so far as to fly over whole, free-range turkeys from Italy, then have a local butcher prepare them.

And say you've managed to find a whole bird, how do you cook it? In France, ovens tend to be much smaller—too small to fit an American-size turkey inside. And, of course, deep frying them was out of the question.

The more I thought about all this, the more panicked I got. I just didn't see how I was ever going to save Thanksgiving.

Then a very special email arrived.

It was mid-October when I received some great news: Lindsay was able to get time off from work to come over and do our Thanksgiving dinner! Knowing we couldn't afford to pay a lot (the holiday wasn't much of a moneymaker due to the extra food and labor costs, as well as having to close early on the big day), Lindsay was fine with the deal: I would personally pay for her plane ticket, lodge her for free, then give her a "per diem" for each day she was in Paris, including extra days if she wanted to take a little vacation.

The Sunday before Thanksgiving, Lindsay arrived at the diner with two huge suitcases full of American supplies. They included restaurant-size bags of mini marshmallows (for the sweet potatoes), dried onions (for the green bean casserole), and fresh cranberries (for, well, the cranberry sauce). Looking at the menu she'd planned, it was almost a mirror image of the Kettles' Thanksgiving feast—but several notches up, as if served at a Michelin-starred restaurant. (Thankfully, Lindsay eschewed the green Jell-O with floating fruit galaxies.)

However, the meal would not be served buffet style. Instead, it would be made up of three courses, starting with a choice of soup or salad (roasted butternut squash soup or harvest salad), followed by the main turkey plate with all the fixin's, and finally ending with a choice of dessert: either Lindsay's delicious homemade apple pie or pumpkin pie.

Julien got very excited when he saw Lindsay's recipe for pumpkin pie and decided to bake a batch.

"Hey, I thought you weren't into Thanksgiving," I teased him.

"That's because you never told me about the magic of nutmeg!"

Watching Lindsay work her magic, I was reminded why I hadn't been able to take the risk of hiring a cook from the outside who wasn't familiar with BIA's kitchen. There were just too many logistical problems, starting with the space itself. Not only did Lindsay have to wait until after the restaurant closed at 11:00 P.M. to start prep, there wasn't enough room in the refrigerators to store everything. She ended up having to do some prep back at the apartment, ultimately pulling three all-nighters in a row.

Given the limited space, Lindsay also had to be very precise when gauging the quantities of soups, salads, and pies she should make, depending on what 150 customers were likely to order on Thanksgiving night. At the same time, she had to be careful not to *over*prep, so that there'd be a minimal amount of waste. This left her very little room for error.

Lastly, Lindsay had to deal with the challenge of an all-male—and sometimes macho—kitchen staff, most of whom were not used to having a woman in charge. But Lindsay *was* used to it. I watched in awe as she empowered them, giving each kitchen member a task they were responsible for, ultimately getting them motivated in a way I never could.

Of course, the front of the house also had its own share of challenges. When it came to the three seatings of fifty-plus people each—at 5:00 P.M., 7:00 P.M., and 9:00 P.M.—we had to be careful which customers were put into which time slot, especially the first two, since they required a fast turnaround. We tried to make sure that the 5:00 P.M. seating consisted mainly of American tourists—with children—since they tended to eat quickly and leave early.

The 7:00 P.M. time slot was the most difficult to manage. When taking a customer's reservation, we had to make sure they understood—and were okay with—finishing their meal in under two hours. We definitely didn't want to rush them, but at the same time, we didn't want to make the 9:00 P.M.-ers have to wait outside, either. Knowing that French people liked to take their time, we encouraged them to reserve for the last time slot. The same for expats, who had gotten used to eating late in France.

By the time the big day arrived, we had a waiting list of over one hundred people. All day long, the phone rang off the hook with customers who'd realized at the last minute they'd forgotten to plan ahead. After closing the place at 2:00 P.M. to set up the main dining room, I went down into the cellar and pulled out a huge box containing all of the special Thanksgiving paraphernalia I'd brought back from the States: politically sensitive Native American and Pilgrim decorations to hang on the walls; special Thanksgiving settings for each table, including mini cornucopias and special "Tom Turkey" napkins; and candles posed on decorative fall leaves for each table.

When we were done sprucing up the place, BIA felt like a fancy restaurant, which meant we had to dress the part. I wore a snazzy suit and tie, while my servers chose to dress in elegant black. Best of all, I was able to get three of my original staff members to make a special guest appearance and work with us that night. They all knew Lindsay and were dying to see her again. As I watched my "old-timers" hug each other, it felt like a special reunion episode of *Friends*.

A half hour before opening, with the tables set and the team ready to go, I dimmed the lights and put on a classic American jazz mix on the sound system. Ella, Louis, Nina, and Billie set the mood as they sang songs about loving Paris in the springtime, dancing cheek to cheek, having plenty of nothin', and finding love *at last*.

Then, just as customers were staring to line up outside, we had our first glitch. The world-famous Kayser Bakery, whose original location was just around the corner from the diner, was supposed to have 120 freshly baked dinner rolls ready for us. But for the first time in fourteen years, they'd somehow forgotten to make them. Not a good way to start off the night. Luckily, Julien showed up just in time and went straight to the bakery and in that French way I still needed to master, somehow got them to promise they'd have the rolls ready before our first order was taken.

After seating the first round of customers, I told my staff to just take drink orders first, to stall for time. True to their word, just as we were about to put in the orders for the first course, two employees from Kayser came running up to the diner, each holding large bakery bags full of piping hot dinner rolls. I discreetly carried them inside, placing them into bread baskets along with pads of *demi-sel* butter. As I served them to our customers, I proudly exclaimed, "Here you go! Fresh out of the oven!" (Only I didn't say *whose* oven.)

The rest of the meal went without a hitch. My favorite part: going from table to table with a big black-pepper grinder that I'd pulled out of storage—just for the occasion.

"Fresh ground pepper?" I'd ask before grinding away and ending with a flourish—tap-tap!—on the back of the shaker.

My second favorite part: the stalking customer, Noah from New York, had worn me out so much with his constant calls and emails I gave him a table the moment there was a cancellation. He turned out to be the nicest guy, as did his family. He was so grateful in fact, that a few weeks later, after he'd gotten back to NYC, he sent me an original album cover of Supertramp's *Breakfast in America*. Not only had he gotten it framed, he also included a picture of his family enjoying their Thanksgiving feast at BIA. The incident made me think of a line from one of my favorite Katharine Hepburn movies, *The Philadelphia Story*: "The time to make up your mind about people is *never*."

In the end, it was by far the best Thanksgiving BIA had ever had. And certainly much better than *my* past Thanksgivings back in the States. There was no family drama. No blaring TV. No football. No politics or religion. No sobbing preacher man or junkyard free-for-all. And since I was in France, no usurping of Thanksgiving by Christmas. (Mercifully, the French waited until December to roll out the holiday decorations—unlike the U.S. where, months earlier, my friend had sent me a picture from his local Target showing Christmas decorations side by side with Halloween decorations. In *September*.)

After the last customer had left the diner, my staff and I pushed the tables together to make one big one so that the ten of us, including Julien, could have *our* Thanksgiving dinner together, buffet style. As I served wine to everyone, I couldn't help but feel moved, recalling all the BIA weddings and baby showers I'd attended. I then held up my glass. "To Lindsay," I said. "Thank you for saving Thanksgiving!"

Forever modest, Lindsay smiled, then gestured toward the piles of food. "Eat up, everybody! Before it gets cold."

I waited until everyone had served themselves before I took my turn. Famished, I piled my plate high with turkey, stuffing, and mashed potatoes, smothering it all with gravy. But when I got to the sweet potatoes, I froze up. In my mind, I was suddenly transported back to the orphanage when I was just four and a half. It was Christmas Eve. I was the only kid left in the cafeteria. All the others had gone back to their dorm rooms to open their gifts. When I stood up to leave, the stern administrator said, "Uh-uh. Not until you finish your meal."

I looked down at my plate. *What's she going on about?* I thought. I'd already polished off my Christmas ham, baked beans—and even my broccoli—but I just couldn't stomach the sweet potatoes. (It was a texture thing.) When the administrator turned her back, I decided to be clever. I smeared the sweet potatoes into the plate, willing them to "disappear." *She'll never see them now*, I thought.

When the administrator turned back around, I cowered slightly, afraid that she would scold me. Instead, she cracked a thin smile and said, "Go ahead. You can open your gifts now." I sprang up out of my seat, elated. But as I rushed back to my dorm, a pang of sadness began to rise up inside me. All of a sudden, I felt so alone. I missed my mom. My Grandma Lizzy. Even my dad. Anyone to share the holiday with.

Back at the diner, I looked at the sweet potatoes, then at Julien, who was surrounded by my makeshift BIA family. Emboldened by them, I decided it was time to create a new "food association"—not one of trauma, but of gratitude. I scooped a glob of sweet potatoes onto my plate. Took a bite. I still didn't like them, but they no longer held the same power over me.

Food can scar. But, man, can it heal.

TWELVE

Supertramping

Could we have kippers for breakfast,
Mummy dear, Mummy dear?
They gotta have 'em in Texas
'Cos everyone's a millionaire

—from Supertramp's multiplatinum album,
Breakfast in America

For years, whenever I heard the lyrics to Supertramp's mega-blockbuster hit song, "Breakfast in America," I would always think, "What the hell's a kipper?" (It's a small oily fish that the Brits eat for breakfast. One word: *Euw* . . .) Then, with the image of the disgusting fish swimming around in my head, a wave of panic would suddenly come over me, followed by a second, even more dreadful thought: "Is Supertramp going to sue me?"

There's an inherent danger when the name of your restaurant is the same as that of a multiplatinum best-selling album. Such is the case with my diner in Paris. Ever since I opened it in 2003, I've lived in constant fear that a mega rock band from the '80s would take me to court and put me out of business.

"But I'm innocent!" I'd imagine myself telling an imaginary judge in my mind. Truth be told, I'd often rehearsed what I would say if I were summoned to court and had to tell the truth and nothing but the truth: the inspiration for the name for my diner, Breakfast in America, had absolutely nothing to do with Supertramp.

It was 2001, and I'd just finished working on an international TV show in Paris. When I returned to LA, my friends asked me what was the one thing I missed while I was away. "Breakfast!" I said without having to give it a second thought.

The next thing I knew, I was sitting in an historic, downtown LA coffee shop with my friends Tom and Corey, feasting on a delicious breakfast consisting of a ham steak and eggs, home fries, sourdough toast and buckwheat pancakes (smothered with butter), all of which I lovingly washed down with a bottomless mug of joe.

"Can you believe it?" I said to my friends as I wiped maple syrup from my mouth. "It's impossible to get an American breakfast in France."

"Who cares?" Tom the musician mused. "You're in France!"

"Yeah, but believe it or not, having croissants and pains au chocolat every day for breakfast gets old fast. And get this: Some of my French friends don't even do breakfast. Instead, they have what they call the *three C's:*" I held up a finger for each *C*: "Café . . . cigarette . . . and caca."

"Ooooh, that's brutal!" Corey the gaffer said.

I returned to my breakfast feast, staring at my buckwheat pancakes, when suddenly I had an aha moment that would change my life forever. "Oh, my God. That's it!"

"What?" Corey asked.

"I know what I'm going to do next: open an American diner in Paris!"

I had never had such a lucid moment in my life. So much so I even knew what I was going to call the place: Breakfast in America.

"But how can you prove you didn't come up with the name for your diner because of the Supertramp song?" the imaginary judge in my mind asked.

"It's easy, Your Honor. Think about it. What was I having that day . . . ? *Breakfast*. And where was I having it . . . ? *In America. Voilà!* I rest my case!" I was so sure that Supertramp and their song had never entered my mind, I was willing to take a lie detector test to prove it.

"Okay, fair enough," my lawyer said when I met with him to work on the business plan for my future diner. At the time, he strongly advised me against using the name Breakfast in America, saying, "Look, even if a judge accepts your claim that you weren't consciously thinking of Supertramp when you came up with the name, he or she could still make the case that you were thinking of them *subconsciously*. And given Supertramp's fame worldwide, that might be enough grounds for a judge to order a cease-and-desist."

My lawyer had a point. If you had grown up in the late '70s and early '80s as I had, it would have been virtually impossible *not* to have heard at least one Supertramp song. They were *that* popular. From Casey Kasem's *American Top 40* to any AM/FM radio station playing in my dad's car, their songs made up a big part of the soundtrack of my youth.

But the thing is, since I had never owned any Supertramp albums—nor did any of my older siblings—I never actually paid attention to *who* sang those songs. It wasn't until I visited France for the first time that I made the connection.

It was the summer of 1984, and I had just arrived in Paris for my junior year abroad. One evening, as I was strolling through the Latin Quarter, I saw a large group of people—mainly international tourists—standing in front of La Fontaine Saint-Michel. They were gathered around a trio of young Frenchmen with guitars who, in perfect three-part harmony, were in the middle of singing a beautiful rendition of Simon & Garfunkel's "The

Boxer." Because I had owned a copy of S&G's *Greatest Hits* album, I knew the lyrics by heart. But I wasn't the only one. By the time the trio got to the refrain, most of the international crowd was singing along: *"Lie la lie, lie la la la lie lie, Lie la lie . . ."*

I'd never seen anything like it. People from all over the world, gathered together in a circle, united in song. I don't know why it should've surprised me that people from different countries, who spoke different languages, could somehow know all the words to a song that had meant so much to me. But surprised I was. And in awe.

But then the tables turned. When the street performers launched into their next song, everyone in the crowd knew the lyrics *except* me. Even though I'd never heard the song before, it moved me. As an American who had no home to return to, it somehow made me feel homesick. Especially when I heard these lines:

> *Take a jumbo across the water*
> *Like to see America*

I felt an instant connection with the person who had written that song. I imagined him growing up as a penniless street urchin—much in the same way I imagined myself as a child—longing to escape from his miserable, one-horse town and see the world. And to think: I'd actually done it! Here I was in Paris, living the *dolce vita*! At that moment, I felt so fortunate. And at the same time, a little confused: *How does one say "la dolce vita" en français?*

In any case, after that magical moment at Saint-Michel, I still didn't know the name of the song nor who sang it. I would have to wait an entire year before I accidentally stumbled upon the answer.

With the school year over, most of the other students in the study abroad program raced back home to the States to be with their families. I stayed behind in Paris, finding a part-time job and an apartment to sublet for just 1,400 francs a month—or $140, thanks to the record-breaking exchange rate.

The studio belonged to a French law student who was on vacation for the summer break. Although it was the size of a shoebox, the studio couldn't have been in a better location—smack in the middle of the Latin Quarter on rue Monsieur-le-Prince. The street was aptly named because for the next two months, I felt like royalty as I lived the life of a real *flâneur*, sitting in cafés for hours—people-watching and catching up on my reading of classic novels. (*Ah, oui*. I was a geek.)

As luck would have, I kept running into the same street performers I'd seen the year before. Their repertoire hadn't changed much, nor had the makeup of their international audience. And as before, I felt the same joy when they played the mystery song whose title still eluded me. I tried to guess it from certain lyrics. Was it: "Don't You Look at My Girlfriend?" Or: "Take a Jumbo?" Or how about: "Never Seem to Get a Lot?" Whatever the title was, it certainly wasn't popping out from the lyrics.

Then one evening back in my apartment, I decided to put on some music while I ate my dinner. The law student had left behind a large box of LPs, only half of which I recognized. As I fingered through them, one album caught my eye. On the cover was a sassy-looking waitress named Libby (I could tell from her name tag). Dressed in classic diner garb, Libby held up a small plate with a glass of orange juice on it. Behind her in the background was a rendition of the New York City skyline—except it was made out of cups and saucers and other diner paraphernalia stacked on top of each other. The *faux* skyline even included two stacks of boxes meant to represent the Twin Towers.

Intrigued by the cover, I decided to put the album on, not sure if the cheap plastic turntable in the apartment worked or not. It did. As I listened to the LP, I couldn't believe how many of the songs I recognized, starting with track #2: "The Logical Song." The moment I heard the opening lyrics, I was instantly transported back to the summer of '79. I'd just finished the ninth grade and was hanging out by the local lake with my older brother, Eddie. It was one of those rare occasions when he let me tag along with him and his "freak" friends. (In my hometown, you were either a jock or a freak. There was no third choice—except maybe "none-of-the-above," which was what I secretly considered myself to be.)

When "The Logical Song" came on the radio of my brother's beat-up Ford van, he turned the volume way up. Then he and his stoner friends took long tokes off their joints as they listened intensely to the lyrics:

> *Watch what you say,*
> *We'll be calling you a radical,*
> *A liberal, fanatical, criminal . . .*

"Man, that shit is SO right on," one of the stoners said.

"Yeah, for sure. *'Watch what you say'*—or they'll lock your ass up. Just for speaking the truth."

"Totally, man," I said, having no idea what the hell they were talking about.

Back in my Paris apartment, I recognized the next track on the Supertramp album: "Goodbye Stranger," yet another hit from my youth. Next thing I knew, I was singing along, surprised by how many of the lyrics I knew.

But the *crème de la crème* came on the next track—track #4. At long last, here it was. The song I'd first heard performed by three talented French singers just a few blocks from where I now lived. *No wonder I couldn't figure out the title*, I thought. *It's never mentioned once in the lyrics.* Yet the name of the song—as well as the album—couldn't have been more clear. For in her left hand, Libby the waitress was holding a menu on which was written three words: Breakfast in America.

For the rest of the summer, I played that album over and over until I practically wore out the grooves. But just like a summer fling, by the time the fall came around, and I'd returned to UConn to finish my senior year, I had moved on to other albums. I wouldn't think about *Breakfast in America* again for another twenty years, not until I was sitting on the 23rd floor of a high-rise in downtown LA talking to my lawyer.

"So, about this subconscious thing," I said nervously to my lawyer, recalling how many times I'd listened to *Breakfast in America* that summer in Paris. "Even if they can prove it, I still don't see how Supertramp can sue me.

I mean—a restaurant and an album are two totally different things. Isn't there some kind of legal defense for that?"

"Yes," my lawyer said. "It's called a 'non-compete,' but it doesn't apply in cases where the name recognition of something is so huge it enters a totally different category. For example, you can't call your company 'Coca-Cola Rental Cars'—unless you're Coca-Cola."

"I get that. But I still don't see how it applies in my case. Coke is a brand name. Whereas 'Breakfast in America' is a description: 'I'm eating *breakfast* . . . in *America*.'"

"Let me give you another example: Have you ever heard of the song, 'Margaritaville?'"

"Sure. It was a big hit when I was growing up."

"Well, some poor schmucks in Arizona decided to open a bar and call it Margaritaville. Faster than they could put salt on their cocktail glasses, the singer, Jimmy Buffett, dragged their asses to court. And won."

"Yeah, but that's different. Margaritaville's not a real word. Buffett made it up. There are no made-up words in Breakfast in America."

My lawyer agreed that the two cases did appear to be different, and perhaps there was no need to worry. But after doing some research, my lawyer found out that over the years, Jimmy Buffett had turned into a lawsuit maniac, suing anyone who even remotely used his music (or lyrics), having a particular penchant for going after restaurateurs.

"Take a look at this," my lawyer said, handing me an article about how Buffett had successfully sued a restaurant in Hawaii for the same reason as before: it shared the same name as one of his songs, "Cheeseburger in Paradise."

I couldn't help but think of the argument I'd been using when defending myself in front of my imaginary judge. "What was *their* restaurant serving?" Cheeseburgers. "And where were they serving them?" In Paradise (Hawaii).

Merde. I hated Jimmy Buffett.

Even though my diner hadn't even opened yet, I had no choice but to change its name. And since I was still in the development stage—looking for investors and a location as well as a bank loan—I had to redo everything, including my business plan, company contracts, and saddest of all, my diner swag, items that I'd made as gifts for my investors. When I saw the new name and logo on the coffee mugs I'd made, my heart sank.

"*American Breakfast Diner*?!" one of my investors cried. "That's awful!"

"I know," I said. "It doesn't have the same ring to it, does it?"

What the investors didn't know was that I had a secret plan up my sleeve. It was a long shot, but there was still a chance I could get the original name for my diner back. The only other person who knew my secret plan—besides my lawyer—was the woman I'd been dating briefly at the time, Fiona. As I was getting ready to make the big move to France, she handed me a present.

"Hopefully this'll bring you some luck," she smiled. I unwrapped the gift. It was an original vintage copy of Supertramp's *Breakfast in America* album. "Maybe one day you'll be able to hang it up in your diner."

Being a fairly superstitious person, I wasn't sure if I should bring the album to Paris with me or not. In the end, I did. Long story short, my backup plan worked. Well, *kinda*. The moment I arrived in Paris, I went straight to the Intellectual Properties office where I was happy to see that the name Breakfast in America had never been registered in France—or the rest of Europe for that matter. I quickly registered the name (and logo) under all the categories related to the restaurant business, including food service, food products, and product merchandise—aka *swag*.

However, once my diner had finally opened, I decided *not* to hang up Fiona's gift. Instead, I put the vintage Supertramp album in storage, waiting for the day when I could be 100% sure that I was safe. In other words, even though I technically held the trademark to Breakfast in America, it still didn't prevent Supertramp from coming after me one day with expensive lawyers in tow. I'd heard of copyright cases that dragged on for years—with appeals and counter-appeals. And given the fact that Supertramp's pockets had to be way deeper than mine, if ever the case went to court, I'd probably end up going bankrupt before a decision was even reached.

So for the next twelve years I played dumb.

This was especially hard to do in France, where *Breakfast in America* happened to be the fifth best-selling album of all time. No surprise then that nearly every day one of my French customers would ask if my diner was named after the album.

"What album?" I'd say.

"*Oh-la-la*, don't tell me you've never heard of Supertramp?"

"Can you sing one of their songs for me?"

The French customer would roll their eyes. "Where did the name come from then?"

"That's easy," I'd say. "Look around you. What are customers having? *Breakfast*. Where are they having it? *In America*!" (As if my diner were an embassy located on sovereign American soil . . .)

For the next couple of years, as my Breakfast in America diners became more well-known, it was hard to stay under the radar. This turned out to be a double-edged sword. Although publicity was great for business, it also meant that there was a greater chance that one of Supertramp's band members—or friends, or lawyers—would see my diner's name mentioned in the media. This was less of a problem when it involved guidebooks, such as Frommer's or Lonely Planet. But when Breakfast in America started appearing in mainstream media, such as the *New York Post*, CNN, NBC News—and especially the trade magazine read by *everyone* in the entertainment business, the *Hollywood Reporter*, I really became concerned.

Despite opening a second Breakfast in America in the Marais (which brought us even more publicity), I never heard a word from Supertramp. Instead, there was a new problem I had to contend with: copycat American diners that were popping up all over Paris, with menus that, coincidentally or not, looked strikingly similar to mine. The most popular of these was Happy Days Diner, which opened its first restaurant not far from La Fontaine Saint-Michel. I couldn't help but wonder if Happy Days Diner would run into trouble for using the same name as the hit TV show from the '70s, back when the Fonz was the king of cool.

I got my answer one day when suddenly out of the blue, all of the Happy Days Diners (which was now a chain), changed their name to HD Diner. A rumor circulated around town that Paramount, the studio that had produced the classic TV show, had slapped the diners with a "cease and desist." This alarmed me. *What if someone in Supertramp's entourage hears about what just happened here in France? Would my diner be next?*

I began to calculate how much it must have cost HD Diner to completely change its brand: from their menus, to their signage, to the swag they sold in their shops—not to mention the name recognition they'd so painstakingly built up over the years. *How confusing it must be for a new customer to figure out what the HD stands for,* I thought. *Hard Drive? High Def? Häagen-Dazs?*

In any case, because of what happened with HD Diner, any chance of my hanging up Fiona's Supertramp album in my diner looked less and less likely.

"Great news, Craig!" my manager said excitedly through the phone. "They just arrived!"

"Really? I'll be right there!"

When I stepped into the diner, a box was waiting for me on the counter. I ripped it open. Inside were five advance copies of my book, *Pancakes in Paris: Living the American Dream in France.* I stared at them, my heart bursting with pride. It had taken me two long years to write my book, but it was well worth it. I could now check "Published Author" off my bucket list.

However, the book had the potential to put me in a whole new league of trouble with Supertramp, especially Chapter 4, which recounted how my lawyer had warned me about the risk of having a diner that shared the same name as the band's most successful album. Heck, the title of the book could just as well have been called *The Breakfast in America Story.* The connection was that obvious.

Complicating matters, the publisher was so excited about my book, they offered to finance a big West Coast tour for its release. For Julien and me, it would be the trip of a lifetime. We'd get to drive up the coast from Los Angeles to Vancouver, stopping at over a dozen bookstores and other venues along the way. If all worked out as planned there'd also be interviews with newspapers and magazines, as well as TV and radio appearances.

Soon, there would be no place left to hide.

Of course, deep in the back of my mind, I'd always been waiting for the other shoe to drop with Supertramp. It was already risky enough that my diner had received a ton of publicity in France. But now Breakfast in America (and yours truly) would be getting media coverage in America, starting off in California where, as fate would have it, Roger Hodgson, the cofounder of Supertramp and writer of most of their hits (including "Breakfast in America") just happened to have a home.

Just when I was about to set off on my tour, I received a call from a Hollywood producer who—full disclosure—was also an investor in my diner. He wanted to option the rights to my book and turn it into a TV show. With the advance I received, I hired my own PR person from New York City to help me promote the book.

It was the best decision I ever made. Gail was responsible for getting me on several radio spots as well as tons of local and national media, including Page Six of the *New York Post* and an article in the *Huffington Post*.

Yet despite all the publicity, I *still* hadn't heard a peep from Supertramp. Then one day, shortly after I'd finished my book tour and returned to Paris, I received a call from my publicist Gail who had some "great news." Roger Hodgson, Supertramp's cofounder and lead singer/songwriter was about to go on a world tour and was planning to make a stop in Paris in May 2017. (Incidentally, the name of his tour was "The Breakfast in America World Tour.")

Unbelievable. It had been nearly thirty years since I'd been an exchange student in France and first heard Supertramp perform our namesake song in front of La Fontaine Saint-Michel. And now, as if coming around full circle, the song's creator would be performing it in Paris where there were currently *two* diners sharing the same name of his most famous song as well as a *New York Times* best-selling book telling the whole story.

"I'm going to contact Roger right away," Gail said excitedly.

"Are you sure that's a good idea? I mean maybe, just maybe, he's never heard of my diner. Is it really worth the risk?"

"Listen, Craig, he's going to find out about your place someday. Might as well confront the issue head on!"

I loved Gail. One of the things that made us such a great fit was that, in addition to representing writers, she also had decades of experience working in the music industry. (For years, she's been the PR person for a mega '70s rock band that continues to tour to this day.) There was a good chance Gail might be just one or two "degrees of separation" from Roger and his handlers. Sure enough, one of Gail's colleagues hooked her up with a contact for Roger. Gail sent the person an email inviting Roger to Breakfast in America once he'd arrived in Paris. But the contact never responded.

I began to worry. *Had we done the right thing? Was Roger meeting with his lawyers right now, drafting a cease-and-desist order that would eventually put me out of business?* After doing some research, I discovered that Margarita-ville had actually been open for *ten years* before Jimmy Buffett discovered them and took them to court.

"Have you heard anything back from Roger?" I asked Gail.

"No, but don't worry, Craig. The moment I do, I'll let you know."

As the silence continued, I began to toy around with the idea of coming up with a new name for Breakfast in America. What if I followed HD Diner's example and simply called it BIA Diner? That might work since regular customers already referred to us as BIA. In fact, it had always been my hope that one day, if my diner got popular enough, kids would give it a hip nickname, saying things like, "*Hé, on y va à* BIA!" (Hey, let's go to BIA!)

But of course, besides the expense of having to change the name, what concerned me the most was how it might turn off new customers who would have no idea what "BIA" stood for. *Bureau of Indian Affairs? Base Information Analysis? Brain Injury Association?* I found dozens of examples online, none of them sexy.

Then in March, with Roger's concert just two months away, I received a message from a travel site called Culture Trip. They'd featured my diner in an article about restaurants around the world where tourists could go to celebrate Thanksgiving. The site's rep told me that someone was trying to reach me through them, but he didn't say who.

"Can you please forward me the email?" I wrote back.

A couple days later, Culture Trip sent me back a screen capture of the message:

Lydia
Social media Manager, Public Relations for
Roger Hodgson, Voice and cofounder of Supertramp
Hi, I'm trying to reach Craig Carlson w/Breakfast in America. I'm the Social Media Mgr for Supertramp's Roger Hodgson, who wrote and sang BIA. Roger will be at Grand Rex May 27. I'd like to offer Craig a pair of tkts and I thought maybe he could put a poster up. Lydia.

I read the message several times. *Maybe it's a setup,* I thought. The reason? The "PR person" referred to Roger's most famous song, "Breakfast in America," as BIA.

I quickly forwarded the email to Gail. My suspicions deepened when Gail answered back, "That's not the contact person I wrote to, but I'll look into it." Gail got back to me a short time later, saying that the woman claiming to be Roger's PR person, Lydia, was indeed the real deal. After corresponding with Gail, Lydia even offered to throw in two backstage passes for me to meet Roger in person after the concert.

I was so excited! I felt I had to do something to show my appreciation to Lydia and Roger. I went straight to Ticketmaster and purchased four tickets to his concert. The plan was to hold a contest at BIA where four lucky customers (two from each diner) would have the chance to win free tickets to the show.

Lydia loved the idea and sent over a bunch of concert posters to hang up in the diner. For the next two months I promoted the *merde* out of Roger's concert.

"Please let Roger know that he and his band are invited to BIA," I emailed Gail. She wrote back saying that, according to Lydia, Roger would only be in Paris for the night of the concert, and then he was off to England for more performances.

I wished Roger could have been able to come to my diner. I really wanted to show him that Breakfast in America was not a soulless chain, but rather an integral part of the community where everyone was welcome: locals, regulars, and people from all over the world, much like those who had gathered at La Fontaine Saint-Michel to sing his songs all those years ago.

With Roger's show a week away, it was time to announce the lucky winners to BIA's concert contest. At BIA #2, two female French students, who weren't even born when Supertramp first came out, won the first pair of tickets. And at BIA #1, two regulars, a Franco-American couple who, along with their adorable dog, Nola, ate at the diner almost every day. (The couple told me that the only word that got their dog more excited than "walk" was "BIA.")

On the night of the concert, I was so nervous Julien and I decided to have some champagne in the lobby of Le Grand Rex (the concert venue) to celebrate the occasion—and to calm me down.

Stepping into the enormous concert hall, the first thing I noticed was how packed it was. (The show had been sold out for weeks.) The second thing I noticed was how great our seats were—just ten rows from the stage. Most of the audience seemed to be made up French people in their forties and fifties, many of whom brought their children, and in some cases, their grandchildren.

As soon as we settled into our seats, the lights dimmed and out stepped Roger and his band. They were greeted by a standing ovation. At sixty-seven, Roger looked twenty years younger, as fit as a yoga instructor, his long hair in the same style he wore back in the day. Much to my surprise, Roger opened the concert with my favorite Supertramp song of all time: "Take the Long Way Home."

Once again, I was transported back to another time, back to the tiny apartment I sublet in the Latin Quarter when I was just a twenty-year-old kid. Now here I was, in my fifties, all that time having passed by in the blink of an eye. I couldn't help but tear up when Roger sang these lines:

When you look through the years
And see what you could have been
Oh, what you might have been,
If you'd had more time.

I wasn't the only one moved by the song. Half the baby boomers and post–baby boomers in the audience were sniffling into their hankies. And that was just from the first song!

Of course, the best was yet to come. About halfway through the concert, the familiar two-chord ostinato keyboard introduction opened THE song I'd come to hear: "Breakfast in America."

Since Julien's phone had much better image quality than mine, I asked him to turn on his video camera so he could film Roger while I cheered and sang along. Once the song was over, Julien went to shut off the camera on his phone.

"Wait," I said as I watched Roger standing by his piano, sifting through a stack of papers on top. "Keep filming."

"Why? Nothing's happening."

"Please. Just do it," I said, acting on a hunch.

Roger continued to finger through the pages, finally stopping on one. He then looked at the crowd and said, "Craig Carlson? Are you here, Craig?"

"*Yeeeeah!*" I screamed.

"You have a restaurant called Breakfast in America?"

"Yes, I do!"

Then Roger said in nearly perfect French, "*Je visite.*" (I'll visit.)

By now, I felt like I was going to pass out from all the excitement. But Roger wasn't done yet. He continued, *en français*, "*C'est un bon nom pour un restaurant.*" (That's a good name for a restaurant.)

"*C'est vrai,*" (it's true) I said with a whimper, completely overwhelmed.

As Roger went into his next song, I turned to Julien and said, "Did you get that?"

"*Absolument!*"

That night, May 27, 2017, would easily go down as one of the happiest days of my life. After the concert, Julien and I were escorted to a private area upstairs where we joined a dozen or so people in line waiting to meet Roger. A no-nonsense, take-charge woman in her fifties stepped up to where Julien and I were standing.

"Thank you all for coming. Please note that Roger does not give out autographs." I quickly hid the concert poster I'd brought along for Roger to sign. "But he is happy to have his picture taken with you."

The woman then looked at me and stepped over. "Hello, Craig."

"Lydia?" She nodded. Gail must have sent her a publicity photo of me, I thought. How else could she have recognized me?

"Thank you for promoting Roger's concert in your diners," she continued. "We really appreciate it."

I couldn't believe that Lydia was thanking *me*. "I'm the one who should be thanking you!" I said.

Lydia smiled and continued on her way. With just two people ahead of me before I met Roger, I could feel myself starting to shake.

"You need to calm down," Julien said, slightly annoyed. He and I had been together long enough I could tell that he was a little embarrassed to see his fifty-plus-year-old husband acting like a teenage groupie. I was fine with it, but clearly he was not. We almost got into a little spat when suddenly a voice from behind said, "Craig, it's your turn." It was Lydia. She pointed to the opposite end of the room where Roger was standing, waiting.

I stepped up to Roger and shook his hand. "Thank you so much for the shout-out, Roger!" I said nervously, unaware that I hadn't introduced myself. Instead, I held up a bag with two gifts inside, pulling out the first one. "Here's a little something for you—a mug from my diner."

"Ah, yes, of course," Roger said. "You're the guy with the restaurants."

"Uh-huh," I swooned. Julien looked more embarrassed than ever.

"Nice mug," Roger said, holding it up. "I'll think of your place every time I have my tea."

"Oh! Thanks!" I said in full fanboy overdrive. Julien gave me a tough love tap, which helped me regain my composure. "I have another gift for you," I said, pulling out a signed copy of my book. "It tells the story of BIA. My BIA."

"Yes, I know," Roger said. From the tone of his voice, I sensed that my diner wasn't a recent discovery for him; that he'd probably known about it for a while. I took this to mean that, after all these years, he was finally giving me his blessing.

"You must come to BIA the next time you're in Paris!" I said. "Breakfast on me!"

"Well, I *do* love breakfast," Roger smiled.

"Me too," I smiled back.

Figuring that Roger was probably tired from performing all night—not to mention there were still several people waiting in line to see him—I decided it was time to move on. As I turned to go, Roger seemed to want to continue our conversation. But before we could, Lydia intervened, saying, "Would you like me to take your picture?"

I nodded. In the picture, Julien is on one side of Roger and I'm on the other. Two of us look calm and collected. One of us is sweating like a pig. I'll let you guess which one.

Almost a year to the day after that unforgettable night, I received an email announcing Roger's upcoming world tour celebrating the fortieth anniversary of his "mythic album," *Breakfast in America*. In the bottom right-hand corner of the poster there was the image of the famous album cover, featuring Libby the waitress. It got me thinking . . .

I ran to my storage and pulled out the gift Fiona had given me all those years ago. I dusted off the album cover and smiled. *I think you've waited long enough.* The first thing on my to-do list: hang up the album cover on Breakfast in America's wall.

As they say in French, *"C'est pas trop tôt."* (It's about time.) Knowing I had Roger's blessing, my heart filled with love and gratitude.

Merci, Roger. I didn't have to play dumb anymore.

PART FOUR

LOVING IN FRANCE

Photo by Lisa Anselmo

THIRTEEN

Love Is Not a Lock

Finnish people hate to say, "I love you." I learned this from watching Morley Safer on *60 Minutes* back in the '90s when I was still living in LA. I felt such relief, I immediately called my best friend Debbie in Connecticut to share the good news.

"Can you believe it?" I said. "For all those years, the reason my family never said they loved me wasn't personal; it was *cultural!*"

It was also practical. According to my Grandma Lizzy, in her heyday nobody had the time—nor the luxury—to get all worked up about something as foolish as love. Case in point, after my Grandpa Hans abandoned her during the Great Depression, my gram's only thought was how to feed my dad and uncle until they were old enough to join the military.

Ironically, it wasn't until my gram was an empty nester that she finally found someone to share the rest of her life with. Or rather, her friend, Shirley, found someone for her.

"Why don't you marry Noel," Shirley said to my gram one day as if the two were at Woolworth's picking out a pair of socks.

"Noel?" my gram said, looking across the tobacco field where she and Shirley worked. Standing next to a brand-new '51 Oldsmobile parked in front of a tobacco barn was Noel, a balding bachelor in his early forties. He worked for the tobacco company as well, but in their main office.

My gram noticed that even when he was visiting the fields, Noel was always impeccably dressed, his fat, colorful tie standing out against the pale, sunbaked earth.

"I don't know, Shirley," my gram said. "Noel doesn't seem like the marrying type."

"Listen, Lizzy, the longer you wait for some Rhett Butler to come along and sweep you off your feet, the less chance you've got of finding a husband."

My gram's eyes followed Noel as he pulled a pipe out of his pocket and stuffed it with tobacco. He then lit it with a match and took several long, soulful puffs.

Shirley shook her head. "I admit he's a little odd," she said. "But I guarantee you one thing: he'd be a good provider."

Try as she might, my gram couldn't think of a single argument to prove otherwise.

"So the next thing you know, we got married," my gram would say years later as I sat in her living room—all within the earshot of my Grandpa Noel who sat silently in the next room, puffing on his pipe.

For more than fifty years, the two would sleep in separate bedrooms, rarely expressing any outward affection toward each other. But my Grandpa Noel *did* provide. Right up until the day my Grandma Lizzy passed away at home, in her own bed, *not* in a nursing home, just as he had promised her. Doctors said it was a miracle my gramp had outlived her, since virtually every organ in his body had long since shut down. A few months later, with a feral cat he'd adopted lying on his chest, my grandpa joined my gram in the big tobacco field in the sky.

Whenever I think about my grandparents and their tender relationship, a variation of that line from the classic, tearjerker film from the '70s comes to mind:

Love means never having to say I love you.

I wish I'd had that bit of wisdom back when I was a kid living with Fast Eddie in Frenchtown. With my mom having moved 2,000 miles away with her new husband, I was craving to hear those three magic words. But Fast Eddie wasn't biting.

"Of course, your dad loves you," my fourteen-year-old neighbor, Gay, insisted. "He just doesn't know how to show it."

Just two years older than me, Gay seemed so much wiser. Thin and awkward in her coke-bottle glasses, Gay was subjected to constant ridicule from the other kids in the neighborhood, especially when it came to her name. I felt bad for her. Back then, I never could have imagined going through life being called Gay.

Fortunately in our neighborhood of misfits, Gay had loads of company. Just around the corner lived a young girl whose parents were constantly fighting. On the day she was born, they couldn't even agree on what name to give her. Aggravated, the husband turned to the nurse and asked what day it was.

"Tuesday," she said.

"Fine! That's it!" the father shouted. "We'll call her Tuesday!"

"Fine!" the wife shouted back. "Anything's better than your stupid names!"

If I could travel back in time, I'd return to Frenchtown and console Gay, telling her, "Hey, it could have been worse. You could've been called 'Gay Tuesday.'"

Gay would have laughed at this. (I loved making her laugh.) And *she* loved trying to convince me that my father really *did* love me. I can't say I blame her for being so optimistic. It was the '70s, after all. You couldn't turn on the radio without hearing that pesky four-letter word repeated at least a dozen times in practically every song. And Gay was feeling it in her bones.

"The times are a-changing, Craig," she exclaimed as we listened to Bread's "Baby, I'm-a Want You" on her orange, portable phonograph. "It's the age of Aquarius! The dawn of a *new* and more *sensitive* male!"

"It is?" I said, my eyes watering up as I listened to the schmaltzy lyrics blaring from the phonograph, "*You're the only one I care enough to hurt about.*" Somewhere deep inside me, the seed of gayness was starting to sprout, only I didn't know it yet.

"Yeah," Gay continued. "But not everybody is as *enlightened* as we are."

"They're not?"

"Uh-uh. That's why your dad needs your help."

"He does? How?"

"*You* have to help *him* free his feelings . . ."

"Far out . . . And how do I do that?"

"Easy. *You* be the first to say that you love *him*."

Gay must have seen the look of dread on my face, because she took my hand in hers and said, "Don't worry, Craig, I got your back." She then squeezed my hand so hard I had to bite my lip to override the pain. "When your dad comes home tonight, I'll be watching from the front steps, sending you good vibes, okay?"

I nodded then gently wiggled my throbbing hand away from hers.

Later that night, I heard the sound of a dragging muffler echoing among the tenement buildings just as Fast Eddie rounded the corner and pulled up in his multicolored love-mobile featuring a bright yellow racing stripe that he'd painted on himself. The door opened and out stumbled Fast Eddie, his nose bright red as he balanced a large pizza box in his hand like a waiter's tray.

I watched from across the street, then looked over at Gay who was sitting on the front stoop to our apartment building. She jerked her head in the direction of my dad, mouthing, *Say it!*

I took a deep breath and crossed the street, catching up with Fast Eddie as he made his way along the sidewalk. "Uh, dad . . . ?" I said, my mouth struggling to form the words. Fast Eddie stopped and looked at me, expressionless. "Um . . . I just wanted to let you know . . . I love you."

Fast Eddie suddenly looked sober, eyeing me suspiciously. "What do you want?" He pulled the pizza box away. "If you're after this, you can forget about it. It's mine."

My dad chuckled to himself, then stepped around me as if I were a big pile of poop, humming as he shuffled down the sidewalk to our apartment, pizza box in hand. Upon seeing Gay on the stoop, Fast Eddie tipped his "Keep on Truckin'" baseball cap, then said in his deep, Ted Baxter–like voice, (which he only used for addressing "women of the female persuasion"): "Good evening, young lady."

With that, he disappeared into our building. I looked at Gay who was grinding her teeth. Literally. The enlightened Zen master in her was gone, the fourteen-year-old girl back with a vengeance. "*Ooooh*," she growled. "Your dad is *such* an *asshole!*"

Gay got up and stormed into her apartment, slamming the door shut behind her. "Gay, wait!" I yelled as I followed after her. "He was only kidding!"

Of course, Gay wasn't buying it. And I'm not sure I was, either.

In any case, looking back now, I can see that Morley Safer was only half right; not only do Finnish people hate saying I love you, but judging from my father, apparently they don't like *hearing* it, either.

So much for the Finnish side of my family. As for the Polish side, it was a bit more complicated.

"Bullshit love!" my Grandma Mary would say in her thick Polish accent every time I brought up the subject.

But who could blame her, really? By the time she'd turned thirty, my gram had been married twice—and widowed twice. Her last husband, my Grandpa Frank, ultimately succumbed to mustard gas poisoning, which he'd been exposed to as a soldier in World War I. On his deathbed, and only a few months after my mom was born, he turned to my gram and said, "After I'm gone, promise me you'll never marry again."

My gram was taken aback by the comment, not sure how to respond. Fortunately, my Grandpa Frank saved her the trouble. "If you do marry again, you'll lose my military pension. Do you understand that?"

"Yes, Frank," my gram said. "I promise. I'll never remarry."

And damn if she didn't stick to her word, raising four kids on her own and supplementing her late husband's pension by working grueling, twelve-hour shifts at the local garment factory.

Bullshit love, indeed. In my family, nobody had time for that *merde*. But in France, it was a completely different story . . .

When I first arrived in Paris in 1984, I couldn't believe the number of PDAs (public displays of affection) taking place everywhere I looked. On a bench across from Notre-Dame, a couple barely my age was passionately engaged in what I could only imagine was "French kissing." At twenty, I'd never made out like that with anyone. Anywhere. Ever.

Of course, I had my reasons. Naturally, there was my family, who weren't exactly the best role models when it came to love. But there was also my *environment*. I'd grown up smack in the middle of New England Puritanism, thanks to the Shakers, a religious sect that a century earlier had settled in my hometown. (According to Fast Eddie, the Shakers eventually died out because they weren't bright enough to foresee the consequences of not being allowed to procreate.)

In any case, watching the French couple on the bench shoving their tongues down each other's throats, I was full of conflicted feelings: *exhilaration* that humans could express themselves so brazenly in public. *Is that even legal?* I wondered. And *squeamishness* as I watched the couple's hands wander all over their bodies, grabbing onto every bump and bulge within reach.

"*Get a room!*" I wanted to shout at them. But unfortunately, I didn't know how to say that in French yet.

As it turned out, this kind of thing wasn't just happening on city benches. *Amour* was *everywhere*. I'd walk down the street and see a French couple standing in the middle of the sidewalk, their arms wrapped tightly around each other, their faces buried in each other's necks, completely still, as if propping themselves up. Either they were dead and rigor mortis had set in, I surmised, or they were like those marathon dancers from the 1930s, where the last couple standing wins. I'd circle around them, examining their stiff, motionless bodies, looking for signs of life, not sure whether to call the *SAMU* (an EMT) or slap a numbered bib on their backs.

During those first weeks in Paris, I learned that, as a guy, I was only seeing half the picture. One afternoon I was strolling up Boulevard Saint-Michel with two girls from my study abroad program, Sandy, a tall, leggy blonde, and Caroline, her brainy, acerbic sidekick. I'd stopped to take a picture of the famous Saint-Michel fountain. When I looked back up, the wolves had come out: a pair of horny French guys started following the girls, begging them to come back to their place.

I caught up with Sandy and Caroline just as they were shooing the guys away. "Wow," I said. "How often does that happen?"

"All the time," Sandy said. "A girl can hardly walk down the street without hearing '*voulez-vous coucher avec moi!*'"

"What do you do when that happens?"

"Ignore him," Caroline said.

"But you know what the funniest thing is?" Sandy said. "Since arriving in Paris, I've never been told 'I love you' so many times in my life!"

"Yeah," Caroline chimed in. "And Sandy was prom queen!"

Listening to the girls, I felt as if I were living in an alternate universe. How come I never heard the French say, "*je t'aime*?" And in particular, why wasn't I hearing it said to *me*?

But according to Sandy and Caroline, such *declarations d'amour* were *très* commonplace in Paris. They'd be riding on the *métro* and a panhandler would come up and ask for money. When they refused, he'd say, "*Ça ne fait rien* (no biggie). How about coming back to my bridge? We can watch the Bateaux-Mouches go by as we make mad passionate—"

By this point, the girls had moved on to the other end of the train. "Hey, where are you going?" the panhandler would yell after them. "*Mais . . . je t'aaaaime!*"

If *60 Minutes* were to do a segment on the French, they could easily call it: "The French Can't *Stop* Saying I Love You."

I thought about this nearly thirty years later as I stood beside the same park bench where I'd see the couple making out in front of Notre-Dame. Only now the stately 19th-century bridge connecting the Île de la Cité with the Left Bank, *le Pont de l'Archevêché*, was covered with thousands of love locks.

It was 2012, and back then the locks were still considered *très* romantic. Lovers would come from all over the world to declare their devotion to each other by latching a padlock onto one of the many picturesque bridges in Paris. Most couples would purchase an overpriced lock from a seedy vendor squatting like a troll at the corner of the bridge. The couple would then mark their names on the lock with a pen, or better yet, a Sharpie (so it would be more permanent). Some would draw a sappy symbol like a heart with an arrow going through it, or their anniversary written in Roman numerals. Other couples would arrive with their own fancy locks, their names already engraved in medieval-style calligraphy.

No matter how cheap or ostentatious the lock, every couple would follow the same routine. They would search for the best available spot on the bridge to hang it. Then they'd give each other a big fat kiss before snapping the lock shut and throwing the key into the Seine, their love imprisoned for all eternity.

Doing a quick survey of the locks, I noticed that there were a lot of Bobbies and Sues, Fernandos and Gabrielas, Natashas and Vladimirs—but nary a Matthieu or Margaux in sight.

"Why do you think there are so few French names on the love locks?" I asked Julien one night, after coming home from another hard day at the diner.

"*Ah, quelle horreur!*" he said, summing up what most of his compatriots thought of the gesture. "That's because love is *not* a lock! They might as well hang straightjackets from the bridge, too. It's the same thing."

"I totally agree," I said, my mind racing back to the previous month when Julien, who had been my boyfriend for just six years at the time, had asked me to marry him. He'd caught me completely off guard; I wasn't expecting the question—or at least not while we were brushing our teeth before going to bed. After a long and awkward silence, I blurted out the first thing that popped into my head. "Hey, wait'll you hear what happened at the diner today! Remember that lesbian couple I told you about . . . ?"

Julien removed the electric toothbrush from his mouth and tilted his head up to prevent toothpaste from running down his chin. "That's the second time you've said *non*."

"That's not true!" *I'd just changed the subject, that's all.*

"Well, you didn't say *oui*. So I'm telling you now, if I ask you a third time and there's no *oui*, I will *not* ask you again."

Mon dieu. The pressure was on. I quickly changed the subject to, I don't know, Picasso or something, so that Julien wouldn't pop the question a third—and final—time. Truth be told, there was a reason why I'd gotten so tongue-tied; the two of us had such a good thing going, I didn't want to jinx it. But was that the *real* reason? Or was it just an excuse to preempt any chance of my name being added to the slew of failed marriages that adorned my family tree? Or perhaps it was something more.

I couldn't put it into words at the time—neither in French nor English—but deep down, I didn't feel I was worthy of Julien's love.

The next day, I thought about what had happened with Julien as I watched the lesbian couple at the diner. They were regulars who, every time they came in, would practically make love with their clothes on at booth thirty-three. *Their grabby paws could certainly use some love locks right now*, I thought as I watched them go at it with wild abandon, barrel-rolling onto the table and knocking over milkshake glasses. But then I thought: *Wait, maybe I can learn something from these gals.* After all, neither of them had the slightest hang-up when it came to love. The same could be said about two other customers from the diner, both of whom had recently come to me with a very special request.

The first was Thibault, a young Frenchman who had sent me an email with the heading: "Marriage proposal (yes, it's weird)." In the email, Thibault said that he had had his first date at Breakfast in America and wanted to propose to his girlfriend there. "The thing is," he wrote. "I want to make 1,000,000% sure we get the same table we had back then. If there's one thing I've learned from going to BIA, it's that it's very crowded and you don't take reservations. But I would be extremely grateful if we could have the same table for us. I can even pay for everything in advance if that'll make it work."

I wrote Thibault back, telling him how much I loved his story and that we could certainly make an exception for him. But first I would need to know two things: the date (I crossed my fingers, hoping it wouldn't be on a weekend, since those were our busiest days); and the table—hoping it wouldn't be a booth, since they were reserved for parties of three or more. I won't go into all the gory details, but for a small diner like BIA, it's very hard to hold a table on a busy day, especially when hungry customers are lined up outside, staring through the window at an empty table, waiting for the customer who reserved it to show up.

Thibault answered my email within minutes. "Sorry, I forgot to mention, it would be on May 11, which is a Sunday.☺ As for the table, I couldn't think of a good way to describe it, so I drew the BIA instead.☺"

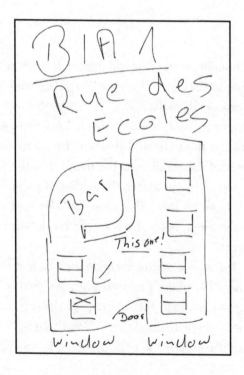

Well, one out of two ain't bad, I thought. Sunday was definitely the worst day Thibault could've chosen, but I let it slide. On the plus side, the table he requested was a two-top, not a booth.

She better say 'oui,' I said to myself as I sent off an email letting Thibault know we were good to go.

The other special request came from Pascal, a wiry Frenchman from head to toe, right up to his wire-rimmed glasses. I'd noticed that he'd been coming to the diner by himself lately.

"That's what I want to talk to you about," he said.

Turns out, Pascal's relationship with his girlfriend was on the rocks. (She'd caught him cheating on her.) He asked if he could tape a message onto the *Pulp Fiction* poster that hung on the wall beside their favorite booth.

"*Pas de problème,*" I said.

"I'm begging her to forgive me," Pascal said as he handed me a note with his girlfriend's name written on it.

"I'll put it up right away," I said. "And if it's any consolation, we have an excellent track record here at BIA when it comes to love."

"I hope so," Pascal said, his eyes tearing up. "I can't live without her."

Ironically, while all this was going on with Thibault and Pascal, the public opinion on love locks was starting to sour, thanks in large part to a grassroots campaign started by two American expats living in Paris, aka "the two Lisas." Through their blog, nolovelocks.com, the two Lisas argued that fastening an ugly padlock to one of Paris's cultural and historic *patrimoines* (heritage sites) had nothing to do with romance and everything to do with ego—and in particular, *vandalism.* Their motto: *Free your love, save our bridges!*

But try as they may, the two Lisas couldn't get City Hall to take any action and stop the city's cultural icons from being defaced. *Was it because the locks attracted so many tourists?* they wondered.

Fortunately, the press was quick to hop on board and support their cause. The *Guardian* proclaimed: "Love locks are the shallowest, stupidest, phoniest expression of love ever!"

Helping the movement gain even more momentum was the harsh reality that—*quel surprise!*—sometimes love is *not* eternal. Former lovers who'd suffered a nasty breakup would return to the bridge where they'd once declared their *amour éternel,* and with huge bolt cutters in hand, they'd chop off their repressive symbol of love. *Free at last*!

Not to be outdone, savvy lock sellers came up with even more enterprising ways to profit from the love lock frenzy. After selling a padlock to an unsuspecting couple, they'd wait until they were gone, then pull out the spare key they had hidden away, remove the lock, scrub off the names written on it, then resell the lock to the next pair of romantic suckers who wandered onto the bridge.

Unfortunately, I'd forgotten to warn my Cuban friends about this scheme when they came to Paris for the first time on their honeymoon. After spending the day strolling through the city, Alejandro and his wife met up with me for a drink. "Hey, Craig, have you heard about those love locks?"

"Of course," I snorted. "They're the shallowest, stupidest, phoniest expression of love ever!"

Alejandro and his wife looked at me as if I'd just popped their heart balloon.

"Or . . ." I continued, realizing they probably hadn't heard the news about the media storm surrounding the love locks back in their native Cuba, ". . . they're the most romantic thing on the planet. You decide."

Alejandro perked up. "I'm so glad you said that, because we ended up getting one! And get this—we were able to find the perfect spot to hang it on the bridge behind Notre-Dame."

"Wow, you actually found a free spot among all those locks! You're so lucky!" (I didn't have the heart to tell them there was a pretty good chance their lock had already been resold to another tourist.)

"It was the most beautiful moment of my life," Alejandro's wife said as she hugged her husband. "After we threw the key into the river, we held each other and cried like babies."

Boy, did I feel like a schmuck. If love locks made couples feel this way, who was I to judge?

Not that my opinion mattered, really, because in May 2014, a near-tragedy occurred that would seal the fate of love locks forever. Due to their tremendous weight, a huge panel fell off the *Pont des Arts* bridge and crashed into the Seine below. Realizing that the locks could have landed on a Bateaux-Mouches and killed a bunch of tourists, the French government decided it was time to take immediate action.

But, as per the French government, it would take a year before that immediate action actually took place.

Meanwhile, back at the diner, my manager Bruce was busy preparing for the big day: Thibault's marriage proposal.

"I hope it's all right that I bought a bottle of champagne on BIA's dime," Bruce said through the phone. "Just in case Thibault's girlfriend says yes."

"Sure, no prob," I said, even though what I really wanted to say was *prosecco* would've been just as good—for a third of the price.

"Oh, by the way," I said before hanging up. "Is Pascal's note still on the *Pulp Fiction* poster?"

"Nope."

"Really? Since when?"

"Hmm, let me think . . . A few nights ago."

"Any news from Pascal?"

"Uh-uh. Haven't seen him in ages."

I was starting to worry about BIA's nearly perfect track record when it came to love. Fortunately, that afternoon I received a text from Bruce: *She said yes!* It was followed a few minutes later by an email from Thibault. "Everything went so well! Thank you guys! And thanks for the bottle of champagne! I clearly didn't expect that."

"Don't mention it," I replied. "Congratulations!"

I only hoped Pascal's story would have the same happy ending.

That night in our apartment, as Julien and I climbed into bed, I thought about something that had been on my mind since the first time I'd come to Paris. "Why do French people say they love you when they don't really mean it?" I asked Julien.

"I don't understand. *Explique.*"

"You know . . . the way they chase after tourists who they don't even know, shouting like a lunatic, '*Je t'aime*! *Je t'aime*!' Why say it if you don't mean it?"

"But they do mean it."

"Oh, come on. In America, you gotta be dating a person for months, sometimes *years*, before you finally work up the courage to utter those three words. It's a pivotal moment for us. That's why you never hear any character say I love you until the *end* of a film. When the music swells."

"You Americans. Such big children. What you need to understand is that in France, we have two kinds of love: *l'amour sensuel* and *l'amour universel*. When a guy says I love you to someone he's just met, what he's really saying is, 'I love your style, the way you walk, the way you dress, the way you move your hips. So get ready to swing, baby!'" Julien wrapped his arms around me and started moving his hips in a very non-Puritan way.

"Okay, okay, got it!" I said. "Don't let this get to your head, all right, but . . . that kinda makes sense. In a weird, pathetic, ridiculous French-kinda way."

"*Exactement.*"

"So in other words, what you're saying is: when it comes to the French, everything that doesn't involve getting into a woman's panties—"

"Or a man's—"

"—is considered a different kind of love?"

"*Et oui*," Julien nodded. "*L'amour universel.* Love between parents and children, brothers and sisters. Friends even, you name it."

This made me think about my own family—especially the Finnish side—and how difficult it was for them to express any kind of feeling—be it sensual, universal, or otherwise. "I'm curious," I said. "How many times has your mom said 'I love you?'"

Julien held up his thumb and index fingers, forming a big, fat zero.

"No way!" I said. "I was sure she'd said it to you a thousand times."

"Oh, but she does. Only not with words, but through her actions: spending time together, cooking a good meal, giving me a call to see how I'm doing, asking my advice about something she's bought. All the things that show you matter to that person."

"*C'est beau ça*," I said. (That's beautiful.)

"*N'est-ce pas*, kiddo? And since you're practically a Frenchie yourself, you can start saying '*je t'aime*' the French way, too. By making the bed. Doing the dishes. Ironing your *chéri*'s pants . . ."

"Hmm . . ." I grumbled. "It's a lot less work to say I love you the American way."

I'd completely forgotten about Pascal when I ran into him one rainy day near the Hôtel de Ville. He'd put on a little weight and had changed his wire-rimmed glasses to rimless ones.

"Well?!" I said excitedly. "Did she take you back?"

"*Non*," he said with a Gallic shrug. "She filed a restraining order."

On a hot summer day in 2015, Julien and I stood on the *quai* overlooking *le Pont de l'Archevêché*. A huge crane struggled to remove tons of love locks from the bridge, one panel at a time. In total, an estimated forty-five tons of rusty metal would have to be gathered up from Paris's iconic bridges before being melted down, thrown away, or turned into modern sculptures. The only thing that would remain were the 700,000+ keys resting at the bottom of the Seine, left for the catfish and other bottom-feeders to choke on.

As I watched the crane dump a huge chunk of locks onto a truck, I felt a slight pang of sadness. I turned to Julien. "I think I know why Americans were so in love with the love locks."

"Yeah? Why?"

"Because they were a way of staving off our mortality, to give us a sense of permanence, something that's very foreign to our country, where it's out with the old, in with the *nouveau*."

Julien smiled and took my hand. "Speaking of permanence . . ." Of course, he didn't have to ask me a third time for me to know what he was referring to. For once, I didn't change the subject. Instead, I looked at Notre-Dame, all 850 beautiful years of her. If that didn't represent permanence, I don't know what did.

"I'm almost there, Julien," I said. "I just need a little more time."

FOURTEEN

Operation Escargot

Mothers-in-law get a bad rap. It doesn't help that we call them mothers "in-law"—as if we're forced by a judge to accept them into the family. Compare this to the French version: *Belle Maman*. Beautiful Mama. Honestly, which one would you rather have?

I first met my Belle Maman long before she was officially my mother-in-law, just my boyfriend's mom. I'd been going out with Julien for only a few months when, unable to resist my rugged American charm, he made his *déclaration d'amour* in a Sri Lankan restaurant near the *Gare du Nord*, professing his love over palak paneer and a delicious paratha cheese set.

"I can't wait for you to meet Elisabeth," Julien said as he smiled and held my hand.

Ever since I'd known him, Julien always referred to his mom by her first name. Apparently when he was just nine years old, he decided one afternoon—and for no particular reason—that he would no longer refer to his mom as his *mère* but his *pair* (or "peer" in French).

It was odd to hear—and a little unsettling. My dad, Fast Eddie, used to call his mom by her first name, too—and in the same deep voice as Julien. (It's a bit disturbing when your boyfriend sounds exactly like your old man.)

"It won't be long before they're putting you in a box, Lizzy," Fast Eddie would say to my gram every year on her birthday. "Just letting you know right now, I'm not going to your funeral. I hate those damn things."

"I don't blame you, Eddie," my Grandma Lizzy would say in the sweetest voice ever. "I'd skip my funeral too if I could."

Ironically, Fast Eddie got his wish; he didn't have to attend my gram's funeral after all since she ended up outliving him by nearly seven years.

Back in the Sri Lankan restaurant, I smiled at Julien. "I can't wait to meet your mom—I mean . . . *Elisabeth,* too," I said, suddenly feeling a little anxious. "Have you . . . um . . . come out to her yet?"

"Oh, yeah, years ago. With my first boyfriend. In fact, she's Facebook friends with all my exes."

All his exes? Jeez, how many did he have? I barely had the good fortune of having one—although I'm pretty sure Luis would argue that holding hands and kissing a couple times did *not* constitute a relationship worthy of being labeled an "ex."

In any case, I was relieved to hear that Elisabeth was so open-minded. When it came to my own family, I dreaded the day when I would have to tell them about Julien. That is, if we actually ended up staying together long enough. Back then, I was so fatalistic, I was convinced that it was just a matter of time before Julien wised up and dumped me. *If that* does *happen,* I tried to comfort myself, *at least his mom and I can still be Facebook friends.*

"Nice to meet you, Grack," Elisabeth said with a warm smile when I met her for the first time a few weeks later in Dijon—the mustard capital of the world. Julien and I had taken the TGV (high speed train) down to meet her at a restaurant *gastronomique* for lunch. Elisabeth was wearing white linen pants and matching blouse that made her raspberry-tinted hair and girlish freckles really pop out.

"That's *Craig*," Julien said.

"*Oh, pardon . . .* Greg-*errr*."

"Ccc-raig," Julien repeated. "With a 'C'."

"Ccc . . . rrack-*errr*."

"Ah, c'mon, Elisabeth, it's not difficult," the language teacher in Julien said. "Watch my lips: 'Cu-rai—'"

"It's okay, Julien," I said. "Close enough," which was the honest-to-God's truth. I was used to French people massacring my name way worse than his mom had done. Besides, I actually loved the way Elisabeth pronounced it. Having lived in Burgundy her whole life, she had a way of rolling her R's, especially at the end of words, (*errr*), that gave them a lovely, lilting quality—like listening to *pure beurre*.

Unlike most French people her age, (Elisabeth was in her mid-sixties, but looked at least ten years younger), my future Belle Maman invited me to address her using the familiar form of you (*tu*) instead of the formal one (*vous*). She made me feel part of the family right from the start.

"Elisabeth chose this restaurant because she wanted to introduce you to some of the region's specialties," Julien said.

"Have you ever been to Burgundy before?" Elisabeth asked in her beautiful lilting French.

"Once," I said. "Back when I was an exchange student in Rouen. Some French friends and I piled into a van and drove all night to Dijon to attend the Gastronomy Fair."

"Oh, what a coincidence," Elisabeth said. "I used to take Julien to that fair every year, ever since he was a little boy. Do you remember, Julien?"

"How could I forget," Julien said as he took a bite of his *coq au vin* (rooster in red wine sauce), being careful to avoid one ingredient—the rooster. Back then, Julien was a strict vegetarian, save for a few glaring exceptions—such as *foie gras* and *escargots*—both of which we'd just enjoyed as our starters.

Julien smiled as he scooped out the last morsel of *coq* from his *coq au vin* and placed it on my plate. "Wouldn't it be funny if Craig was there at the same time as us, but we didn't know each other yet?"

"Ah, *oui*," Elisabeth said excitedly. "And now here we are together, all these years later, enjoying the same delicious dishes that were offered at the fair!"

The romantic in me just couldn't resist: "Almost feels like destiny, doesn't it?"

Julien reached under the table and put his hand in mine. *Oh, my*. I thought. *This is getting serious*. I glanced at his mother, wondering if she'd seen the move. If she had, she wasn't letting on.

"What shall we have next?" Elisabeth said as the waiter took our plates. "Cheese or dessert?"

"Hmm," I grinned. "Must we limit ourselves to just one?"

"*Oh-la-la*," Elisabeth smiled. "*Quel gourmand!*"

Gourmand literally means a person who loves to eat and drink. But as Julien happily pointed out, it can also be a subtle way for a French person to suggest that you're being a glutton.

Right on cue, the waiter rolled a cheese cart up to our table. On it sat more than a dozen of the 300+ varieties of stinky cheese that exist in France, including camembert, comté, bleu d'Auvergne, chèvre, vacherin, and a specialty *fromage* from Burgundy, époisses—all served with bite-sized morsels of a crispy baguette. I could feel myself starting to drool.

"How many of these cheeses do we get to try?" I asked. Elisabeth smiled as Julien gave me a quick kick under the table.

As my relationship with Julien got more serious, my culinary adventures with my future Belle Maman got more numerous. Much to my great fortune, Elisabeth turned out to be a wonderful cook, so much so that, if I chose to, I would never have to go to a pricy restaurant *gastronomique* again.

Having grown up in the lush Burgundy countryside, Elisabeth literally took her first steps in the vineyards of *la Grande Route des Vins*, one of the most famous regions for wine connoisseurs. But Elisabeth's early days were not all wine and roses. One night, when she was just fourteen years old, she overheard her parents arguing while her younger siblings slept. Her mother had just broken the news to her father, Pépé, that she had a lover and was going to move in with him.

"The children will have to be placed in an orphanage," her mother said without a hint of remorse.

Pépé, a towering man of few words, looked at his wife and said, "You go. I'll take care of the kids."

Elisabeth's eyes would water up every time she told this story. "Can you imagine? Pépé raising us four kids all by himself and never complaining once."

In contrast, Pépé had never known his own father, who was killed in World War I when Pépé was just a baby. Following in his father's footsteps, Pépé was drafted into World War II in 1940, when he was in his late twenties. Shortly thereafter, he was captured by the Germans. Strong and fit, Pépé survived the Nazi death march to a concentration camp as many of the less fortunate were left to die by the side of the road.

As the war raged on, the Nazis desperately needed laborers to keep up their war effort. Pépé was subsequently moved from the concentration camp to a German household where a middle-aged couple trained him to be a cobbler so he could make boots for the German soldiers. The couple took to Pépé right away, confiding in him that they were completely against the war and wanted nothing more than to see their son come back from the front lines as soon as possible.

Then in 1944, with allied forces closing in, the German couple risked their own lives to help Pépé escape back to France just as the Nazis, who were enraged to be losing the war, massacred as many prisoners as they could. For the rest of their lives, Pépé and the German couple would remain friends. (Their son survived the war.) Elisabeth showed me some of the letters the couple had send to her father over the years, written in perfect French. I wondered if Pépé had taught them the language.

"I suppose so," Elisabeth said. "They loved France. And they loved Pépé."

It goes without saying that Elisabeth worshiped her father. He continued to be her rock as she went through a series of difficult relationships, starting with her first marriage to a local vintner at the tender age of eighteen, which ended in divorce. Not long after, Elisabeth met Joël, Julien's father. Unfortunately, Joël preferred hanging out with his buddies at the local dive bar than being a responsible parent. When Julien was three, Elisabeth wrote Joël a heartfelt letter, saying he had to make a decision: either be a father to Julien or move on.

After reading the letter, Joël took Pépé aside and said within Elisabeth's earshot, "Your daughter doesn't want me around anymore." Elisabeth's heart sank; this was *not* the response she was expecting. Pépé turned to Joël and said calmly. "You go. I'll take care of the kid."

Now a single parent, Elisabeth focused her energy on building her career. Thanks to the experience she gained working in her first husband's vineyard, it wasn't long before Elisabeth had become an accomplished sommelier (wine expert). However, to be a true sommelier, one must be familiar with what wine pairs with what dish, which meant that Elisabeth was required to know all the ins and outs of fine cuisine. Fortunately she already had a strong foundation thanks to Pépé who had taught her how to make nearly every classic French dish from Burgundy. And fortunately for me, that tradition continued.

By the time Julien and I had moved in together, my Belle Maman was already spoiling me rotten with her delicious culinary creations. Every month or so she would take the TGV up from Dijon to visit Julien and me in Paris. On her first visit, we went to meet her at the Gare de Lyon train station. After giving each other the customary *bises* on each cheek, I tried to lift up Elisabeth's king-sized suitcase, only to keel over, almost getting a hernia.

"*Oh-la-la*, Belle Maman! What's in here? It weighs a ton!"

"That's exactly what the nice man on the train said when he was helping me get my valise up onto the overhead rack: '*What do you got in there, Madame? A chopped-up body?*'"

The man wasn't that far off the mark.

Once we got back to our apartment, Elisabeth unloaded the contents of her valise. Like Mary Poppins and her magic bag, she reached inside and pulled out stacks upon stacks of cookware—a Le Creuset "cocotte," a braising skillet, dessert molds and metal escargot trays (replete with ghastly "de-snailing" tools)—all of which was a not-so-subtle way of pointing out that Julien and I did not have the necessary equipment to match Elisabeth's culinary skills.

But that wasn't all. Elisabeth had already prepared most of the meals for the weekend ahead of time, sealing them up in her pots and pans for the one-and-a-half-hour trip from Dijon. After making sure that nothing had spilled out, Elisabeth dug into her purse, pulled out a decorative piece of parchment paper and began reading the note she had written on it.

"*Voici le menu*: On Saturday, the starter will be a scallop *tartar* with a white wine *coulis* followed by the main course, *Parmentier de canard* topped with *comté* cheese *au gratin*. Sunday's menu will include *foie gras* on mini toasts with a *gelée de* Gewürztraminer as the starter, bœuf bourguignon (with my secret ingredient, *bien sûr!*) for the main course, followed by a selection of seasonal *fromages*. And if you still have room," Elisabeth smiled at me. "*Dessert!* A recipe I've been wanting to try out for some time now: *Miroir au cassis* (a blackcurrant flan)."

Mon dieu. This was exactly what I'd craved when I was a student in Rouen. And to think, Elisabeth hadn't even gotten to the wine list yet.

The only thing better than Belle Maman carting her delicious creations to Paris was the rare occasion when Julien and I were able to get away from work and visit her in Dijon. (After all, there were only so many delicacies Elisabeth could fit into her suitcase.)

One Sunday afternoon, Julien and I spent four lovely hours seated at Elisabeth's dining room table, which was perfectly laid out with her father's gold-laced china, linen napkins, and heavy-in-the-hand silverware. After enjoying a scrumptious five-course meal, the three of us desperately needed to move, lest we fall into an unrecoverable food coma.

"Shall we go for a walk?" I said as I held my hand atop my plump belly, not sure where *gourmand* ended and glutton began.

Although summer had officially started two weeks earlier, it was still unseasonably chilly. A light drizzle soaked through the trees as we strolled through the wooded area not far from Elisabeth's place. Thanks to the fresh air and exercise, it wasn't long before we started building up an appetite again—or at least I did. Just when I was about to ask Elisabeth what was on the dinner menu, something caught her eye, and she made a beeline to the base of a large oak tree.

"*Oh, comme il est beau!*" Elisabeth said as she crouched down and picked up . . . an *escargot*. A Burgundy escargot, to be exact—aka *the* snail that's used by the French to make their most famous delicacy.

Elisabeth held up the snail and turned to Julien. "What's the date today?"

Julien looked at his watch. "July 5."

"*Parfait*! Stay here. I'll be right back." Elisabeth set the snail back on the ground and rushed back to her place.

"What was that all about?" I asked.

"Elisabeth wanted to make sure hunting season has started already."

"Has it?"

"Yep. Four days ago."

Sure enough, France actually has a hunting season for snails. According to the *Arrêté du 24 avril 1979* (the government decree of April 24, 1979), escargot hunting season begins on July 1 and ends on March 31—with one stipulation: the captured snail must be at least 3 centimeters (1.18 inches) in size.

After a few minutes, Elisabeth returned holding a large plastic shopping bag. She gently picked up the snail from before and placed it into the bag. Then she looked around the woods, her eyes lighting up. For the first time I noticed there were snails everywhere, as if appearing out of thin air.

"Where did they all come from?" I asked.

"Who knows," Julien shrugged. "But apparently the weather conditions are just right for them to . . . how do you say in English—*s'accoupler*?"

Thank God for Google translate. A few taps into the keyboard of my phone and, *voilà*!—I learned a new French word: "*S'accoupler*" or "to mate."

"You mean to tell me, your mom . . . I mean, Elisabeth, is hunting down a bunch of horny snails?"

"Yep." Julien smiled. "Horny snails who've just laid their eggs and are ready to *faire l'amour* all over again!"

"Well, at least they're going down happy," I said. I then turned and watched Elisabeth, youthful and fit, as she crouched down from one tree trunk to the next. In less than an hour, she had gathered more than 250 snails!

"*Bon*, that should do it," she said, her shopping bag bursting at the seams.

"Impressive," I said. "Is there a limit to how many escargots you can catch in a day?"

"Hmm, that's one of those gray areas in France," Julien said. "As long as they're for personal consumption—and not for sale—there shouldn't be a problem."

"But what if an *inspecteur* comes along and asks why you have so many?"

Elisabeth pondered the question for a moment then looked at me and said, "Well, I'll just tell him we have a big family."

I've always wondered how so-called delicacies got their start. For example, who was the first person in Cambodia to say, "Hey, I got an idea: Let's fry up some tarantulas for dinner!" The same goes for ants, grasshoppers, frog legs, corn fungus, maggot cheese, and chocolate-covered locusts. For me, these "delicacies" have one thing in common: they're all so disgusting, the first humans to even consider eating them must have been either desperate, starving, or both.

My hunch appeared to be correct when I heard the gruesome process Elisabeth went through to prepare *le délice* known as escargot. (And here I thought making *foie gras* was horrendous.) It reminded me of the first time I saw my Grandma Lizzy prepare the trout my dad had just caught in the nearby (soon-to-be classified "toxic") Scantic River. With the fish still alive, my gram grabbed a big, scary knife, then with one quick flick, gutted the sucker, blood and intestines splattering all over the place.

"How do you want it cooked, Eddie?" she asked my father. "Broiled or fried?" I stared wide-eyed as my sweet, doting grandmother held the dead fish in one hand and the killer knife in the other, blood dripping off her face and apron.

Recalling that memory, I didn't have the heart (nor stomach) to watch my elegant Belle Maman physically transform something so hideous as a snail into something so delicious as an *escargot*. Instead, I asked her to describe for me each step, which I'll share here:

Step 1: *Place the snails in a box or jar that's punctured with little holes so air can get in but the snails can't get out. Let sit for eight days until the snails' digestive tracks are completely empty of food and poop.*

"Hold on a sec'," I said. "Are you saying you *starve* them to death?"

"Yes," Elisabeth said. "Except for one *petit* detail."

"Oh, no. Don't tell me . . . they're still alive?"

"*Et oui.*"

> **Step 2:** *Take the snails out of the box or jar and rinse them with tap water. Place them in a new container filled with* gros sel *(coarse salt). Add 2 teaspoons of vinegar per 48 snails and let sit for two hours, causing them to drool.*

"Are they dead yet?"

"*Pas encore* (not yet)."

"How is that possible?"

"Because *les petits* (the little guys) are tough cookies!"

> **Step 3:** *Rinse the snails with running water a second time in order to get rid of any excess drool. (FYI, sticky drool is not good for snail meat.)*

"Okay, they've gotta be dead by now, right?"

"*Non*, they're very much alive."

"But . . . it's been, like, eight days of nonstop torture!"

"*Et bien*, (yeah, well)." Elisabeth gave me one of those Gallic shrugs I've come to know so well.

> **Step 4:** *Boil the snails for 10 minutes. Using a corkscrew, remove the snails from their shells, making sure to separate the intestines from the muscles.*

"Okay. *Please* tell me it's over! That the little guys have been put out of their misery!"

"*Ah, oui! Les escargots* are definitely deceased now."

"Thank God! I couldn't bear to hear one more grisly detail."

Elisabeth smiled as she put the prettiest snail shells aside to be used later on.

"By the way," I said, "who taught you how to do all this?"

"Why, Pépé, of course."

Step 5: *Rinse the snail meat one last time before boiling them on low heat for three hours in a "court-bouillon"* (vegetable-based broth), *consisting of thyme, bay leaf, carrots, onions, shallots, garlic, white wine, salt and pepper.*

"Mmm, sounds yummy!" I said voraciously, managing to shock myself with how quickly my Paleo brain had forgotten the horror the poor snails had been put through.

Step 6: *Remove from heat and let cool down. You are now ready to*:

a) Stuff the prettiest shells with snail meat and garlic butter. Bake and eat;

b) Freeze the snails in ziplock bags for all eternity—or at least until the zombie apocalypse arrives;

c) Preserve the snails in jars of 48 each (240 total) so they can be transported to, say . . . I don't know . . . *California?*

With my Belle Maman having successfully transmuted the mushy mollusks into a fancy French delicacy, it was now on to our next mission: smuggling those 240 snails past U.S. Customs. Or as Julien and I lovingly called it: "Operation Escargot."

As is often the case with government edicts, the language used can be a tad confusing. In other words, it's impossible to know exactly what's "legal" or not. Take these excerpts I found on the U.S. Customs and Border Protection page of the Department of Homeland Security:

"Many prepared foods are admissible. However, bush meat made from African wildlife and almost anything (my emphasis)

containing meat products, such as bouillon, soup mixes, etc., is not
admissible . . . (Furthermore), because rice can often harbor insects,
it is best to avoid bringing it into the United States."

What exactly did the U.S. government mean by "almost anything" and "it is best to avoid?" For me, it screamed of the dreaded *gray area*—a world where nothing is black or white. I'd been grappling with this ambiguity ever since I received my first French green card years ago. But now that very same ambiguity felt so reassuring. After all, I certainly wasn't bringing in "bush meat," *n'est-ce pas?* And if pressed by a border control agent, I could simply say that I'd done my "best to avoid" bringing in 240 dead snails.

"The problem is, officer," I'd explain to the agent, "I have an important social engagement that, frankly, *can't* be avoided." For months, Julien and I had been planning a dinner party in LA with twelve of my closest friends, all of whom couldn't wait to meet the woman I'd been raving about so much: my Belle Maman.

To minimize the risk, Julien, Elisabeth, and I decided to spread out the five jars containing forty-eight escargots equally among us. Well, kind of. Julien and his mom ended up with two jars each, which left me with just one. However, I made up the difference by volunteering to smuggle in several vacuum-sealed packages of stinky (unpasteurized) French cheese—along with a few jars of *foie gras*, which was illegal in California at the time.

The morning of our flight, Julien, Elisabeth and I gathered our suitcases, then held out our hands like the three Musketeers, vowing: "All for one and one for all!" But there was one *petit* detail I hadn't taken into account, which didn't rear its ugly head until the moment we arrived at U.S. customs:

"U.S. citizens and legal residents to the right!" the Homeland Security agent shouted at the throngs of jet-lagged passengers. "Foreigners to the left!"

"Oh, *merde!*" I said, suddenly noticing the worried look on Elisabeth's face. This was her first trip to America, and she didn't speak a word of English.

"*C'est pas grave*, Belle Maman. (Nothing to worry about)," I said reassuringly. "Just smile and say '*yes*' to everything the agent says. Unless, of course, he asks you about *you-know-what* . . ." I whispered. Elisabeth looked even more worried than before. Clearly, I was *not* helping.

"Sir, you're holding up the line!" the Homeland Security agent snapped. "Make a choice: left or right"

I nodded then turned right. My heart sank as I realized I was leaving my two musketeers behind to fend for themselves. Making matters worse, I had "Global Entry," which meant that I was able to whiz past the border control agent, waving my American passport at him as I forced a cheerful, "Ah, it's good to be back!"

I glanced over at Julien and Elisabeth waiting in the impossibly long line of foreigners. Before disappearing into baggage claim, I mouthed back to them in French, "See you on the other side!"

Or so I hoped.

For the first time since I could remember, my suitcase was the first to pop out at baggage claim. This left me way too much time to imagine nightmare scenarios of Julien and my Belle Maman being arrested and thrown in the slammer, a sadistic border control guard laughing hysterically as he flushes Elisabeth's snails down the toilet.

By the time I'd imagined Elisabeth and Julien strapped to an electric chair, the baggage claim area had cleared out and their suitcases *still* hadn't arrived. Just when I was about to give up hope, I noticed something at the far end of the room in a blocked-off security area. Through frosted panes of glass, I saw what I could swear was raspberry-tinted hair.

After a moment, the door swished open and out stepped my two musketeers wheeling their suitcases in front of them as they galloped toward me. Julien had a Cheshire cat grin on his face while poor Elisabeth was as white as her pantsuit. Before I had a chance to say a word, Julien whispered in French, "Outside."

As we waited to pick up our rental car, Julien filled me in on what had happened. As they were getting their passports stamped, a TSA agent stood on the sidelines, scrutinizing Elisabeth. After a moment, he motioned for her to join him for "a random check." Since Elisabeth didn't speak English,

Julien convinced the agent to let him join her. The two were taken to a holding area where the agent, wearing rubber gloves, opened Elisabeth's suitcase.

"Did the agent have a sniff dog?" I asked.

"No," Julien said. "The doggie was busy with another suitcase."

"Oh, thank God! Go on."

Julien continued. "You should've seen the look on Elisabeth's face when the agent, who had a big gun strapped to his belt, started digging through her personal belongings."

Like a lot of foreigners, Elisabeth had heard way too many horror stories of trigger-happy Americans just itching to unload on anyone who looked even remotely suspicious. "You should've seen Elisabeth's expression," Julien continued. "It was like, 'Please don't shoot me, officer?' Right, Elisabeth?"

"Ah, *oui*!" she said. "That would have been a *catastrophe*! We've got dinner plans tomorrow night."

"*Exactement*," Julien nodded at his mom.

"Did the agent end up finding the snails?" I asked.

Julien paused, getting great pleasure out of drawing out the suspense for as long as he could. "Well . . . the agent ended up looking everywhere, except . . ." Julien turned to his mom, letting her finish his sentence.

"*Dans mes chaussettes*! (in my socks!)," Elisabeth beamed.

"Bravo, Belle Maman!" I said, breathing a huge sigh of relief. "*Mon dieu*, I hope this little incident doesn't tarnish your first visit to America."

"*Au contraire*," she said. "Think of the marvelous story I have to tell!"

With the 240 snails successfully smuggled into the United States, the three of us went straight from the airport to the Organic Farmers Market in Santa Monica, next to our friends' place. With the big dinner coming up the following night, Elizabeth and Julien wanted to find ingredients that were as close in quality to what could easily be found in France: grass-fed, hormone-free beef (for Elisabeth's bœuf bourguignon), and fresh, non-GMO produce.

Needless to say, Elisabeth's dinner was a huge hit. That afternoon, as she and Julien prepared the four-course meal for fifteen people, I stood back and watched in awe. As someone who only knows how to make breakfast, I was impressed with how easy they made it look.

"Is there anything I can do to help?" I asked.

"Yes," Julien said. "Get out of the kitchen."

That night at the dinner table, my friends were enthralled to hear the story of how Elisabeth had hunted down their appetizer herself—not to mention their astonishment to hear that there was actually a snail-hunting season in France.

"Oh, Elisabeth, these escargots are delicious!" my foodie friend, Kimberly, said as she sopped up the melted garlic butter with the closest thing we could find to a baguette in Southern California. "You'll have to tell me how you prepared them."

"Actually," I said, thinking of the six-step torture process that resulted in the snails being on Kimberly's plate. "Probably best if you *don't* know."

I looked at the guests, half of whom sat there frozen, holding their snails midair in front of their gaping mouths.

"*Bon appétit!*" Julien grinned as he shoved the drippy mollusk down his throat.

After the appetizer came *la pièce de résistance*: Elisabeth's very own bœuf bourguignon, the recipe of which she had learned from her father—but with her own special touch. As my friends devoured their meal, the room fell silent, save the sound of knives and forks scraping against their plates. Once they had finished, Elisabeth asked, "Who would like seconds?"

Everybody's hand shot up. "*Oh-la-la*," Elisabeth said. "What shall we do?" She held up the cocotte. "There's only one portion left."

"I have an idea," Julien said. "Whoever guesses Elisabeth's secret ingredient gets the prize."

"Ooh, ooh, ooh!" I yelled, waving my hand in the air.

"Uh-uh," Julien shook his head at me. "You can't play. You already know the answer."

My hand dropped as I sunk in my chair, pouting like a six-year-old.

I was surprised how long the guessing game went on. For a good ten minutes, my friends debated what the secret ingredient could be—everyone except Gerhard, who sat silently at the end of the table. Gerhard, a direct descendent of Austrian royalty, handed his spoon to Elisabeth and said, "May I have one more taste please?"

"*Bien sûr*," Elisabeth smiled.

Gerhard slurped the red wine sauce from his spoon, letting it saturate his palette. After a moment, his eyes lit up. "I got it! Is it—"

"*Oui!*" Elisabeth said before making us promise never to tell anyone what her secret ingredient was.*

I watched from the sidelines, green with envy, as Gerhard lapped up the last helping of bœuf bourguignon that I had so coveted.

Fortunately, the meal wasn't over yet; we still had vacuum-sealed stinky French cheese to unwrap, followed by dessert, another of Elisabeth's family recipes: *cake aux escargots*. (Or as Julien liked to call it: "snails loaf.")

However, unlike the three courses that had preceded it, the reaction from the guests regarding the snails loaf was "*comme si, comme ça*" (so-so). *Not a problem*, I thought. *That leaves more for me*! As I held out my plate for a second helping, Julien kicked me under the table. "Easy, Craig. Don't forget we're going for a jog tomorrow morning." (That was Julien's code for saying I was being a glutton.)

"Oh, Julien, it's okay," Elisabeth said. "Remember what Pépé used to say?"

The room got quiet as Elisabeth told the story of her father's experience in the concentration camp; how he and the other prisoners were fed only one potato a day—if they were lucky. Sometimes at night he would hide half of the potato under his pillow, saving it for another time.

Years later, after Pépé had retired, he would often serve himself two or more helpings at each meal. At first, Elisabeth said nothing. But one day, after she had taken Pépé to the doctor for a checkup, she couldn't keep silent any longer. As she watched her father pile a second helping of steak and potatoes onto his plate, she said, "*Doucement*, Pépé. Don't forget your cholesterol. And your high blood pressure."

Pépé looked at his daughter and said, "*Laisse le vieux manger. Tu n'sais pas ce que c'est de mourir de faim.*" (Let an old man eat. You don't know what it's like to die of hunger.)

---

* Okay, I'll spill! Elisabeth won't mind. It's two to four squares of extra dark chocolate, to your taste.

Elisabeth made a zipping motion across her lips. "After that, I never uttered another word to Pépé about it again." I glanced around the table. All my friends were visibly moved by the story.

At that moment, I realized that all this time Elisabeth had been feeding us the way she had wanted to feed her father.

"To Pépé," we all said, raising our glasses.

My Belle Maman smiled as she served me a second helping of snails loaf.

FIFTEEN

Wedding Day Bleus

On a drizzly Sunday morning in Paris, Julien and I sat in our breakfast nook, Chopin's *Fantaisie-Impromptu* playing softly on the radio in the background. I bit into my shrimp and Swiss cheese omelet, my eyes half-closed in culinary ecstasy as I savored every buttery, cholesterol-laden bite. After having a heart scare two years earlier, I only allowed myself to have eggs once a week, usually on the weekend, before Julien and I headed off to work.

The life-changing incident had happened at the height of the most difficult period at BIA. Julien and I were jogging along the Seine, near Pont Neuf, when I collapsed onto the *quais*. After spending a day in the hospital getting a battery of tests, the cardiologist couldn't find anything definitive to prove I'd had a heart attack. The most likely culprit, he said: I'd been overcome by stress. Shortly thereafter, afraid of losing me to the big diner in the sky, Julien quit his job at the Asian Cultural Center and came to work at BIA, helping to lessen my load.

Back in our breakfast nook, grateful for the life I had with Julien, I placed my hand on his knee, my heart welling up with *amour*. "So . . . um . . . that question you asked me twice . . ." I said, struggling. "You know, the one where you said you would only ask me one more time. . . . Does that offer still stand?"

Julien looked up from his cellphone. He was in the middle of posting pictures of the community garden where he volunteered so it took him a moment to figure out what I was trying to say.

"*Attend* (wait)," he said, squinting slightly. "Are you suggesting a *proposition de marriage?*"

"Sure, I mean, yeah, if you're still okay with it . . . I mean."

Julien savored the opportunity to tease me. "Wow, it's really hard for you to just come out and ask, isn't it?"

He was right. I was tongue-tied. Why couldn't I just say to Julien that I wanted to share breakfast with him every morning for the rest of my life?

After letting me stew in my own juices for a few more seconds, Julien said, "Okay, *mon petit. Marrions-nous!*"

I leapt out of my seat and onto my *chéri*, giving him a big ol' American hug and slobbering him with French *bisous*.

Whew, I thought. *That went* really *well!*

I wished my dad were still alive. Back when I was in college, he'd been living with his blond-wigged girlfriend, Linda, and her two young kids. After four years together, she gave him the ultimatum: either agree to marry by a specific date—or hit the road.

I found Linda to be likeable enough, although her bouffant, Dolly Parton–sized wig always made me a little uncomfortable, compounded with the fact that my dad moving in with her had rendered me homeless at sixteen.

"Linda's got fantastic hair underneath," Fast Eddie would tell me when we were alone. "She only wears a wig because it's easier for her to maintain."

I noticed that Linda always went out of her way to be overly nice to me, as if auditioning for the role of stepmom. For me, it was obvious that she had just one thing on her mind: getting her hooks into Fast Eddie and slowing him down. Way down.

Despite everything, however, I had to admit that Linda had been good for my dad. Besides getting him out of the house so that she and her kids could participate in a myriad of activities—from picnics to whitewater rafting—she also helped him cut down on his drinking. She even got him to cover up that embarrassing yellow racing stripe he'd painted on the side of his station wagon.

When U-day arrived—as in "the ultimatum"—Fast Eddie wore a collared shirt and even put on some pants. (Like many men of his generation, the moment he passed over the threshold into his "castle," Fast Eddie would strip down to his boxer shorts.) Alone in their living room, with Linda's kids away at their grandparents, Fast Eddie put a bottle of bubbly on ice and lit two candles, using the flame of one to light his cigarette. After pouring the champagne, he raised his flute into the air. Linda quickly followed suit, her eyes lighting up in anticipation of his proposal.

Turning on the charm, Fast Eddie smiled. "Here's to the end of a beautiful relationship."

Before they had a chance to clink their glasses, Linda went ballistic, immediately throwing Fast Eddie's ass out to the curb. Ever the narcissist, my dad couldn't understand why she'd truly "flipped her wig." "But I bought an expensive bottle of champagne!" he'd say for years after. "And I meant what I said. It *was* a beautiful relationship. But she and her two brats were costing me a fortune—driving me to the poorhouse!"

Ironically, my dad would spend his remaining years renting a cheap room in a former Civil War Hotel turned boardinghouse for single men. If he'd stayed with Linda, perhaps he might have been a little poorer, but I'm pretty sure his life would have been much richer. And who knows, maybe he wouldn't have passed away quite so young, at sixty-three.

"Marry her, dad!" I would have said if I could go back in time. "Some things are worth the risk."

The moment Julien and I stepped into the marriage office of the *Mairie du 4ème* (Mayor of the 4th *arrondissement*), a jittery *fonctionnaire* in her forties, who looked as if she'd had one too many espressos for breakfast, lurched at him before he had a chance to utter a word.

"Stop! Do you have an appointment?"

"*Non*," Julien said calmly. "Where can we make one?"

"Why *here*, of course," she said as if speaking to an idiot child.

Barely ten seconds in and already I could feel my blood pressure going up. Julien, of course, was unfazed. Being a Frenchman, he intuitively knew how to handle *fonctionnaires*. "Just stick to the facts," he'd said to me before we left our apartment that morning. "Never question or contradict them. And the absolute cardinal sin: never show weakness or emotion. That's when they go in for the kill!"

Mon dieu, *were we big game hunting or trying to get a marriage license?*

"When's the next available appointment?" Julien asked Freida the *fonctionnaire* (as I came to call her).

After ten minutes of complaining about how busy she was—especially now that the French government had passed same-sex marriage, which doubled her workload (the office was located in the heart of the gay-centric Marais)—Freida finally put on her reading glasses and looked at her old-school paper agenda. "Unfortunate news, *Monsieur*," she said. "The next opening's not until three weeks from now."

"*Parfait*," Julien said. "We're not planning on getting married until September anyway. Six months should give us plenty of time to get our dossier together, *n'est-ce pas?*"

As Freida stood there stone-faced, I felt a pang in the pit of my stomach. Saying we had "plenty of time" in France was like saying the *Titanic* was unsinkable.

"One last thing before we go," Julien said. "Do you have any special documents to give us?"

Freida gave Julien another long, cold stare. "You'll have to wait, *Monsieur*," she said. "They're in the other room." She turned and disappeared into an adjacent office.

I whispered to Julien. "Why doesn't she just keep copies out here at the front desk?"

"*Sssh.* No questions. No emotion."

"*Et les voilà*," Freida said when she returned, handing Julien two forms. "Be sure to follow everything *exactly* as written. *Si non . . .*" she let the sentence trail off menacingly.

I couldn't get out of that office fast enough. Outside in the hallway, I could feel my heart racing as I watched Julien stuff the forms Freida had given him into his backpack.

"Hey, good luck with that," I said.

"Wait. What are you saying?"

"I am *not* coming back here."

"Why not?"

"Doctor's orders, remember? The cardiologist said to stay away from *fonctionnaires*."

"He did not say that. He said to avoid *stress*."

"Exactly!"

Julien shook his head. "Uh-uh. No, you don't."

"C'mon, Julien," I said. "It only makes sense. You take care of the French wedding, and I'll take care of the American one. It's the perfect deal!"

After a moment, Julien shrugged. "Okay."

Actually, it was a *terrible* deal. For Julien, anyway. I didn't know it until sometime later, but on my end, I only had to supply two documents, both of which needed to be translated into French: my birth certificate—notarized within the last three months; and proof from the American Embassy that I wasn't committing bigamy, meaning I didn't have other husbands stashed away somewhere.

Julien took care of everything else. However, it wasn't the paperwork that was the most frustrating; it was dealing with Freida. During their first meeting, Julien pointed out to her that we'd already supplied all the paperwork on her list back when we'd gotten our domestic partnership—or PACS (*pacte civil de solidarité*)—five years earlier, before France had legalized same-sex marriage.

"Since you already have everything on file," Julien said. "Can you simply transfer the documents to our marriage *dossier*?"

"*Non!*" Freida snapped. "You must get each and every one of them all over again!"

The fidgety *fonctionnaire* also loved to pull out a slew of made-up rules from her *derrière*. Anyone who's ever lived in France knows the value of the dreaded electric bill (or EDF). It's the first document required to do just about anything: open a bank account, get a visa, purchase a monthly *métro* card, and yes, get married.

"Your EDF bill only has your name on it," Freida said to Julien. "But since marriage concerns *two* people, I need *both* your names on it."

"But EDF doesn't allow two names on the same bill," Julien said calmly, sticking to the facts.

"Then bring me another *justificatif de domicile*—with *both* your names on it!"

The madness continued for several long weeks. Julien had to return to the office seven more times because, among other things, Freida kept losing the copy of his passport. On his eighth visit, the frightful *fonctionnaire* had the day off, so Julien met with her colleague instead. A newly formed bureaucrat who looked as if he were fresh out of high school (which meant he was still relatively unscathed), the young man patiently went through the dossier with Julien, item but item.

"Is it complete now?" Julien asked.

"Yes, it is, Monsieur Chameroy. Congratulations!"

The next day, Julien got a call from Freida. "My colleague was mistaken! Your dossier is *not* complete!"

"Why is that?" Julien asked. I was amazed that he could *still* remain calm.

"Because your fiancé's birth certificate is not valid!"

"Yes, it is," Julien said. "If you check it carefully, you'll see that it has the official seal from the notary—and is dated less than three months."

"But that is not sufficient!" her voice blasted through the phone. "The rules clearly state that it needs to have an *apostille* stamp from the Secretary of State where the birth certificate was issued." (There was no such rule on the list Freida had given him.)

My poor *chéri*. He had to go back to the office for the *ninth* time to retrieve my birth certificate. Even worse, the three-month date on it was about to expire—in just *three* days! Since it was *my* birth certificate, I took over from there. To beat the ticking clock, I had to FedEx the doc to Connecticut, with a prepaid return envelope. If the certificate didn't make it back to Paris in time, I'd have to get a new copy and start all over again.

The day of the deadline, we waited on pins and needles for the FedEx truck to pull up to our apartment building. It didn't arrive until the late afternoon. With minutes to spare, Julien grabbed the envelope and raced over to the mayor's office for the *tenth* time. Being only human, my future husband broke his cardinal rule and showed emotion: pure, unadulterated anger, to be exact.

He slapped the apostille-stamped birth certificate onto the counter. "Here's the *putain de* certificate!" he snarled. "And here's the *putain d'*invoice from FedEx. Who's going to pay for it? You? Or You?" Julien pointed to the young colleague, then to Freida.

Fearing the wrath of my handsome Frenchman, Freida's tone suddenly took a 180, sounding like the sweetest kindergarten teacher ever, which was somehow even more irritating.

"*Je suis désolée, Monsieur,*" she said in the purest honey voice. "But the mayor's office is not authorized to pay outside invoices."

"So you're saying *I* have to pay 90€ for *your* mistake?" Freida and her colleague turned away, looking out the window at the fancy courtyard of the *Mairie* outside.

"*Ecoutez bien,*" Julien continued. "We are done here, understand? I've come ten times. I am *not* coming back again!"

That was wishful thinking.

The next day, Freida called back bright and early, her bubbly voice coming through the phone. "*Bonjour* Monsieur Chameroy! I'm calling because I need just one last, teeny, eensy, weenie thing—then your dossier is complete!"

"All right. Spit it out."

"A copy of your passport."

Julien's face turned redder than a French flank steak. "Uh-uh-uh-uh-uh, Madame. Give me your email address."

"*Pardon?*"

"I told you I'm *not* going back there again."

"But it's a government email. It's extremely complicated."

"*Peu importe!*" (Whatever!) Just give it to me.

Freida rattled off a long string of letters, numbers and characters. Twenty-six in all.

Julien stared at the address, then took a deep breath. "Madame . . . Please take a moment to look at your email address again. Is it, by chance, missing something?"

"*Non,*" she said. "I told you it was complicated."

"I'll give you a hint. What does every email address have in common?"

"*Je ne sais pas.*"

"An '@' sign! Every email has an @ sign! Where's your @ sign?!"

"There isn't one," she said. "Oh, wait! There it is! Right between *4e* and *gouv.*

"*Excellent!* Hold the line while I send you the email."

A long—*très très* long—pause. "Did you get it yet?"

"*Non.*"

Julien read the email address aloud to Freida again, making sure it was correct. It was. He hit send again. "How about now?"

"*Non plus.*"

After ten more minutes of this nonsense, Julien hung up the phone, grabbed his passport and stormed off to the Mayor's office for the *eleventh* time.

But it wasn't over yet. The next day, Julien's phone rang. He groaned as he recognized the number.

"*Coucou,* Monsieur Chameroy! Me again!" Freida's sing-songy voice came through the phone. "Good news! Your *convocation* (the final French official document) is ready! I just need to confirm one last, *petit détail.*" Julien and I braced ourselves. "On what day would you like to get married?"

By now, Julien and I just had to laugh. It was all so absurd—even for France.

"Madame . . ." Julien said, back to his former, calm self. "If you look at the very first form you gave me . . . on the very first line . . . what date does it say?"

"Oh! September 17!"

"And what day is today?"

"September 7."

"That gives me just ten days to get my *entire* wedding ready. How am I supposed to do that in just ten days?"

"You're resourceful, Monsieur Chameroy! I'm sure you'll figure it out!" she said. "Oh, and don't forget to come by and pick up your *convocation*. Otherwise, you risk losing your date."

After Julien hung up the phone, I put my arm around him and gave him a big *bisous*. "Bravo, *chéri!*" I said. "I owe you one."

"Actually, you owe me *twelve*—one for each time I had to go back to that *putain de Mairie!*"

"Deal!" I said, hugging him nice and tight. "And that was so sweet of you to pick September 17—the same day we got our PACS!" (Domestic partnership.)

"What can I say? It's a special day."

"And here I thought you were just making it easier for me to remember one date instead of two," I smiled. Me, the king of forgetting important dates.

"Anything to help, amnesia boy."

Needless to say, with just ten days to prepare everything, it was going to be a very small, intimate wedding. None of my family was able to make it over from the States on such short notice. But a dozen or so of our closest Parisian friends had requested the day off from work weeks in advance, just in case.

As for the reception, my Belle Maman, Elisabeth, came to the rescue, offering to cater the affair. She hopped on the high-speed TGV train from Dijon, her suitcases packed with goodies as usual. Her menu for the big day consisted of a savory collection of *amuse-bouches* to go along with champagne for the starter, followed by a buffet (with an enormous cheese plate), and the *coup de grâce*, a three-tiered carrot cake for the *gâteau de mariage*. Elisabeth knew it was my favorite, experimenting for weeks until she'd refined her homemade cream cheese frosting, making sure it would taste as good—and certainly better—than in the States. For my part, I found two plastic tuxedoed figurines in a small boutique on Île Saint-Louis, which would serve as groomsmen on top of Elisabeth's cake.

The day before the wedding felt like a dream sequence in a movie. After getting out of my Belle Maman's way so she could prepare the buffet (and *gâteau de mariage*), I swung by the Abbey Bookshop, an expat institution, to get Julien a small wedding present: Eckhart Tolle's follow-up book to *The Power of Now*. Its sage advice had helped me get through the toughest times at BIA.

"I know I've seen that book somewhere," the friendly owner, Brian, said. "If you have a moment, we can take a look."

Brian led me down to the 16th-century vaulted stone cellar. With virtually every square inch stacked with books from floor to ceiling, I feared the search could take hours. As Brian started to go through each tome, one by one, I looked to my left. There on top of a stack at eye level—as if waiting for me—was the book I was looking for.

"Hey, Brian . . . ?" I smiled, pointing at it.

"Huh, whaddya know," he said. "I think it's a sign." He handed me the book. "Here. My wedding gift to you and Julien."

I was feeling positively giddy as I made my way back to our apartment, book in hand, singing the classic tune from *My Fair Lady*: *"I'm getting married in the morning!/Ding dong, the bells are gonna chime!"*

Right on cue, just as I approached the Saint-Nicolas du Chardonnet church near Maubert Mutualité, its 16th-century bells began to chime. *Ding dong, ding dong.* I stopped dead in my tracks. *How was that possible?* It was a Wednesday, not a Sunday, with nary a holiday in sight. And at an odd hour in the middle of the afternoon.

What next? I thought as I crossed the street, singing the song anew as the church bells continued to chime. On the other side of the road, I looked down. There on the pavement was a crisp 20€ bill. I looked heavenward. *Oh, c'mon, this is too much.* I picked up the 20€ bill, stuffed it in my pocket, and raced back to the safety of my apartment, lest my magical dream sequence end with me being struck by lightning or hit by a bus.

Every marriage in France must pass through City Hall. Julien and I couldn't have asked for a more lovely one than the *Mairie du 4ème*. Built in 1887 during the reign of Napoleon III, the grand *Salle de Mariage* was adorned with beautiful hand-painted frescos and an enormous white marble fireplace.

About twenty guests were able to attend. For the ambiance/background music, Julien and I selected two Cat Stevens songs. First, "If You Want to Sing Out, Sing Out," from one of my favorite movies, *Harold and Maude*. And the other, "Morning Has Broken." Much to my surprise, Freida the *fonctionnaire* was in charge of manning the CD player.

As our guests mingled, I reviewed the game plan with Freida. "When I nod, that's your cue to softly fade out the music. *Ça marche?*" Freida gave me a look as if to say, *What do you think I am? An idiot?*

The guests took their seats as the *adjointe du maire* (deputy mayor) entered the *grande salle*. From our introduction earlier, Julien and I were thrilled to learn that the *adjointe* was half-French, half-American, kind of like us. And not only that, her colleague in the 3eme *arrondissement* had a teenage daughter who was a huge fan of BIA and ate there regularly.

As Cat Stevens's raspy voice echoed against the marble walls, my heart filled with joy. "*You can do what you want, The opportunity's on, And if you find a new way, You can do it today. . . .*" The whole time, I couldn't stop my feet from tapping to the bouncy beat. I was cloud-nine happy.

Before the end of the song, I nodded to Freida, her cue to softly fade the music out. Instead, she abruptly cut it off mid-lyric, somehow creating the sound of a cringe-inducing record scratch.

The wedding ceremony itself was short but beautiful. Elisabeth made a very touching speech. Earlier that morning she had promised Julien she wouldn't cry. But two lines in and already she was blubbering. I tried my best (unsuccessfully) to not follow suit.

One thing that stood out from an American wedding were the vows. When asked the question, "Do you take *such and such* to be your lawfully wedded husband?" instead of saying "I do," the French simply say, "*Oui*." However, when it was my turn, and the *adjointe* asked me, "*Voulez-vous prendre Julien Chameroy pour votre seul et légitime époux?*" she winked at me, and somehow I knew to answer, "*Oui* . . . and . . . I DO!"

The guests erupted in laughter. From that moment on, whenever I would do something stupid or embarrassing, Julien would say, "I can't believe I said '*oui*' to this guy!"

Once the ceremony was over, we gathered to take pictures at the back of the *grande salle* next to the magnificent marble fireplace. Our accountant at BIA, knowing how much I appreciated the intricacies of the *Code de Travail*, came over to Julien and me and said, "Hey, guys, I looked it up and by law, you're entitled to *four* paid days off for getting married. And it's not even subtracted from your normal five weeks of paid vacation!"

"Wow, did you hear that, Julien?" I said, putting my arm around his shoulders. "It's Thursday. We don't have to go back to work until Monday!"

Julien, our accountant, and I stared at each other for a moment, then burst out laughing, knowing full well we had to be back at the diner the following day.

As "Morning Has Broken" played in the background, the *adjointe* mayor came over to Julien and me. In her hand was a document covered with soft blue velvet and embossed in gold leaf: The *Livret de Famille* (The Family Booklet). The official record book was so important to French life, everyone knew that if you lost it, or it got stolen, or it burned up in a fire, it was impossible to replace.

"Congratulations," the *adjointe* mayor said, handing Julien and me the *Livret de Famille*. "You're officially a family now."

As I held the booklet in my hand, my eyes began to tear up. The first page I flipped to was for children. It contained a numbered list for up to eight *enfants*. I wondered what the French did for nine or more.

But by far the best part: at the top of the page, where it was listed Father and Mother, a ballpoint pen had been used to update it, crossing out Mother so that it now read: "Father and ~~Mother~~ Father."

I took a deep breath and looked at Julien. "How about that? I'm finally French."

"Yep," he grinned. *"Almost."*

"What do mean, 'almost?' I have my *Livret de Famille*! What else do I need?"

"Just one last, teeny little thing: your French nationality."

Bon dieu. That would be another story . . .

SIXTEEN

From France to Frenchtown

"Wake up, Julien!" I said, tugging on his blanket. "It's time for breakfast!"

Julien groaned and rolled over on his side, covering his head with his pillow. "Not now, *mon petit*," he said. "We can have breakfast anytime, remember?"

"Not on this train we can't!"

Sure enough, even though Julien and I were in America—on a rickety Amtrak train from Chicago to LA—breakfast was only served from 6:30 A.M. to 9:30 A.M.

The trip was half honeymoon, half book tour. Three days earlier, back in Frenchtown, Connecticut, I'd finally done *the* big book presentation I'd been so anxious about ever since Mrs. O. made a surprise visit to Breakfast in America. The event turned out to be quite emotionally intense, so I needed some time to process it. The train seemed like the perfect place to do that.

After Connecticut, Julien and I continued on to Madison, Wisconsin, and Chicago for a few more book signings. Thinking it would be more romantic than taking a plane, Julien and I hopped on the Southwest Chief in the Windy City—destination LA—for one last event. After that, it was back to Paris, where I still had to cull together about a year's worth of official documents in order to complete the *dossier* for my French nationality.

Julien crawled out of the *couchette*, ran a comb through his hair, then groggily followed me down the hallway as the train gently rocked us to the dining car. Much to Julien's surprise, the car was completely empty.

"Wait . . . what time is it?" he asked.

"6:20 A.M."

Julien groaned. "I am going to kill you."

After we were seated, I ordered a stack of pancakes and a side of sausage patties. Julien ordered the "healthiest" thing on the menu: breakfast quesadillas filled with Monterey Jack cheese and topped with scrambled eggs and tomatillo sauce. It also came with a "flaky croissant." I couldn't wait to compare it to the real deal.

In the fastest turnaround time ever, the server came over and placed our breakfasts on the table in front of us.

"Oh, man," I said with excitement. "Sausage patties! I haven't had these in years!"

Julien stared at the round hockey pucks of processed pork. "Those look disgusting."

"They are," I said, shoving a piece in my mouth. "Yet sooo delicious!"

As for Julien's croissant, it turned out to be much better than either of us expected, moist and buttery and going quite well with a dab of grape jelly, something Julien had never tried before.

One thing I loved about dining on an Amtrak train was that the crew made you sit with total strangers, filling up one table at a time as passengers arrived. Halfway through our breakfast, the server sat a friendly couple from Wisconsin next to us. We soon learned that they hadn't left their dairy farm in years and were on their way to visit their son who had moved to Hollywood to become an actor.

"How's his career coming along?" I asked, tearing open a packet of "Table Syrup"—whatever that was—and squeezing it onto my pancakes.

"Not so good," the mom said, the worried look in her eyes magnified by her horn-rimmed glasses.

Her husband smoothed out his long white beard, then looked at his wife, speaking in a soft tone. "Ma here's gonna try to convince him to come back home. But there ain't no work, 'cept on the farm. And our boy don't wanna have nothing to do with that anymore."

The mom started getting a little teary-eyed. The old farmer noticed and changed the subject, asking Julien and I where we came from. When we told him France, he chuckled and said, "By gum, that's *far*! At least our boy's in the same country, right Ma? Otherwise, we'd *never* get to see him 'cause me and the missus don't fly."

I gave the woman a warm smile. "Don't worry," I said. "I followed a similar path as your son's. And although there were a lot of twists and turns, ultimately it led me to where I needed to be—living my dream—even if it wasn't *exactly* the dream I'd planned on."

The woman nodded slightly, then turned and looked out the window, lifting her glasses and wiping her eyes.

Later, as the Southwest Chief snaked its way through a snowy mountain pass, Julien and I sat in the viewing car. The décor was straight out of the '70s, as if formed by a gargantuan lava lamp that had spilled over and congealed into groovy plastic swivel chairs and honeycomb-shaped windows. But the train cars hadn't been designed that way for nostalgic reasons; they were the *actual* cars from the 1970s, the last time the U.S. government had properly funded the country's rail system. It was a far cry from the network of ultramodern, high-speed train lines that crisscrossed the French countryside.

"Amtrak will get there one day," I said to Julien, optimistic. "Just probably not in my lifetime."

Julien smiled, then uncorked a bottle of California red that we'd purchased on the train, filling two plastic cups with a hearty Paso Robles Cabernet.

"*Santé!*" we said in unison as we raised our cups and clinked them.

"So . . ." Julien said after taking a sip of his wine. "Now that your book tour's winding down—and we're doing *absolument rien*—are you ready to talk about what happened at your book presentation in Frenchtown?"

"Yeah, I think so," I said, taking a big gulp of my wine.

I gazed through the viewing window at the snowy white canvas outside as I recalled the events from that day.

After landing at JFK airport from Paris, Julien and I picked up a rental car and raced up Interstate 91 to the last town in Connecticut before the Massachusetts state line. Between the heavy traffic and torrential rain, we arrived at the Barnes & Noble with just minutes to spare.

I parked at the far end of the parking lot, shut off the engine, and took a deep breath. Julien looked out the window at the huge complex full of retail stores.

"Hmm. Frenchtown doesn't look so bad," he said.

"That's because this is a *mall*," I said. I turned and pointed west. "French-town is five miles that way, near the toxic river and the abandoned railroad tracks."

Julien smiled and took my hand. "What are you so worried about, *mon petit?*"

"I don't know . . . you know, when you're an adult and you think you've got your *merde* together? Then you visit your family and suddenly you feel like a ten-year-old kid all over again? It feels like that."

"Hmm, might be an American thing."

"Or, maybe you've always had your *merde* together?"

Julien gave a Gallic shrug then grabbed the door handle. *"On y va."*

As Julien and I got out of the car and made our way across the enormous parking lot, I whispered to him, "What if nobody shows up?"

"Doesn't matter."

"Or worse yet, what if they get all weirded out because I have a *husband?*"

"Doesn't matter even more."

At the entrance to the Barnes & Noble, I looked through the window. The place was packed. "Oh, my God, Julien," I said. "Look. There must be at least a hundred people in there."

"Ah, my *'enfant prodige'* (prodigal child) has returned home," Julien grinned.

Staring at the crowd inside, I recognized so many faces, many of whom had played important roles in my life—both good and bad. (I was relieved to see that Todd Ferguson, the kid who had traumatized me when I was ten by telling me that nobody liked me, was *not* there.)

Julien gently took my arm and led me inside. When the crowd saw us in the doorway, they whooped and hollered.

"Craigie!" Mrs. O. said as she stepped over to greet Julien and me. It was the first time I'd seen her since she'd popped into BIA months earlier. "I have a big surprise for you," she said. Standing next to her was a blond woman in her late sixties, wearing cool shades. Mrs. O. beamed, "I was able to track Jan down and drag her out of retirement!"

Jan . . . ? Wait. Oh my God. "Mrs. Robataille?" I said, hardly believing my eyes. My fourth grade teacher nodded and smiled.

"Hold on a second," I said. I ran over and grabbed a copy of my book off the display table, then came back and flipped to the second to last page.

"Look," I said. "I thanked you in the acknowledgements."

"You did?" Mrs. Robataille said, flattered—and a little embarrassed. "What for?"

"Are you kidding?" Once again, like most heroes, the public school teacher was incredibly modest. I thanked her for having seen potential in me as a kid—even when I couldn't—and then fostering it. Mrs. Robataille blushed. Saving her any further embarrassment, the manager of the store came over and said it was time for my presentation.

Stepping up to the podium, I noticed that off to the side, a TV camera from a local cable access show was filming the event. I could feel the butterflies flapping around in my stomach as I looked out at the sea of familiar faces, most of whom were shining as brightly as the beacon atop the Eiffel Tower.

Mrs. Robataille, who was seated in the front row, surveyed the crowd, then gave me a big smile of encouragement. I could practically hear her voice from over forty years ago saying, "See, Craig? Told you the kids liked you!"

After my presentation, Mrs. O. insisted that Julien and I stay at her place instead of paying for a hotel. "But I have to apologize ahead of time," she said, as we exited the Barnes & Noble. "I didn't get a chance to iron the sheets."

"Oh, well, in that case, maybe next time . . ." I teased, pretending to head off in the opposite direction.

Actually, Mrs. O. had already planned for the next time.

The following morning over a delicious breakfast in her blue and yellow, French Provençal–style kitchen, Mrs. O. told us that she was itching to organize a big dinner party for our next visit. Having lost her husband recently, she said her home felt empty and could use a little life in it.

Happy to take her up on her generous offer, Julien and I would return the following year, but this time with my Belle Maman, Elisabeth, in tow. Mrs. O. would insist on doing all the cooking herself for twelve guests, which included yet another of her wonderful surprises: my two French teachers, Mme. Thompson from junior high school and Mme. Bueker from the AP class that had changed everything. Most touching, Mrs. Bueker and her husband ended up driving for seven hours, all the way from Virginia, just to see Julien, Elisabeth, and me.

After breakfast, with our suitcases packed and waiting by the door, I told Mrs. O. how much it meant for me to see her again. I also thanked her for tracking down Mrs. Robataille, who'd been such a guiding light for me as a little boy. For some reason, I decided to tell her the story about

Todd Ferguson, and how I'd run away from school only to be picked up later by a kind stranger.

Mrs. O.'s face lit up. "You know, Craigie, that stranger was . . . *Mister* O."

I don't know what moved me more: that Mrs. O. knew my story already; or that her late husband had been the one to bring me home safely that day. Turns out, he was the principal of the school at the time, and when Mrs. Robataille told him I hadn't come back from recess, he'd decided to go out and search for me.

"*C'est magnifique ça*," Julien said, touched.

"*Oui, c'est magnifique*," Mrs. O. replied with a near-perfect French accent. Julien looked at her, impressed. Mrs. O. blushed. "We can stop right there, okay," she said. "I know just enough French to get myself in trouble!"

After saying our goodbyes and promising to come back the following year, Julien and I set aside enough time to visit Frenchtown before continuing on my book tour. As we pulled onto Chapel St. the first thing that struck me was how deserted the neighborhood was. It reminded me of the science fiction film, *The Omega Man*, where Charlton Heston is the last man on Earth. Only there wasn't even a Charlton Heston.

Nobody was sitting on their stoops chitchatting like they used to. No kids riding their bikes or playing kickball. There wasn't even a single, solitary soul in sight for aliens to zap into oblivion as they'd done in my Super 8 masterpiece, *Invasion on Chapel St.*

I parked the rental car in front of my old apartment building, a split-level, two-family duplex built in the late 1800s. My old *chez moi* was hardly recognizable. The porch had been ripped off, making it look even smaller and more run-down than I remembered. But at least it was still standing, I thought, unlike all the buildings across the street, which had been razed, leaving a dusty, vacant lot.

"So what do you think of Frenchtown?" I asked Julien.

"*C'est un peu triste, non?*" (A little sad, no?)

"Yeah, but . . . it was a *lot* better back then, I swear."

I looked up at the second floor apartment where I'd lived with Fast Eddie all those years ago. I thought about the cutouts of Impressionist paintings he'd plastered all over the walls, wondering if the new tenants had kept any of them after we'd gone.

I then remembered the time I'd gotten together with Fast Eddie for a coffee and Bavarian cream donut right after I'd come back from my junior year abroad.

"Did you get to see any of the Impressionist paintings while you were in France?" Fast Eddie asked, perking up in his seat.

"Oh, yeah. A ton."

"How 'bout Van Gogh? Did you get to see *Sunflowers*? And *The Potato Eaters*?"

I nodded, knowing that the Dutch painter was my dad's favorite. "But those two are in a museum in Amsterdam," I said. "I had to go there to see them."

Fast Eddie nodded, then took a long drag off his cigarette, thinking, imagining. "I bet they're *spectacular* in person," he said, exhaling.

Back on the Southwest Chief train, I looked out the window at the snowflakes swirling around like the strokes of Van Gogh's brush. "It's a good thing you got out of Frenchtown," Julien said, his voice bringing me back to the present.

I nodded, but couldn't help thinking about all the kids who hadn't.

The train hugged the edge of a cliff, rounded a corner then entered a long, dark tunnel. It came out the other side along the banks of the mighty Mississippi River, crossing over a magnificent iron bridge and into the state of Missouri. The sky cleared, and for the next 1,000 miles, the train would *chug-chug-chug* along the flat, endless plains of America's heartland.

I swiveled around in my groovy '70s chair and examined the viewing car. It was full of people from a broad section of the country rarely seen on the two coasts, including a family dressed in traditional Swiss-German–style garb.

"Are those the Amish?" Julien asked in French.

"I think so," I replied. "Or the Mennonites. I always get them confused. I just know that neither can fly, so you always find them taking the train."

Julien smiled then went to hold my hand.

"One second," I said. Seeing that the train was also inhabited by a bunch of beer-swilling guys from the deepest of red states, I unwrapped the scarf from my neck and covered our hands with it. "Just to be safe," I said. We wouldn't see another blue state for two days.

Long after the sun had set, Julien and I were still sitting in the viewing car, secretly holding hands, totally hypnotized by the scenery floating by.

The deeper we went into the plains, the more I noticed how many run-down, industrial ghost towns there were. They reminded me a lot of where I'd grown up. As we passed one Frenchtown after another, I wondered how many kids were out there like me, longing to see the world, yearning to breathe free. I hoped that they had a Mrs. Robataille, or a Mrs. O., or a wise and worldly foreign-language teacher in their lives.

And if they didn't, I hoped that one day, in the not too distant future, there wouldn't be any more Frenchtowns. In the world I envision, every kid would have the chance to experience the quality of life I've come to know in France, no matter where they live.

Sure, there are constant strikes and social unrest; the Pigeon Man and Kafkaesque *dossiers*; not to mention the occasional savvy and unscrupulous employee who can't be fired. But there are also weeks and weeks of paid vacation; a deep appreciation of history, art, and cuisine, including all the fresh, delicious snails your mother-in-law can hunt down.

But more importantly, France is a place where no citizen will ever go bankrupt just because he or she has the misfortune of falling ill; where no young person will ever be crushed by the massive weight of student loan debt; and where study after study shows that a kid from my background has a much better chance of social mobility, of having a better life than his father's.

Ah, oui. From my own personal transformation in the City of Light, I can proudly proclaim: *Vive la Révolution!*

ACKNOWLEDGMENTS

A hearty *merci* to all those who helped make this second helping of my adventures in Paris as rich and rewarding as the first. To my agent, Joelle Delbourgo who found the perfect home for *Let Them Eat Pancakes* at Pegasus Books. To Lisa Anselmo for introducing me to Joelle. To Andrea Hurst who was there from the start. And above all, to Jessica Case, the Deputy Publisher at Pegasus who was a complete joy to work with, striking the perfect balance between guidance and creative space, inspiring me to push myself as far as I could.

Thanks also to Lori Thicke who, on the recommendation of Linda Hervieux, invited me to join her Paris writers group. If it weren't for Lori and fellow members Laurel Zuckerman, Anca Metiu, Marissa June McCants and Janet Skeslien Charles, all of whom pushed me each week to write new chapters, I'd probably still be sitting in a Paris café by myself, working on this book.

Last but not least, thanks to my gang of trusted readers who offered their valuable and constructive criticism every step of the way, including my "ideal reader," Paula Sewell, who was back for round two, as well as Tim Maloney and Greg Huson who, under intense time pressure, helped me to fine tune the final manuscript.

And, of course, my story would not be complete if it weren't for my better half, Julien. *Chéri, je t'aime plus fort que jamais.*

ABOUT THE AUTHOR

New York Times bestselling author **Craig Carlson** first came to France as an exchange student in 1984 and instantly fell in love with the country. He never could have imagined that some thirty-five years later he'd be the owner of two American diners in Paris and be nicknamed *"Le* Pancake Kid" by the French. With a background in journalism, Craig studied cinema at the prestigious USC School of Cinematic Arts, using his experience as a screenwriter to pen his debut memoir, *Pancakes in Paris: Living the American Dream in France*. Craig and his husband Julien currently split their time between Paris and Los Angeles. Well, at least they try to. With two busy diners that can't be left alone for too long, their lives lean heavily on the Paris side, which, of course, is not such a bad thing, *n'est-ce pas?*